Beclouded Visions

SUNY series, INTERRUPTIONS:
Border Testimony(ies) and Critical Discourse/s

Henry A. Giroux, Editor

Beclouded Visions

Hiroshima-Nagasaki
and the Art of Witness

Kyo Maclear

State University of New York Press

Cover: *Observers, Operation Greenhouse, 1951.* (Anonymous). Photo courtesy of U.S. Department of Defense.

Published by
State University of New York Press, Albany

For information, address State University of New York Press,
State University Plaza, Albany, N.Y. 12246

Production by M. R. Mulholland
Marketing by Nancy Farrell

Library of Congress Cataloging-in-Publication Data

Maclear, Kyo, 1970–
     Beclouded visions : Hiroshima-Nagasaki and the art of witness /
Kyo Maclear.
          p.   cm. — (SUNY series, interruptions—border
testimony(ies) and critical discourse/s)
     Includes bibliographical references and index.
     ISBN 0-7914-4005-2 (hc : alk. paper). — ISBN 0-7914-4006-0 (pbk.
: alk. paper)
          1. World War, 1939–1945—Japan—Hiroshima-shi. 2. World War,
1939–1945—Japan—Nagasaki-shi. 3. Nuclear warfare in art. 4. Art
and nuclear warfare—Japan. 5. World War, 1939–1945—Art and the
war. 6. Hiroshima-shi (Japan)—History—Bombardment, 1945.
7. Nagasaki-shi (Japan)—History—Bombardment, 1945. I. Title.
II. Series: Interruptions.
D767.25.H6M22 1999
940.54′25—dc21
                                                                        98-3383
                                                                        CIP

10 9 8 7 6 5 4 3 2 1

Dedicated to the memory of Osamu Masaoka
1953–1994

Contents

Illustrations

Acknowledgments

There are many individuals who contributed to this project along the way. Many of these people provided invaluable resource support, others made equally precious creative and intellectual contributions. This book is dedicated to all these people.

I would like to extend my gratitude to Kazuyo Yamane, members of the Japan Council Against A- & H-Bombs (*Gensui-kyo*), and Hiroshi Harada (Director, Hiroshima Peace Memorial Museum), for providing otherwise inaccessible historical documentation. To Amy van der Hiel (Exhibitions Department, Massachusetts College of Art), Brydon Smith (Curator, National Gallery Ottawa), Takaya Narama (Maruki Bijutskan), Ritsuko Hirao (Curator, Hiroshima City Museum of Contemporary Art), and especially, Kazumi Sakamoto (NHK-Japan Broadcasting Corporation/Hiroshima), for their ongoing correspondence on art commemorating the atomic bombings.

My heartfelt thanks to Setsuko Thurlow and the family of Yamashita Sohoh for entrusting their memories to me and for their profound belief in the importance of learning from the past. My thanks also to participants at the 1995 "Powell Street Festival" (Vancouver) for giving my preliminary thoughts on the art of witness a warm and considered hearing. I am also indebted to members of the History/Memory Workshop (University of Toronto) for continuing to rouse me with their own unique perspectives and commitments to this field of research. Thank you to Professor Harlon Dalton and the Yale Law School for inviting me to participate in your "Bearing Witness" seminar. Your questions and offerings came midway in the process of writing and helped guide me through.

My love and appreciation is extended to Mario Di Paolantonio, Tamai Kobayashi, Nancy Friedland, Naomi Klein, Avi Lewis, David Buchbinder, Seth Klein, Mio Adilman, Naomi Wall, Jude Binder, Brenda Joy Lem, Richard Fung, Kerri Sakamoto, Megan Wells, Haruko Okano, Roy Miki, Amy Gottlieb, Nourbese Philip, Hiromi Goto, and, in particular, David Wall for providing companionship, discussion, and helpful criticism. My thanks to the artists who encouraged me to view art as a life force, an indescribable breath of hope and sorrow, exhaled toward stirring compassion and learning. This book is above all dedicated to my parents, Mariko and Michael, for their constant faith and loving encouragement. I would not be writing today were it not for my father's eagle eye and always considerate suggestions. I would not see art the way I do were it not for my mother's teachings. (My first lesson—that words often fail us—has stayed with me.)

Last but not least, I would like to acknowledge Roger Simon, Henry Giroux, Priscilla Ross, and Cathy Caruth for their support and thoughtful comments throughout this project. In particular, I would like to thank Roger Simon for always pushing me further with his insights. As novelist Anne Michaels writes: "The best teacher lodges an intent not in the mind but in the heart." Your love of teaching will be remembered, having inspired me to chase the question of learning into the future.

Introduction

The true picture of the past flits by. The past can be seized only as an image which flashes up at the instant when it can be recognized and is never seen again. . . . For every image of the past that is not recognized by the present as one of its own concerns threatens to disappear irretrievably.

—Walter Benjamin

Clouds gather visibility, and then disperse into invisibility. All appearances are of the nature of clouds.

—John Berger

Black rain literally paints the face of a Nagasaki child survivor in one photograph. He looks out to the camera, riceball in hand, a homemade cloth air-raid hood on his head. Another photo captures a human shadow permanently stained on concrete steps. It is a cold silhouette. Yet another picture outlines a crater left by someone who was once there: a carpenter, a librarian, a student?

A half-century later, there are various images associated with the atomic bombings. Some are stranded in limited-edition monographs. Some have circulated more widely as Press Agency photos. Some capture the ocular distance of an aerial bomber, the killer plane. Others have a horror of intimacy, settling on minute traces of destruction, scalding the optic nerve with glimpses of bodies stiffening into death.

Images flare up from the sites of Hiroshima-Nagasaki alerting us to the scope of violence wrought by those original explosions. Lending tangible form to intangible events, they insinuate the need for historical recollection and understanding, particularly with respect to events of such magnitude. We have the capacity to destroy the earth in seconds! To lose sight of the consequences of history is to condemn us all to oblivion! *Let the pictures speak*, we are adjured.

Every war has produced its share of unforgettable, mind-searing pictures. But just as strategies for waging war have changed, so have the strategies used to imagine war. A majestic struggle between Home-

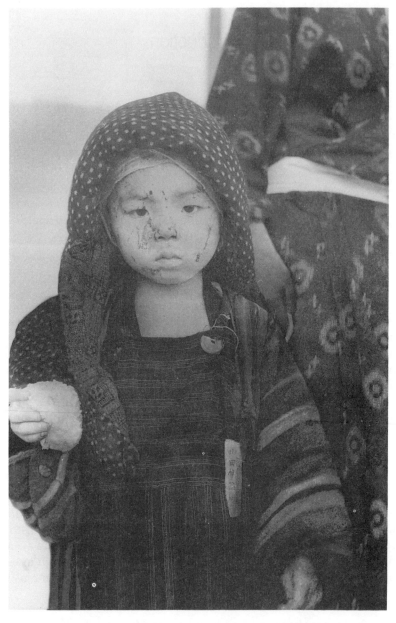

FIGURE I.1. *Nagasaki Child, August 10, 1945*. Photo by Yosuke Yamahata. Copyright: Shogo Yamahata.

ric soldiers—chiseled into a tympanum—gives way, in a leap spanning millennia, to a photograph of a naked Vietnamese child running down a highway from a napalm explosion. In lieu of mythic battle scenes of old, rendered from a lofty distance, the introduction of the camera to the war-front invited the possibility of full immersion and culpability. More than any prior method of depiction, photography offered front-row seats to the most lurid and vivid scenes of violence. Blood spatterings and gut spillings could be conveyed through graphic tableaux vivant. Caught under the glare of a camera, one could die in static pose.

The introduction of photography, which dates as far back as the American Civil War, precipitated a tremendous shift in our ways of seeing and potentially responding to warfare and human suffering. In extending the limits of the visible world, photography ushered us from the theater of the living into that of the dead. From images of corpses in morgues to x-ray shots of human skulls, photography brought to light the face of mortality as a kind of pure seeing. The body in shock, the body damaged, could be posed and poised in a moment of visual notation.

Through photographic access, we continue to experience the prospect of vicariously inhabiting events and experiences hitherto remote. Like Auguste Comte, who in the year of the camera's invention, 1839, was penning his *Cours de Philosophie Positive*, our conception of photography has been guided by the idea that total knowledge of the world is attainable. Through observable and quantifiable facts, carefully recorded through words and images, we might slowly penetrate even the most perplexing and elusive problems of existence.

Dramatic social and cultural changes have occurred, not least in visual technology, since Comte wrote his paean to positivism. Yet despite the test of time and change, many of us remain captivated by the basic lure or idea of photography: remain in thrall to its promises of easy immediacy and facsimile, rather than its historical context. Like Comte, our ethics of seeing, as suggested throughout this book, continue to be largely conditioned by a positivist faith in the correlation between vision and knowledge. As belated witnesses to historical trauma, many of us continue to turn to images in order to elucidate meaning about events that seem to otherwise defy understanding. We wait, so memoried are we, for artifacts to provide assurance, to swing us past our lapses of faith and reason. The act of sifting through visual records lends a sense of order and continuity, allowing us to confront our uncertainties by giving them a shape, a profile. A sense of secular religiosity surrounds many of these images. They have been haloed by time.

In the case of Hiroshima and Nagasaki, however, simple acts of seeing take on a significance exceeding any apparently simple transparency. These events, as we shall document, have produced a unique crisis of witnessing. Again and again, the atomic bombings force an encounter with the limits of vision as a paradigm of knowledge and ethics. Again and again, we return to the questions: How does one grapple with the decimation of tens of thousands of people in a momentary flash? How *can* one imagine the sudden obliteration of an entire city? At the deepest level, images of nuclear disaster turn upon themselves to question the very notion of imaging itself.

It is profoundly difficult to fully imagine what happened in Hiroshima and Nagasaki. From survivor accounts, we can gather only a sparse chronology. We know, for example, that the bomb fell upon residents of Hiroshima and Nagasaki from a serene sky—just after an all-clear siren had sounded in the case of Hiroshima. We know, too, that civilians who survived the three-second blasts were left to wander the ruins in states of extreme shock and disfigurement, many literally blinded by the event. Beyond this, accounts are muddy and dispersed, connected only by their common evocations of temporal and spatial disruption.

It is profoundly difficult to fully imagine what happened in Hiroshima and Nagasaki, for the terror in both instances was compressed into a single instant, which left strange—even illegible—visual traces. The physical force of these disasters overwhelmed comprehension by virtue of their sheer and sudden magnitude. The devastation was not experienced as the cumulative result of protracted battles. There was no gradual interval in which to wrestle with the disruptive rhythm of "conventional" war on everyday life.[1] Like Hamlet, interminably haunted by his father's sudden death at Elsinore, many atomic survivors were abruptly severed from their pre-trauma identities. Neither past experience nor immediate perception could prepare the citizens of Hiroshima and Nagasaki for what they were about to experience. Exactly at 8:15 AM on August 6, 1945, the people of Hiroshima were irrevocably jolted from their social, emotional, and physical moorings. Three days later, the people of Nagasaki suffered a similar fate. Stripped of a sense of stable chronology, time ever since would be "out of joint."

A wristwatch forever stopped at 8:15 AM is among other atomic artifacts on display at the Peace Museum in Hiroshima. Every battle, it seems, leaves a retinue of stranded objects: a soldier's diary from Normandy, shattered crystalware from Dresden, a Mickey Mouse doll from Bosnia. Strewn in trauma's aftermath, these artifacts help us divine a sense of the human dimensions. Novelist Tim O'Brien suggests we file these ruins and remnants in a composite archive called "War," thus registering the commonalities rather than the discrepancies between battles waged through the ages. O'Brien suggests that in gathering such an archive, we might find that even the extremes of war are unalterably mundane—even inevitable. "Staying alive, burning a village, watching the bombs fall, being scared, being brave," writes O'Brien, "those are the things that go back to Homer. Those are ancient things." Or survival by any extreme.

O'Brien is a humanist, albeit a cynical one, whose comments unfortunately disclose a wider tendency to naturalize war's wreckage; to absorb unprecedented traumatic events within a *telos* of history. Humans, he tells us, have always killed other humans for conquest, for ideals, for domination. Thus, he sees in war something eternal: the primal expression of human aggression and suffering.

While acknowledging how the excesses of battle have tragically persisted, *Beclouded Visions* departs from such interpretations. Some aspects of war remain agonizingly consistent over time, but *Beclouded Visions* finds in the scale and scope of modern warfare unique challenges to witnessing. In Homer's time, mass murder was refined into theater. In our own century, it became an industrial process, a murderous test of technological capacity.

World War II, significantly a war of aerial perspective, introduced a new standard of vision to combat. The 1990 Persian Gulf War extended and exploited the strategy of battle at a remove, leaving television's watching world with scant evidence of war's human detritus. In each instance, aerial warfare has proven itself to be an impersonal, even incalculable, business. The manner of waging, representing, and witnessing war is altered dramatically when mass death is delivered from a height of thirty thousand feet or by missiles launched hundreds of miles away. The traditional notion of some final battle—symbolized as the iconic denouement of war—is now replaced by the use of the reigning weapon of the day.

Significantly, the old rationale of military honor in face-to-face combat, characterizing famous scenes of war since Greco-Roman times, cannot be applied to Hiroshima or Nagasaki—or even this era of smart weapons, guided from afar. With scarce depiction of the American airmen who had been enlisted to drop the bombs, the almost complete vaporization of Hiroshima and Nagasaki appeared to take place in the absence of any *outside* witnesses. Moreover, those who survived the atomic bomb experience, those who might have acted as *inside* witnesses to the actual occurrence, were left confounded by an event that had no historical precedent. There was little in the way of prior imagery that could help lend form to the sudden destruction of an entire city by a single weapon. Even the tragic effects, which included invisible radiation disease, extended beyond the bounds of photodocumentary representation.

Indeed, what remains unique to Hiroshima is its message of total and unbounded annihilation. "Hiroshima," writes Robert Jay Lifton, "had not only exceeded all previous limits in destruction but had, in effect, declared that *there were no limits* to destruction" (Lifton and Mitchell 1995, 314). Thus, Lifton suggests a need to register the symbolic and ethical significance of *limitless* warfare. The optics used in waging and representing war must become ongoing matters and means of witnessing. No matter how comprehensive, factual liturgies to the dead cannot justly account for the sudden disappearance of entire populations. Hiroshima and Nagasaki, in their intimation of limitless destruction, have posed a crisis of witnessing that tests the limits of our moral vision, while begging new ways of seeing.

These unique events raise enduring issues about the nature of traumatic loss and the role of visual culture in commemoration. They pose evocative questions about perception, imagination, and our relationship to the visual world: How are Hiroshima-Nagasaki to be remembered and to what end? What is the role of visual culture in mediating historical consciousness about the bombings? The terms for witnessing, as Hiroshima-Nagasaki illustrate, cannot be reduced to simple sight.

Notwithstanding the distinctive mushroom clouds of atomic warfare, retinal memory has carried no guarantee of the contours and consequences of remembrance. Reliance on the power of pictures overlooks that their meaning and significance cannot be decided in advance, cannot generationally appeal to consciousness or conscience. To be sure, the images associated with Hiroshima-Nagasaki continue to yield a cluster of competing messages: the celebrated end of World War II, and with it the lasting specter of global annihilation. Historical interpretations are aided by pictures. Sharing a certain didacticism, they diverge in purpose. A hortatory slogan "No More Nagasakis!" is affixed to a photograph of a "Nagasaki Child." An American postage stamp makes selective use of a mushroom cloud with its victory caption: "Atomic bombs hasten war's end, August 1945."[2]

The memory of Hiroshima-Nagasaki continues to buttress different lessons. In this sense, the war is not over, it is simply reincarnated in a less bloody battle over representation. Taking a familiar image as an example, we might trace the contradictory ways it has been narratively reconfigured. Among some, the Mushroom Cloud has admonitory resonances: advancing a warning, looming as an ominous symbol of modern warfare and technocracy. Among others, the cloud is used to advance a narrow victim discourse that justifies Japanese wartime atrocities.[3] Among others still, the Cloud becomes a symbol of "necessary evils": reinstating the view that *merciless* means secured a *merciful* end to a brutal war.

The Mushroom Cloud swells with each new interpretation. Immaculately conceived in some eyes, it looms as a phantasmic metaphor of the sublime. For others it pivots and juts beyond any imaginable containment, leaking through descriptive captions like noxious gas, interminable, obscene. Interpretations of the Mushroom Cloud, such a nodal image in postwar consciousness, should alert us to the fact that meanings are not uniform. Images evoke competing memories, informed in part by shifting social and political requirements.

The Mushroom Cloud—beyond its traditional use as a factual, even picturesque, document—has proven that photographs are vastly manipulable and infinitely communicable. The image remains static and changeless. The same cloud billows from the earth to the sky. But the significance of the image changes as a result of historical and personal developments. As John Berger puts it, "Clouds gather visibility, and then disperse into invisibility. All appearances are of the nature of clouds" (1993, 219).

All images rely on narrative hooks for their meaning. These hooks can be sharply pointed, about protest or patriotism, or as diffused and dulled as rationales on human nature. Hiroshima's Mushroom Cloud, while periodically stamped with fierce meaning, has also inspired as much trite imagery as any other twentieth-century phenomenon. Cited in advertisements for jeans, used for special effect in video games, its potential to rouse historical meaning, suggests artist Satoshi Furui, may be exhausted. For Furui, the weight of the historical subject cannot be easily tailored to an image that has, in the end, become sadly conventional. Sheer ubiquity, he suggests, has allowed an archetypal image of dread and anguish to be domesticated as a commodity symbol. The collective shiver once induced by this image has passed into a pervasive sense of ennui.

Furui's *Mushroom Collection* (*Mind Games of the 20th Century*) (1995), by deliberately engaging repetition, registers an important concern about retinal fatigue. His motion of replay confesses a certain col-

8

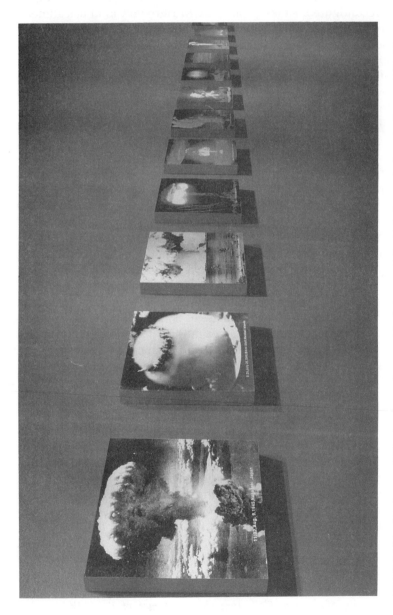

FIGURE I.2. *Mushroom Collection* (partial view, *Mind Games of the 20th Century*). Satoshi Furui, 1995. Photo courtesy of the artist.

lective tiredness, while still hoping for a renewal of meaning. Like Walter Benjamin, Furui wants us to create conditions that might allow the "tidings of the past" to be witnessed. More specifically, Furui hopes to pique the interest of those who see all images of nuclear war as stereotypical; those spectators caught looking within a mild boredom of order.

Like Satoshi Furui, many of the artists discussed in this book have cast aesthetic and visual concerns into the wider net of thinking about trauma history. As a result, their art is deeply infused with problems of witnessing: *How are we implicated in our looking? How can we create a living context for memories and meanings generated through art?* At various levels, these artists reflect a desire to reshape imaginations too willing to grasp for the familiar, too eager to isolate events through freeze-frame, too apt to rely on the world of appearances. The atrophy of meaning, they suggest, is the central challenge facing witnesses of trauma.

The trauma of Hiroshima and Nagasaki, as we will see, provides a compelling basis for revisiting our ways of seeing the past through representation. The crisis of witnessing posed by the technocracy of war calls us to forfeit the notion of a single all-encompassing perspective and the comparative security this offers. Hiroshima and Nagasaki suggest that we must release ourselves of the ambition to see and know it *all*, while attending to the ethical consequences of our partial perceptions. But the space of witnessing is elongated or abbreviated in part by how we define our role as participants in the making of memory and meaning. How we frame questions about what we are seeing invariably shapes our answers: What kinds of witnesses will we be?

Cultures of Vision

The ultimate expression of spectatorial distance is captured by a shot of impassive observers, high-ranking American personnel, sitting complacently in beach chairs as they witness "Operation Greenhouse," a 1951 atomic detonation in the Pacific. This is a stunning moment in visual history because it so succinctly portrays the inert and unaffected onlooker. In retrospect, the act of watching a nuclear test—as if watching some 3-D 1950s movie—seems tragically naive. We know too much about radioactive fallout nowadays to assume this viewing position. The image of stolid test observers (shown on the cover of this book) captures a lethal apathy. Looking has never been so casually dangerous. Yet, the photograph also evokes a danger exceeding the immediate frame. In distilling a moment of passive spectatorship, it has the power to remind us that all casual forms of looking may involve complicity. In this regard, the very passivity inherent to the image is its message, its aggression.

The militarization of vision—which enforces a physical and, arguably, aggressive distance for viewing—is not unique to this photograph. This standpoint was facilitated in extreme manner during the Gulf War when weapons of destruction were camera equipped. Smart bombs with electronic eyes made us spectators to satellite, real-time images in such manner as to tacitly approve the mass killing of civilians from the air. With its spectacle of visual bombing, late-twentieth-century warfare has increasingly fashioned the terms for detached and cruel viewing. How many of us traded in beach chairs for cushioned sofas only to watch brilliant green lights streaking through the Iraqi night sky in the wake of mass aerial attacks?

So as not to abet this dehumanizing perspective, many artists and educators have sought to introduce what David Michael Levin has called "countervisions" (1993). In the case of Hiroshima and Nagasaki, such interventions have looked to substitute hard-scrabbled images of ground zero for the aerial panoramas of scorched earth that have been more frequently associated with the atomic bombings. These countervisions lend human context to depictions that have tended to disembody and, hence, dehistoricize the effects of the bombs. As the liberal antinuke consensus gained momentum in the early 1980s, for example, many North American high schools introduced history units that featured extended newsreel footage and documentary photographs of post-Bomb Hiroshima and Nagasaki.

I do not wish to diminish the value of such evidentiary interventions. Yet, I do believe that our current use of visual culture needs to be broadened, not simply by replacing old images with new images, but by altering our habits of looking. Such shifts are necessary if we are to evolve new values and criteria for responding to events which, on many levels, represent a more profound crisis of vision and meaning. The demands of trauma witnessing, as I will later argue, surpass descriptive commentary and the documentary impulse. Trauma cannot be resolved through the gathering of chronological facts and information because it produces effects that—belated and recurring—elude historical closure. Trauma lingers at the actual sites where communities have been violated and people survive in states of displacement. It strays into the moments when experience and comprehension become irreconcilable and communication breaks down. As Cathy Caruth writes, "The trauma is the confrontation with an event that, in its unexpectedness or horror, cannot be placed within schemes of prior knowledge—that cannot, as Georges Bataille says, become a matter of 'intelligence'—and thus continually returns" (1995, 153). Trauma is precisely the open gash in the past that resists being healed or harmonized in the present. It is the prophecy of memories and truths yet to be symbolically, socially, or politically achieved.

The far-reaching attempts to represent the atomic bombings reveal something about trauma's ongoing legacies. Despite an outpouring of visual and verbal documentation, for example, many *hibakusha* (survivors) express the need to keep testifying to their experiences; many artists and writers continue to wrestle with this historical atrocity imaginatively.[4] Indeed, a strikingly persistent theme in the work of both *hibakusha* and non-*hibakusha* artists relates to the enormous barriers the atomic bombings pose to all attempts at recreation. So overwhelming are their memories, so unprecedented are their visions, that many artists and writers have tried to find new forms and a new language to convey their testimonies. Some describe the atomic bomb experience allegorically: the explosion was like an *electrical earthquake*, survivors resembled the *walking-dead*, *hell-fires* torched the cities. Others have turned to mythological and spiritual sources for images that might place these events within some prior framework of understanding. To merely view these artists and writers as unflinching recorders of the calamity, grief, and suffering that enshrouded Hiroshima-Nagasaki may devalue their struggles for meaningful representation.[5]

Therefore, taking these representational struggles as serious matters of witnessing requires expanding our notions of what is topical for pedagogy, and what counts and passes as knowledge. This is not a matter of rejecting the potential value of visual testimony, as much as loosening its links to notions of transparent access. As testimony, these images provide fragmented and incomplete channels through intersections crowded with ethical, historical, and aesthetic intent. They address themselves to the imagination, to the internal ruin of the survivor. Trafficking slowly through these intersections may demand a gear-change for those of us used to acquiring quick and certain information from images.

The art of witness exists, after all, within a visual field inundated with promises of direct access. We live in a culture pervaded with images, pictures, and spectacle, which together offer instant and rapid entry into events and experiences. Rather than alleviating demands on witnesses, however, I propose that our increasingly absolute culture of vision raises formidable ethical questions about the role of visual rep-

resentation in the formation of collective memory. The covenant
between pictures and events needs to be reconsidered perhaps now
more than ever before. As we enter a new millennium, visual culture
takes on growing prominence and sophistication.

Satellite television provides us with seemingly unlimited views
of world events. At the same time, the advent of Virtual Reality is further blurring the already hazy line between the real and the representational. Killers can be trained in virtual homicide games that seem
and feel intensely authentic. Sensations of pain and pleasure can be
simulated as we immerse ourselves in new digitalized environments.
We are, in essence, both onlookers and participants with an unprecedented degree of scopic access.

There is reassurance for some in these new forms of sensory and
panoptic power. As First World inhabitants, many of us have attained
a sense of omnipotence in the reach of our gaze. Yet despite our extensive perceptual power, many are also beginning to feel more at sea (or,
for that matter, cyberspace) in this increasingly technologized world.
As more and more information comes to us via new media, less and
less seems to come via direct bodily or sensory experience. We feel
"out of touch" and "immobilized." We are so swamped and stuffed
with quantity that there is little room to evaluate what is there, or what
to spend time on.

When one considers how our contemporary image culture is
evolving amid real-time suffering, the question of witnessing takes on
renewed importance. Our death-saturated world continues to produce
numerous collective traumas, traumas demanding historical awareness yet often defying our usual modes of access. More recently, Bosn-
ian mass graves and Rwandan refugee camps, crowded with the dead
and dying, have begged for forms of witnessing that might exceed
televisually conceived understanding. These collective traumas suggest the need for a prolonged gaze—a gaze that can reach insistently
past the moment when newsmakers and satellite cameras decide we
have reached our saturation point; or when they decide an event has
exceeded its interest value.

Artist Allan Harding MacKay has made an ongoing mission of
exploring the silences surrounding events no longer considered news-
worthy. Contracted to act as Canada's war artist in Somalia, MacKay
spent ten days in 1993 recording the activities of Canadian peacekeep-
ing troops. Six of his charcoal portrait drawings, based on the experience, have become property of the Department of National Defense.
More than five years later, however, MacKay works as an independent
witness artist. His drawings and video-art, curated under the title

FIGURE I.3. Still from *Somalia Series* (detail, video/mixed media). Allan Harding MacKay, 1993. Photo courtesy of the artist.

Somalia Series, are intended to keep the spotlight on a country still stricken by famine and strife. He feels his work is more important now that the river of information that once flowed from Somalia to the Western world runs dry. It is vital now that the initial shock has waned and many people see in the very reference "Somalia" an unbearable replay of a familiar tragedy—a place of "chronic" hunger and violence, a place of "natural" disasters.

The power of the *Somalia Series* is that it keeps open to scrutiny events which the media immediately replaces. Somalia, MacKay insists, is more than its six-o'clock-news identity. Headline news coverage tends to deny the historical continuity of events—the sense of connectedness between everyday life and the "momentous" crises they report—and diminish the relationship between the global North and South. By contrast, MacKay's growing collection of sketches and digital images, featuring western military troops and journalists encountering Somalians, illuminates the connections. He wants us to see Somalia as a human habitat with a continuous history of colonial intervention, which includes a history of our own involvement. His art is meant to protract our attention and activate our interest in the plight of those others we might consider strangers. He addresses the limitations of the camera, stating plainly: "We cannot simply follow the cameras around the world. We cannot use cameras to get us into countries, and we must not use cameras to get us out of countries."

The expanded profile of television and fiberoptic technology in popular lifestyle testifies to the ongoing importance of visual culture and cultures of vision.[6] Images of present and past atrocities continue to play a central role in informing our visual and emotional means of relating to these traumas. They shape our memories and possibly our commitments in responding to events and to daily related experiences of mass violence and disaffection. The excessive emphasis we place on visual connectiveness—as artist Allan Harding MacKay observes—is socially encouraged. (Hence, viewing communities are formed around media events like the Gulf War, the O. J. Simpson Trial, or the funeral of Princess Diana.) And yet, because the visual field is saturated with power investments and commercial interests, which lend priority and value to certain events and perspectives over others, the task of investigating visual culture becomes all the more important. The televisual gaze, however intense, is all too brief and promiscuous.

Beclouded Visions thus pursues a double purpose: on the one hand, challenging dominant practices of vision, while at the same time developing a place for visual culture in situations promoting historical witness. I have chosen to focus on expressive visual forms in order to help trace the philosophical shifts that may be necessary if spectators are to encounter collective trauma as witnesses—that is, if they are to find, in a disruption of conventions of looking and thought, new values and commitments. I have looked specifically at art's potential to convey the unsignifiable, its capacity to provoke questions that can take us beyond what is already understood. Art, I propose, may act as a powerful memory resource. Through art, we encounter the prefigurative movement of memories which test our shrunken imaginings of history, community, and responsibility.

Over time, many of our uncertain encounters with the traumas of Hiroshima and Nagasaki have been assuaged through narratives available in books, exhibitions, and films. Narrative language can provide names for even the most extreme excesses of violence. Metaphor can function as a powerful container of meaning and loss. Yet, at the same time, a photo installation entitled *Broccoli* (1995) reminds us of the randomness and insufficiency of language. Tokihiro Sato's black and white triptych places a broccoli bouquet bundled by a string of fluorescent lights at the center of its commentary. This otherwise benign image is given associative weight by the photos flanking it: on one side, we see a nuclear reactor, and, on the other side, anonymous stone ruins. Here, the artist suggests that "Broccoli" would have been as adequate, or inadequate, as "Mushroom Cloud" in describing a visual event that had no prior name or valence. In doctoring a symbol many of us have taken for granted, Tokihiro Sato has created a work that challenges us not to seal memory within a closed metaphorical loop.

In my exploration of witness art, I have looked to work that, like Sato's, may introduce questions ignored or assumed by methods of historical inquiry. I have considered visual culture produced by artists over the past several decades which confound easy delineations between art and documentation, the metaphoric and the literal, fiction and fact. Several of the artists I will be discussing, for example, have created work that offers no explicit message, work that does not presume to represent something concrete and definite about these events, but work no less concerned with the importance of social mourning and collective witness. Included is a discussion of survivor drawings, a film by Alain Resnais entitled *Hiroshima Mon Amour* (1959), and a series of painted murals by Japanese artists Toshi and Iri Maruki. These diverse visual-narrative forms introduce different resources and parameters for commemoration. They all, variously, invite us to consider different priorities and values in our encounters with visual culture.

16

FIGURE I.4. *Broccoli.* Tokihiro Sato, 1995. Photo courtesy of the artist.

Vivid Witness

Writing with impassioned eloquence, John Berger, in his book *The Sense of Sight*, argues for the primacy of vision and sight as a means of apprehending and reflecting on the world. Berger's final essay, relevantly entitled "Hiroshima," illustrates his thesis about the significance of sight. For Berger, Hiroshima epitomizes the importance of retaining sight as a measure of knowledge and moral vision. The nature of this historical cataclysm makes particular ethical demands on our commitment to justly envision the world. Berger's point of entry is a series of paintings and drawings by *hibakusha*, published in a book entitled *Unforgettable Fire: Pictures Drawn by Atomic Survivors.*[7] For Berger, a renowned art critic, the wretchedness and misery conveyed by these pictures suspends the possibility of explicit critical engagement. He writes, "Clearly, my interest in these pictures cannot be an art-critical one. One does not musically analyse screams. . . . These were images of hell" (1993, 288).

John Berger argues that Western countries have been impoverished by a dearth of meaningful information about the effects of the bombings. He sees the horror as having become assimilated by the slow and systematic suppression of significant facts. We have, according to Berger, been prevented from retaining the original meaning of Hiroshima, a meaning that was once "so clear, so monstrously vivid" (291). For Berger, the *hibakusha* pictures provide renewed access to that severed meaning. He rhetorically challenges the BBC to air these pictures, "without any reference to 'political' and 'military' realities, under the straight title, *This is How it Was, 6th August 1945*" (292). Berger concludes: "the memory of these events should be continually before our eyes. This is why the thousand citizens of Hiroshima started to draw on their little scraps of paper. We need to show their drawings everywhere. These terrible images can now release an energy for opposing evil and for the life-long struggle for that opposition" (295).

Berger's discussion of the survivor paintings reflects the difficulty of obtaining witness art, and, in particular, our assumptions about the mimetic relation between images and the events of history. Most of the visual works I will be exploring in this book test this relationship by breaking to various degrees with direct representation. All the works discussed here are explicitly expressive and imaginative. Nonetheless, they have all been conditioned by certain expectations about literalism. It is as if placing the image on a path of certainty and truth is the only way to ratify the experiences they evoke. It is as if the image, itself, represents a certificate of death and survival.

The preface to *Unforgettable Fire* joins John Berger in emphasizing the documentary character of the paintings over the imaginative. To a large extent the survivors themselves corroborate this emphasis in their framing strategies. Captions that accompany the pictures read as journal entries. Date and time (i.e., August 7, 8:00 AM) are carefully noted in many of the testimonies, calling forth the specificity of these calendrical remembrances. (Clock time is precise. Remembering the exact time may exact the distortions that accrue in time's passage.) And, thus, the preface insists: "The pictures are a vivid documentary of the miserable scenes of that day, although thirty years have passed. The memories, etched in the minds of the survivors, are unforgettable! Photographs cannot express the strong impressions which these pictures, drawn by the actual survivors, portray" (1977, 5). The paintings and drawings are authenticated as pure message—apparently transparent and linear in their communication of meaning.

It is understandable that this construction of art has held our attentions. It gives birth to the idea that everything will one day be known; that once represented, the flux of the dead will cease to haunt us. Such an idea is more than a vain desire to turn the page on history. It has provided the energy for human hope, the undersong of compassion. Seen in this light, the painting gives a face to the disappeared, the drawing turns oblivion into a tangible presence. Art is, thus, a response to the vertigo of nothingness. It is a protest against meaninglessness. The act of creation, which allows one to recover a sense of significance, is equal to a rebirth.

Yet many of the memory paintings retain a central paradox: promising immersion in trauma only to express certain crises of witnessing. As visual elegies, for example, these works are evocative of localized experiences and specific personal losses, turning away from an overall picture of the events. They suggest the difficulty of directing a frontal look at horror. Significantly, many of the contributors have noted their ambivalence about their pictures, feeling that even the most terrifying and graphically descriptive drawings could only reveal a portion of what they had seen and suffered (Gerson 1995, xv).

Art critic Guy Brett, discussing the emotional impact of these pictures, has evoked the stylistic power of art naif: "Undoubtedly one of the reasons they are so powerful is because of their rudimentary, unpolished style which itself seems to echo the way the familiar urban infrastructure had been obliterated and human behaviour reduced to helplessness. All culture—medical, artistic, productive, political—is wiped out" (1986, 119). Brett's response may seem a nostalgic interpretation of stylistic minimalism. But what becomes clear

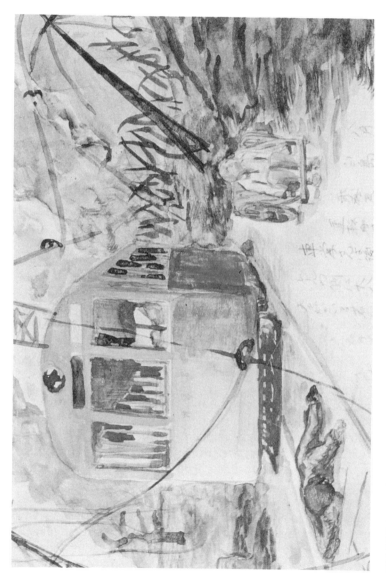

FIGURE I.5. *Hakushima Line, August 6th, 5 PM* (from *Unforgettable Fire*). Hidehiko Okazaki. Copyright: NHK Publishing Operation.

from his description is that he is engaging with much more than evidentiary documentation. Amid the grim horizons of atomic waste, images of flattened landscapes and human carnage, one continues to find indices of art: its ruined and its ruinous language. Which is to say that something slips, surpasses, the frame of the document. The surface of art has, itself, come to matter in the furbishing of meaning and emotion.

The critics make a virtue of saying the memories of survivors are direct because so unadorned and unvarnished; but the first and most unforgettable thing we learn about memory is that it is imperfect and fragile. Memories may be buried, lost, blocked, repressed, even recovered. Other memories may be mythologized by repetition into well-wrought chapters of the survivors' lives. This is not to demote their impact, or the place these formed and unformed memories have occupied in our minds. It is to stress, rather, that memory can be a reluctant volunteer: erratic, unwilling to come at any predictable beck and call. Taken in this light, the paintings are less important for the generic truths they reveal and more significant for what they ask of us. As viewers we are asked to become midwives to memories still caught in the throes of becoming. Our viewing presence—our intentions, blindness, and sight—becomes part of the witnessing activity.

Our response matters all the more because memories of trauma come into the world precariously: out of affliction, in the face of indifference, without cultural precedent. Through art, they attempt to cross the usual (statistical) barriers defining and controlling our knowledge of the bombings. But because they have moved toward the imagination their meanings are tentative. We enter *terra incognita*, only to follow artists as they struggle with and through a language that can evoke their particular experiences and responses. We are left, in many cases, with a floating flash, a testimony to effects that (while definitive), are itinerant and imprecise. Thus, the testimony addresses itself to all the future moments when it will be looked at. It waits to be intercepted and animated with meaning, so that it may continue to exist beyond its function as a souvenir of a past moment.

The capacity of art to motion toward future memories as well as contemporary ones implies an endlessly flexible critical language. It requires being mindful of the places where interpretation sabotages itself, blinds its own vision. And so the questions: When does an awareness of historical fact enrich our interpretive language and when does it impoverish it? How do these images participate in the formation of *our own* memories and towards what possible transformations in consciousness and action?

Criticism as a form of knowledge is capable of robbing art not only of its own implicit and explicit resonances; it can dismiss the painstaking work artists do to make work that becomes and remains part of and significant within a collective memory. I submit that the sensuous aspects of art cannot be condensed into verbal treatises, however radical, without some sense of loss. This is not to mystify art or appeal to notions of artistic transcendence, just to signal the limits to witnessing within narrow evidentiary terms. Eradicating the boundaries between art and documentation, in this sense, may simply eliminate art's unique power of indirection and evocation.

Art may act as a mnemonic device encouraging a type of remembering that is fluid *and* discontinuous. Art may introduce individual experiences to wider constituencies of memory. It may break habits of seeing perpetuated through our cool and detatched trust in photography. For these possibilities to be realized, however, requires challenging certain definitional precepts about the role of art in shaping memory and consciousness. The depiction of a collective and affective subject in art can present *both* a limit *and* resource for witnessing.

It is a common intellectual conceit, for example, to speak of the virtue of the dispossessed. This viewpoint is complicated by the fact that it is understood to be a graceful, even generous, liberal gesture. Yet, to say that the afflicted and oppressed are closer to reality has become a cliché; and a somewhat condescending one, in that it suggests that reality on the social margins is blunt, coarse, obvious, physical. Reality is thus opposed to the aesthetic and to the spiritual, categories from which the marginalized are mostly excluded.

Indeed, when not hailed as an unblemished recorder of historical fact, art that deals with the trauma of survival has tended, more recently, to be dismissed as "victim art." Art critic Arlene Croce's attack on Bill T. Jones's dance performance *Still/Here* serves as a watershed moment in contemporary art criticism. Published in the *New Yorker* (December 1994), Croce's "nonreview" inaugurated a backlash against *all* art commemorating collective resistance and survival. Her argument, that she should be able to attend a dance performance without encountering what she derisively called "dissed and abused" AIDS-survivors performing a "travelling medicine show," employed certain aesthetic codes to divest Jones's work of cultural authority. Croce suggested that Jones's work could not be considered an individuated subject since it was not seen to deliver an aesthetic experience. Croce's comments disclosed a certain globalizing bias toward modernist abstraction in favoring the art of "dislocated signs."

Artists such as Bill T. Jones have imparted options for developing both aesthetic and ethical responses to social trauma. In asking for more interactive modes of witnessing, they have posed a challenge to notions of discrete viewing. They have also challenged the idea that social considerations can be erased from the deliberations of aesthetic criticism. Yet, while there is clearly a pedagogical thrust to this work, it is rarely as doctrinaire as critics might have us believe. It is disquieting that many critics, giving privilege to the dematerialization of art, have simply abandoned the territory of social concern raised by commemorative interventions. If art is to play a role in the construction of collective memory, we must reexamine its pedagogical potential, without dismissing consideration of its aesthetic goals.

One of the distinguishing features of testimonial art is the factoring of the spectator into the actual construction of the work. As spectators, even collaborators, there can be little doubt that our encounters are encircled by an aura of taboo. The circle is netted tighter as we oblige ourselves to consider content and subject matter as divorced from the economy of visual signs and language, and the motives and message of the artist as preeminent in enforcing meaning. Empathy, guilt, pity, neglect, all collude in different ways to restrict our participation, each affective frame differently anticipating what will be seen and not seen. The strident and veerless among us approach these images in search of the missing links, the avowed truths, that can make clear a be-clouded history. Overreacting to conventional and confining priorities of aesthetics and beauty, we have tended to emphasize art's social claims. We avoid responding critically to the art production of those who speak from experiences outside our own for fear of revealing a tacit complicity with the very power structures under scrutiny. We remain silent, even pious, rather than risk responding in an "inappropriate" fashion.

So, while atomic-bomb artists frequently dramatize the elusiveness of truth and clarity, and the limits of their work in evidentiary terms, witness art is often exclusively called up along narrow historical and sociological criteria. The memory paintings and drawings that together comprise *Unforgettable Fire* are acclaimed for proferring a view from ground zero. Similarly, as I will later elaborate, critics of the *Hiroshima Panels* by Toshi and Iri Maruki have tended to focus on their "ideological content," commending these artists, in some cases, for furnishing an honest and realistic picture of the devastation wrought by the bombs. Though many of these artists have called attention to the limits of their own representational practices, the large majority of criticism tends to engage the work *solely* in referential terms: Does the work correspond to or obscure the reality of the atomic bombings? The norms of aesthetic evaluation worked out for testimonial art are tethered to criteria of accuracy and authenticity.

Thus, the criticism and reviewer responses I will be exploring throughout this book sound a common theme and quest. In particular, they indicate the heavy burden of depiction and delegation weighing on artists dealing with historical trauma.[8] These responses lend further context to artists' decisions to stick to realist forms and stay within evidentiary frames. The move to literalize and caption art is, in part, a reflex conditioned by historiographical and sociological conventions that marginalize imaginative and affective expressions. (Signs of creativity are "read" as falsifications, or as *too* subjective: a narrative is "just a story," a mural is "just a painting.") The tendency to value direct over indirect treatments of the events is exacerbated precisely because the effects of the atomic bombs have for so long been eclipsed or representationally marginalized. (The production of ground-zero images in Japan was hampered by censorship codes strictly enforced by U.S. Occupation authorities between 1945–1952.)

Indeed, for many Japanese artists in the immediate post-Occupation period, the choice of realist forms such as memoirs, figural representations, and documentary fiction was strongly influenced by the demand for evidence. Such representations, it was assumed, could help fill the representational void produced through a seven-year-long period of censorship. In addition to providing an alternative to dominant narratives of the bombings, the resulting work helped generate a pool of common symbols. Realizing how generally accessible and appealing realist forms can be, many artists and writers continue to mobilize them in hopes of dramatizing the ongoing significance of the atomic bombings within a matrix of present-day political and social concerns. In optimum educative contexts, this work may help to (metonymically) retemporalize experiences which have been cordoned off in historical time.

Nonetheless, while keeping in mind the value of using these images for resistance and solidarity, I began this book by asking about the limits inherent to corrective visions. The act of correcting the visual record carries certain expectations about what the past can teach us and how this learning will most appropriately take place. While many agree that we have to attend to knowledge of the past and historical trauma, in particular, there are many views on how and why we should proceed. Maxims warning us that those who forget the past are condemned to repeat it often rest on the idea that productive lessons will be garnered once previously neglected or suppressed documents and truths are brought to light. But this assumes that given the right resources the past will be apprehended in the correct way, imparting a sense of collective responsibility. Events of the past half century—a period of increased televisual saturation—have provided sad reminder that making injustices visible does not necessarily lead to a commitment to rectify them. In fact, the visible can become dangerously canonical. That which was fashioned as a votive space for remembrance can become a container locking in the past—signaling a desire for quick closure and reconciliation with trauma memories.

The danger of reduction inherent in any image lends cause for ongoing reflection. The denotative and connotative aspects of art, I suggest, need to be joined in a bifocal way—demonstrably more critical than a fascination with unadorned facts or visual phenomena. As viewers, we need to place what art says *beside* the findings of empirical history—for example, what art says, often explicity, about what is intractable to time, and thus, closure.

Art does not have the power to change the course of history, or even to halt the recurrence of mass violence. It does, however, have the capacity to cast new and even unexpected light on a subject by moving the viewer emotionally and intellectually toward the unknown. Moreover, art may lay bare the contradictory dimensions of trauma memory as it vacillates between the imaginable and unimaginable. Recognizing that some aspects of the work may not be *about* an event in a literal or direct sense, we reevaluate our approaches and criteria for looking.[9]

At the same time, looking must be taken seriously as agency, as world view, involving responses that affect not just ourselves but others. With this in mind, it is not enough to ask whether or not art remembers the atomic bombings, or even how it remembers. We need also ask to what ends *we* have remembered, what actions we are prepared to take in light of our new understandings. Our task is to find a way to approach witness art that respects and opens up venues of collective interaction and dialogue across difference. These events bring us face to face with the consequences of dialogic breakdown. Not to enter dialogue is to isolate, to silence, to render invisible, and, finally, to exterminate. Thus, in later chapters I ask: How have the limited imaginings of communities and nations made mass violence conceivable? What prompts and makes possible a process of entering dialogue with what one is estranged from?

The need to reenvision history, and grapple with its contemporary significance, is preeminent in the case of Hiroshima and Nagasaki. To suggest that memory is an impossibility, to write off the traumas of the atomic bombings as "not our own," is to participate implicitly in reproducing the marginalization of these events and their direct victims. How we engage with this history may in no uncertain terms determine whether or not the marginal status of the subject is increased or lessened. Iwona Irwin-Zarecka, addressing the oppression of *hibakusha*, writes, "In Japan, the language and social practice separated out those 'tainted' by the bomb" (1994, 48).[10]

Many *hibakusha* still live an ostracized, shadowless existence tucked away from the eye's view. Conditioned in part by the unknown effects of radiation, and by Japan's lingering caste system, atomic bomb memories have been corralled into segregated zones of visibility and remembrance. A Peace Museum and an Atomic-Bomb Dome become distilled signs of memory—factual icons—just as they facilitate an exorcism of grief from the body politic.[11] The outward scars betray a need to look into the internal scars left by trauma. They call us to attend to those people still lingering with injury on the borders of power and history.

Thus, a monument to veterans of another war seeks to remind us of the people still hobbled to grief. The Vietnam Veteran's Memorial deserves mention for the way it invites public mourning. Designed by Maya Lin, it aspires to maintain its presence as an elegiac wound on the otherwise suturing memorial landscape of Washington D.C. The polished black granite wall, receding in a V-formation, bears the actual names of the dead (over 58,000 U.S. casualties are listed in chronological order of their deaths). Yet, the tension between its nonheroic form and its honorific promise cannot be synthesized. Because its testimony is both direct and indirect, because it refuses to employ familiar symbols of patriotism and glory (flags, fallen soldiers, tanks), it returns the burden of memory and meaning to its visitors.

The Scope of Memory

It is the eve of the year 2000 and we have unprecedented televisual access. Intricate computer networks and satellite dishes have extended our visual range, carrying our sights to distant parts of the world at warp speeds. At the same time, our ongoing exposure to news of violent events based on the persecution of ethnically and nationally defined groups (as with Bosnia-Herzogovina and Rwanda) has created new demands on our ability to respond to experiences of collective trauma and on our commitment to alleviate mass suffering. In asking what kind of witnesses we will become, I suggest that we distrust any security in simple sight. At the same time, I argue for the need to retain a sense of the value of visual culture in lending tangible form to overwhelming events.

In Chris Marker's film *Sans Soleil* (1983), the narrator asks, "I wonder how people who don't film, who don't photograph, who don't use tape recorders, remember." Marker gestures toward the devaluation of memory and imagination in the absence of *memento mori*. These material inscriptions and artifacts have helped facilitate collective grief-work. The power of commemorative culture cannot be ignored, even as we renounce its transparent link to historical events. The challenge I perceive as central, however, is how to allow for the development of a historical consciousness that does not settle—and ossify—in a stasis of empathetic recognition or nostalgic resolution. By this, I mean the formation of an insurgent memory that seizes upon an image as a starting point for ongoing inquiry and action.

At the heart of this project is a preferred belief that if people "forget" traumatic social events it is often not out of malice or uncaring. Many forget, or choose not to remember, because wanton destruction of the scale visited on noncombatant civilians in Hiroshima and Nagasaki has no fitting place in their system of (humanist) values. Mass death—whether it be the 150,000 estimated killed in the first flash explosion in Hiroshima; the six million Jews murdered by the Nazis in Europe; or more recently, the genocide of hundreds of thousands in Bosnia and Rwanda—is unfathomable. Our grief cannot be multiplied to encompass death of such boundless magnitude. So to both accept and reject mass murder as a part of contemporary life and collective memory, we look for ways to inscribe and materialize these events. We turn to symbols and rituals to lend names to the otherwise anonymous dead. We look to art and literature to help us imagine unimaginable suffering.

But the testimonial relationship is a demanding one. The survivors of atrocity afflict the witness with the openness of their claims, their pain, their vulnerability. They tell us that trauma is not simply absorbed into the flow of history; it recurs, it troubles the very notion of chronology. (Manifest in such concrete effects as hallucinations, flashbacks, nightmares, it presents a psychic burden, pressing down on the humanity and equilibrium of its victims.) They tell us, too, that their experiences of violence are no less haunting for having happened in a different geography. The attempt to reanimate lost worlds is, thus, an expedition without temporal or spatial ligatures.

The work witness-artists do to unfetter the imagination from the demands of mimetic language is complicated, yet in many ways definitive. Trauma inflicts a deep violence to subjective experience. The blurred distinction between direct and indirect representation begins and develops with this violence. (The survivor of trauma often does not discern between external stimuli and stimuli from the imagination. The survivor reacts equally viscerally to events from the imagination as it does to "real" events.)

Grappling with trauma's vestigial lesions through art requires a range of stylistic and ethical strategies—never complete, never sufficient. To say, as some have, that the specter of nuclear violence has been metaphorized out of historical consciousness is a complex statement. Insofar as there is no direct pipeline to the past, testimony can only be circuitous. But how wide we veer, how far we fold into testimony, and with what consequences, is a matter of importance. The question, therefore, is not so much whether or not we can give *Hiroshima* and *Nagasaki* a palpable sense of materiality, but rather whether we, as artists, educators, and viewers can develop strategies that can allow these historical events to *matter* as ongoing problems and concerns of the present. By this I mean strategies that test themselves against the magnitude of our present plights (which are always both symbolic and material): the proliferation of weapons of modern warfare, nationalist violence and genocide, the destruction of the environment, the erosion of basic social-welfare programs in North America, the growing concentration of power in the hands of a few transnational corporations, the increased impoverishment of a majority of the world's population.

These unremitting social and environmental traumas entreat us to *defer* the dubious accomplishment of wresting meaning from the deaths of hundreds of thousands of civilians in Hiroshima and Nagasaki, while exploring the depths and implications of these historical events in relation to ongoing inequities and abuses.

Our vision of mass trauma may never be complete, but the rays of memory we draw forth from existing testimony may lessen the obscurity surrounding these events. Witnessing, thus, may allow us to wrestle with the loss of certainty that disasters like Hiroshima-Nagasaki impose on our models of vision and visually derived knowledge. Taking up historical trauma as "our own," in this sense, need not imply a total absorption of historical meaning nor an appropriation of the experiences of that ordeal. The art of witness, rather, bids us to consider how a remembered image might gain new hold on our lives and actions. Memory work, beyond the ritual gesture of solemnity or nostalgia, involves such forays into social transformation.

This is memory work that invests significant faith in the propensity of sight to stir emotional and cognitive vibrations: "For every image of the past that is not recognized by the present as one of its concerns threatens to disappear irretrievably" (Benjamin 1968, 255). These are flickering images that may, in the words of Chris Marker, "quicken the heart," propelling us to touch the breaks and tears in history upon which these signs of trauma gingerly rest, so that once the body of trauma ceases to exist, the wound is not forgotten.

1

Atomic Visions

The slayers and the slain have memories equally long. That much seems clear fifty-odd years after the atomic bombings of Hiroshima and Nagasaki. Beyond a common passion of remembrance, however, very little appears to be shared. In fact, the bombings continue to be a major source of political contention. Despite a growing reserve of historical documentation, including formerly classified military information, there is meager consensus when it comes to deriving the meaning of these events. History devolves into a brawl of interpretation.

This was glaringly evident in commemorative exhibitions scheduled in Washington and Hiroshima to mark the fiftieth anniversaries of the atomic bombings of Hiroshima-Nagasaki. The Washington curators opted for an airborne perspective. Their objective was valedictory and artifacts were selected with this in mind. The polished fuselage of the Enola Gay was displayed as a trophy to honor the sacrifices of American veterans. The Hiroshima curators, by contrast, were soberingly earthbound in their focus. The photographs they selected were intended to speak to the wound: the civilian victims and human consequences of the bombings. Oceans apart, these exhibitions seemed irreconcilable. But there was an odd commonality between them, a link of method rather than message.

The ideal history is an empirical one, which reflects what is placed in front of it. The ideal history pushes toward certitude. It is ideal because it denies that there is anything visible beyond it: no edges, no resistance, no horizon. While thematically adverse, both exhibitions foregrounded this ideal. Viewers entering the Washington and Hiroshima museums—while traveling through two separate tunnels, following two unequal monologues—were engaged in parallel quests for naked truth.

It is somewhat ironic that projects which have variously sought to remember and forget the victims of Hiroshima and Nagasaki have shared a similar relationship to the visible. There is continuity to be found in their approach to pictorial language, the way they select images to keep a given history company, to demonstrate a thought. Images, in their mere presence, their mime of immediacy, provide proof positive that an argument is credible. They are systematically used to confirm and convince.

In the end, of course, the curators in Washington and Hiroshima remain mimetic rivals. Visual evidence continues to lend form to *both* protest *and* patriotism. Messages deriving from the visible—because tied to ideology—can lead to the inauguration *or* cessation of hostilities. *All things not being equal,* it is important that we maintain sight of how power and institutional relations persist in differentiating among narrations of the visual field—giving primacy to certain memorial visions and interpretations over others. But the tendency among enactors of collective memory to deny ambivalence, to turn away from the unknown and unwitnessed, also warrants consideration. From the point of view of the empiricist, a perspective that recognizes contradiction and uncertainty is ultimately unwelcome, but it is precisely what these events demand.

Thus, while exploring how collective memory has been swayed, even corrupted, through censured atomic-bomb imagery, this chapter queries tactics of protest which have no drive other than the exchange of images. To simply replace old images with new ones is a restrictive enterprise, presupposing, for starters, that images can speak for themselves. In the case of Hiroshima and Nagasaki, however, there has never been unanimity of meaning relating to the visual field. Even the most renowned pictures—the *Mushroom Cloud* being a prime example—have been stamped with contradictory and confusing messages.

Images of Hiroshima and Nagasaki, in other words, have never been transparently or unilinearly "received." Each picture has entered a historically and ideologically saturated field of visibility, only to be interpreted and reinterpreted against the grain of other images, which together constitute our perception of the past. These assorted pictures are further linked and mediated by narratives—narratives that, in the case of the atomic bombings, have doled out memories both triumphant and scorched. What is seen, what is deemed plausible as visual evidence, is clearly tied to what we know and have learned. Yet popular disputes about the accuracy of Hollywood depictions of history regularly remind us that facts and figures are open topics for debate. Directors of films ranging from *Mississippi Burning* to *Nixon* to *Evita* have stood accused of turning erstwhile villains into heroes, of painting glory out of human anguish. Stephen Spielberg's *Schindler's List* has undergone every conceivable analysis for its representation of events surrounding the Holocaust of European Jewry.

It only takes an afternoon on the Internet to realize that discussion groups abound on the very question of how popular culture relays—or, for that matter, distorts—history. These discussions, while sharing fairly predictable terms, reveal in concrete ways that questions of plausibility and truth are ongoing arenas of social combat and power, such that one community's selection of very-important-and-evocative visual evidence may be dismissed by another community as propaganda, trivia, or sentimentalism. That historical interpretation is always a matter of judgment and value does not lessen its impact. In its insights and blindnesses, interpretation is social comment. It reverberates on the lives of the living.

Thus, it becomes important to test the limits of our historical frames: What counts as plausible visual evidence and knowledge? By dint of what assignations, and under what circumstances, does "seeing become believing"? Or, for that matter, "believing become seeing"? The historical frames that shape our encounters with visual culture (whether scrolled on the big screen or mounted on museum walls) imply that there are no "simple" relations of seeing. There is nothing direct or untrammeled about the act of perception.

The task, then, is not one of replacing one visual history with another more truthful one—but of reflecting on the possible uses of visual material in organizing memory practices. Thus, I have provided in the pages that follow an initial exploration of some of the central images and visual metaphors that have coaxed and, in some cases, framed memories of the atomic bombings. At the same time, I have looked to the historical and political conditions of invisibility that have established a unique emphasis on evidence in relation to Hiroshima and Nagasaki.

The Voided Imagination

In the cinematic adaptation of Matsuji Ibuse's *Black Rain* (directed by Shohei Imamura), the theme of a vanished city recurs. Protagonists wander through the desolate ruins, their words echoing loss amid their motionless surroundings: "It blinded me, I could see nothing" . . . "I hear Hiroshima vanished" . . . "Where is Hiroshima? It disappeared."

Hiroshima and Nagasaki represent the sudden "voiding" of human life and its remains. The atomic bombs threatened to devour the visible world in its entirety. To be sure: 13,983 people were missing without trace after the first blast. This is not a toll of the dead, these are humans who *literally* disappeared from the field of vision: "Were they murdered, vaporized, or transformed into shadows, mushroom cloud, or black rain? Were they high school students, children, mothers, or grandfathers, reduced to memory, to physical and emotional voids? Are they now only numbers, transformed into disembodied specters for reasons of state?" (Gerson 1995, 27)

Positivist approaches to representation have been generated on the site of this unfathomable and incalculable loss. They accord with the experience of annihilation. They address a world swallowed up by a single explosion. Their message is potent. If the traces were rendered *unclear*, if American censorship codes *concealed* the human consequences, if the effects of radiation and the deadly atomic-bomb disease had the power to destroy people *invisibly*, if the city was rebuilt before the devastation could be properly documented, then the task is to reconstruct as *total* a picture as possible—a picture extracted from the lingering traces of disaster. Such pictures may act as talisman against the dissolution of memory.

Nothing summarizes this longing for repletion, this desire to compose a pictorial chronicle, more eloquently than an image evoked by Lisa Yoneyama in her essay "Taming the Memoryscape: Hiroshima's Urban Renewal." Yoneyama reminds us that as a result of Hiroshima's fierce and literally blinding flash, many people partially or totally lost their eyesight. She describes a national railway worker, a *hibakusha* (atomic-bomb survivor), who was nineteen when he lost his left eye in the bombing:

> In the ten years since his retirement, this man has been searching on his own for what he calls "the atom bomb claw marks" (*tsumeato*), that is, the relics of the bomb, and compiling their photographs and his detailed handwritten explanations into a booklet. He takes with him almost everywhere a hefty high-tech camera, splendidly equipped with automatic focus and zoom and wide-angle lenses. . . . It is as if, through his tenacious search for the "clawmarks," he is reconfirming his own life, the fact that he had survived, although with irreparable impairment: the camera substitutes for his lost eye. He criticized the city's attitude: "I feel as though I must continue to take pictures of the ruins so that I can help protect the human rights of the dead" (*shinsha no jinken yumon o mamoranya*). (1995, 121)

The precision with which the man goes about mechanically recording a lost world is existential. It is also political. In honoring the dead, he wants to call forth the legacy of nuclear violence. Every picture, he

FIGURE 1.1. *August 10, 1945, Nagasaki.* Photo by Yosuke Yamahata. Photo
courtesy of Shogo Yamahata.

feels, takes on added dimension as these events recede from immediate public concern. Their historical load grows heavier as time and interest passes.

If the memory of things is to deter, where is that memory? Testimony beseeching us to remember Hiroshima and Nagasaki assume a renewed sense of urgency in a world in which eleven countries now have the capacity to threaten nuclear war (Gerson, xvi).[1] Proposing that many North Americans have been beguiled into apathy by relative social calm, nuclear critics from Robert Jay Lifton to Jacques Derrida have advised us not to forget that we continue to live in an atomic age: an age where policy and possibility remain governed by the specter of global annihilation. The tens of thousands of nuclear warheads existing in our global arsenal, they argue, continue to wreak havoc on our notions of peace and order. Even as these missiles remain "safely" esconced in their silos, the mere mention of the Bomb has the power to secure consent and compliance.

The Bomb, without even being used, has, in fact, shaped the terms of virtually every major conflict since 1945. Its presence as a means of absolute destruction has shaped tolerance and acceptance of other forms of warfare—whether it be the use of napalm in Vietnam or carpet-bombing in Iraq. The language of "conventional" weapons as applied to non-nuclear arsenal has made them sound comparatively benign, tame, ordinary.

Military rhetoric continues to pose obstacles to witnessing. From the "precision" bombings of 1945 to the "smart" bombings of 1991, war propaganda has tended to obscure the consequences of civilian death. Suffering has been trivialized through euphemistic battle talk. In the case of the Gulf War, the North American public was left with little incentive to imagine the massive human fallout of "limited-strikes," the messy "collateral damage" left in the wake of this *clean* and *precise* war.

With war trauma persistently submitted to various forms of rhetorical damage-control, the temptation to wholly abandon the field of witnessing cannot be underestimated. How can we maintain sight of the human effects of modern warfare amid the lull of military techno-speak and against the rapid commerce of time? Or more specifically: To what extent can memories of Hiroshima and Nagasaki endure?

The concern that memory of the atomic bombings has been evicerated from public conscience has motivated memorial campaigns venturing to draw increased attention to the clawmarks of war. In March 1977, most notably, a project was initiated to bring Hiroshima and Nagasaki into the imagination of North Americans, to call forth the human consequences of nuclear warfare. This project, culminating in a 350-page book entitled *Hiroshima-Nagasaki: A Pictorial Record of the Atomic Destruction* (1978), was culled from the voluntary labor of thousands of Japanese citizens. In direct response to the legislated suppression of visual records of the bomb by U.S. officials, and increasingly virulent cold-war sloganeering, these volunteers sifted through over four thousand photos by both Japanese and American photographers. The selected photos have been assembled alongside a selection of survivors' paintings (Brett 1986, 120). The book, conceived as a commemorative gift, has since been distributed free of charge. In late 1978, members of the committee that produced the book formed a delegation to take it to the UN General Assembly on the occasion of the First Special Session for Disarmament (Brett 1986, 123). One delegate remarked on the dearth of knowledge of Hiroshima and Nagasaki among the Americans they met with:

> Only a limited number of Americans who were the leaders of the peace movement and their followers had seen a few photographs of the atomic destruction. Two-thirds of the people whom I met at the exhibitions of the panelled photographs held on street corners did not know about the historical evidence of *Hiroshima-Nagasaki*. Namely, they knew nothing about the fact that the government of their own country dropped atomic bombs on Hiroshima and Nagasaki. As a result, I felt keenly the necessity to show them the visual records of the atomic disaster. (Brett 1986, 123)

More recently, photographs of Nagasaki taken by Yosuke Yamahata on August 10, 1945, have been curated into a touring exhibition for international viewers. Yamahata's photos—which include the famous image of a Nagasaki child holding a rice ball—provide the centerpiece for *Nagasaki Journey*, a book published on the fiftieth anniversary of the bombings (Pomegranate Artbooks). The book shows acres and acres of burnt-out landscape, torched buildings, bodies charred beyond recognition. In several photos, the bodies appear lost—buried amid wood beams and mounds of debris, flesh camouflaged by black and white emulsion. Looking at these pictures, the viewer is left to deduce a sense of violence from the stimulus of neutral tones.

Both these book projects communicate how in war, civilians become invisible. They have sought to enlarge the scope of our historical vision by returning the spotlight to the dead and maimed. They are pictorial-based interventions waged against all the weapons and words that contract our understanding of the *embodied* effects of nuclear war.

Instrumental Visions

In 1945 there was some debate about how the atomic bomb should be used. A few scientists held out for a demonstration shot at night over the water rather than the annihilation of a city full of people. But offshore fireworks would have left almost everything to the imagination. War planners knew that this new weapon's devastating power had to be *seen to be believed*. Such was the opening premise of the atomic age, and it was acted on with conviction.

But something curious happened to the new bomb's fresh visibility: it quickly vanished behind a succession of phrases about "breakthroughs in physics," "saving American lives," and "ending the war." (*my emphasis*)[2]

Pictures of war tend to be belated in their arrival—destined, as they are, to record rather than halt the dropping of bombs and the hurtling of missiles. Some pictures, however, come later than others. It was a week before official photographs of the bombings were released to the North American press. The first image to appear before the American public, in *Life Magazine* (August 20, 1945), was a military photograph taken from a cockpit thousands of feet above Hiroshima. This bird's-eye view excluded even the city below, focusing instead on the spectacle of a mushroom cloud, its expanding mass of smoke distorting a still sky. The still-frame image, which would later become a powerful symbol in Cold War power brokering, was undeniably memorable. Its visual power was heightened because it was so immediately distinctive. Yet with no sign of human presence, the mushroom-cloud image seemed to support a technocratic vision. What eye but that of a machine, a camera, could safely gaze upon this calamitous spectacle with such calm tranquility? (Nelson 1987, 32) Detached from flesh and context, the mushroom cloud could be seen by some as the culmination of scientific progress, even worthy of adorning a proposed U.S. commemorative stamp.[3]

The mushroom cloud is, for many critics, a monstrous example of the kind of mind-image that remains lodged at an insulated abstract distance. Photographer and writer Robert Del Tredici, addressing the scarcity of images of nuclear war, has noted: "the only thing that comes to anybody's mind as an image is a mushroom cloud, a little pointy weapon and a cooling tower. That's about the extent of the imagery."⁴ The cloud's iconographic hold, its ability to obscure other views, is seen as a sign and symptom of human absence. The cloud, Del Tredici argues, has vaporized memory of its human target. If only the cloud could be thinned, scattered, we would be able to see the wreckage beyond.

Visual materials censored by the U.S. government, and concealed in large part from the viewing public until 1980, become the necessary precondition for splitting the bomb's representations into two zones of visibility. The one gaze beclouded of any human trace, the other gaze concertedly turned to the irradiated body: the image of affliction and suffering.⁵

This splitting of vision is dramatized in "Ground Zero" (1995), a prototypical documentary made for the Canadian Broadcasting Corporation, which features "the men who dropped the bomb and the people who were under it."⁶ Statements made by Charles Sweeney, a crew member aboard the infamous *Enola Gay*, narrate an eclipse of vision. His voice-over is accompanied by a visual aerial map of the city he describes:

> We could see the city just lying there like it looked in the pictures. A beautiful military target. We picked as close to the geographical center of the population area as we could. And there was a temple right by the bridge, so the temple crossing the bridge in the water gave us a good aiming target. It was a T-bridge in the form of a T itself. And I saw the bomb leave his airplane. I did say to myself, 'Gee, there it goes. It's a live one. It's the first live one I've ever seen. And there aren't any strings on it. We can't pull it back. It's for better or for worse, it's gone . . .'

The documentary subsequently cuts to ground zero. Here, the narrator tells us of a Japanese man who remembers watching the *Enola Gay* as it passed overhead, wondering if it would drop anything. Another *hibakusha* recounts his impressions of the aftermath: "We were in total darkness, we could not see anything." The screen rolls with footage taken at a distance of thirty thousand feet, presumably from the cockpit of the *Enola Gay*. We return to Sweeney's point of view : "Nothing we could see but smoke. A burbling cloud." The final cut in this visual interchange is to a series of photographs. We are told that these were the first photos taken in the aftermath of the Hiroshima bombing. Civilians walk with flesh dripping. Charred human remains and debris litter a desolate horizon. Yet despite the array of disturbing images that flicker across the screen, this documentary, and others like it, maintain that pictures of atomic warfare can only be viewed in *retrospect*, that is, with the hindsight of today. We now have proximate access to ground zero, but, for the bomber pilots involved in the aerial attacks on Hiroshima and Nagasaki, the human ramifications were elusive. From the vantage point of a cockpit, the target was simply too abstract; the explosion too spellbinding.

The message is simple, if deceptively so. Broaching the human consequences of nuclear warfare requires breaking from spectacle: the framing of a city as a "dot" on a bombing map. The horror needs to be brought into sharper focus. To see the aerial maps alone adheres to a perspective that allowed civilians to be dehumanized under the monolithic sign of an "enemy target"—a target fixed within boundaries dividing an *us* from a *them*. That the gulf between the bombers and the bombed had racist, if not genocidal, overtones was made manifest in a statement President Truman recorded a mere two days after civilians perished in Nagasaki: "When you have to deal with a beast, you have to treat him as a beast" (Gerson 1995, 38). Canadian Prime Minister Mackenzie King's official declaration was consonant with Truman's: "It is fortunate that the use of the bomb should have been upon the Japanese rather than upon the white races of Europe."[7]

Blurry reconnaissance photos of Hiroshima, which sketched a damage-radius bereft of bodies, fortified President Truman's initial insistence that the target was military in nature, serving to emotionally and cognitively distance North American viewers from the immediate aftermath of the atomic bombings. The illusion of complete aerial surveillance, while producing allegedly objective and informed spectators, made witnessing virtually impossible. As Joyce Nelson has remarked, the near-total elimination of "the bombings' effect on human beings—a complete exclusion of the irradiated human body from public view—shifted North American attention away from lasting corporeal destruction to what Truman, in his press statement of August 7, 1945, called 'the greatest achievement of organized science in history'" (Nelson 1987, 31). Through a feat of rhetorical alchemy Truman seemed to successfully turn swords into ploughshares. Leaders and generals since Truman have prudently followed his lead, proving that showing nothing or very little of war's human remains can be effective military strategy.[8]

Yet while the Truman administration worked hard to curtail information *after* the bombings, the collapse of witnessing around

Hiroshima and Nagasaki was actually ensured from the beginning—long before the crew of the *Enola Gay* departed for Japan. The thrust toward atomizing knowledge has, in essence, been paradigmatic in the creation of the Nuclear New World since the early days of the Manhattan Project. The inability of workers, whose labor was highly compartmentalized, to imagine the end result (which in itself was an unimaginable horror), was enhanced by an instrumental vision of war and production. Scientists working on the Manhattan Project were isolated and sworn to silence in their research pursuits for reasons of national security. The idea that knowledge was "forbidden" was further enforced by the sudden and total ban in 1940 on any publications about nuclear fission (Ruthven 1993, 7).[9] This history of open suppression deferred the possibility of acquiring testimonies from the inside for many years.

For the majority of us who come to these events as belated witnesses, procuring historical knowledge is crucial. Knowledge is necessary if we are to counteract the mythic characterizations of these events, penetrate techno-babble designed to keep basic information in the hands of elite strategists and researchers. It is vital if we are to see the relationship between various fragmented and dispersed visions—the connections between views from ground zero and from above (from inside and outside of the event). The censorship period, which we will come to shortly, enforced a separation between these visions. We need to find ways of setting them in a moving dialogue.

Nonetheless, the struggle to make relational sense of these events, the desire to gain knowledge, may not be adequately active, ethical acts of seeing. To simply "picture" and "know" the human effects of the bombings has carried no assurance of ethical remembrance. The legacy of the U.S. Atomic Bomb Casualty Commission (ABCC) draws this point back into focus. The commission, which sought to chronicle the effects of radiation fallout on the bodies of the *hibakusha*, turned survivors into objects of research rather than treatment and responsibility. Bodies were taken out of the debris of history—tagged, charted, and coded—and recirculated as silent documents. To add insult to injury, the collected evidence and photographs concerning the irradiated bombing victims was not declassified for several decades.[10] When we look at the ABCC photos today, we can see that they were designed solely for clinical interests. The *hibakusha* who posed for them seem thoroughly uncomfortable, conscious of the fact that they were chosen as specimens.

The history of the ABCC research mission raises the issue of an inherent bias toward objectification in vision itself, which too easily appropriates bodies from their social and historical biographies. The question, thus, becomes: what images can activate a social-biographic imagination on the part of the viewer? Clearly, naturalism and portraiture are insufficient. The ABCC photos perhaps provided a representational form for calibrating the physical suffering of human beings against the generalizing technologies of science. Yet at no point did the use of descriptive naturalism by the ABCC have anything to say of the victims' substantive and historical experiences. The photos did not address the specific historical character of their disfigurement—working instead to freeze understanding of the still-unfolding dimensions of *hibakusha* suffering. Through this aperture, suffering was depicted as *atomic*, that is, discrete and manageable. Researchers were not there to empathize with or support the victims. They were there to sift the evidence, to measure the past in inches and yards.

The purpose of shifting our ways of looking at visual culture would be to provide grounds for challenging the objectification of experience—whether it be undertaken in the name of science or research. Sorting through what is missing, what cannot be envisioned, by a representational practice reveals how images are constructed and invested in historical perspective. Our ways of imagining the past are riddled with inscriptions of power. How might we identify the political agencies and commitments made possible through representational practices? This is a question of preeminent importance to witnessing.

In reclaiming vision as a source of situated knowledge and as a basis for ethical action, the task becomes one of marking the commitments we bring to bear on visual practices. In short, reflecting on the ways we are ethically implicated in our looking would require rejecting a standpoint of transcendent access that seeks to overcome all limits and responsibility. Heeding the call to witness requires that I answer for passivity, that I respond to practices that deny the possibility of being responsible (or capable of response). Representational practices that indulge in a pornography of violence preempt possibilities of envisioning a less oppressive world that rejects the use of subjugation and aggression. What is, thus, called for is a partial vision that understands its contingency, while seeking to understand the social practices and objectifying tendencies that not only facilitated the mass obliteration of civilians under the sign of "enemy target," but made this process inevitable. Because the concept of vision has been so central in securing knowledge about the bombings, it must be heavily scrutinized *and* used.

The Censored Eye

The world will note that the first atomic bomb was dropped on
Hiroshima, a military base. That was because we wished in this first
attack to avoid, insofar as possible, the killing of civilians.

—President Harry Truman

The power to see, the power to make visible, is the power to control.

—David Michael Levin

In September 1945 Japan's major newsreel company, Nichiei Pro-
ductions, sent a documentary film crew to Hiroshima. Ordered by
American authorities to stop shooting in Nagasaki, they prepared for
confrontation as they arrived in Hiroshima. They were finally granted
permission by occupying authorities to complete a nineteen-reel film
entitled *Effects of the Atomic Bomb* with the proviso that upon completion it would be turned over in its entirety to the American Occupation
Forces. The crew complied, but only after several members had
secretly made a duplicate print of more than half of the original film.
This footage was carefully stored in a photographic lab in the suburbs
of Tokyo (Lifton 1967, 453; Braw 1991, 4–5). It was not until July 1952,
shortly after the U.S. Occupation had ended, that the hidden footage
was retrieved and portions of the documentary were screened "with
great excitement" in movie houses across Japan (Lifton 1967, 454). The
footage featured extensive shots of radiation and burn victims. One
section showed the silhouette of a painter on a ladder, with arm and
brush extended: a man etched permanently by the blast onto the surface of a concrete wall (Lifton and Mitchell 1995, 58). For most Japanese civilians, this was their first opportunity to become visually and
affectively immersed in the terrors of the atomic bomb experience.[11]

With scarce exception, representations of the bombings were
guarded from the public imagination for a decade, and several
decades in the case of classified government documents.[12] Between
September 1945 and September 1951, all interpretive responses to the
bombings fell within the jurisdiction of a Press Code. The Code, introduced by American Occupation authorities, imposed *prior censorship*
on anything written for broadcast or publication. The motivations
behind the Press Code are sobering: the U.S. government did not want
any evidence of the bombings to circulate. Suppression of evidence
became the surest means of quelling dissent and garnering support for
any further use of the atomic bombs in the emerging Cold War era, in

which the Soviet Union would also obtain the Bomb.

Atomic-bomb historian Paul Boyer has focused on the censorship period as a pivotal moment in the scripting of atomic-bomb history for the American public: "From the beginning, the entire Hiroshima/Nagasaki story was carefully stage-managed by the American military. The first accounts, written by William L. Laurence, who was in effect functioning as the Manhattan Project's public-relations man, simply recorded the visual observations of the bomb crews" (1985, 187).

What has qualified as visual "evidence," as Boyer notes, has been circumscribed. The U.S. government worked concertedly to organize the visual field surrounding the atomic bombings. We might say that there are many visions of Hiroshima and Nagasaki, but what if there is only one enforced vision? Does this not limit historical interpretation? Reviewing this legacy of censorship and suppression brings us closer to understanding how the war was prosecuted through a discourse of "popular" consent, how it was representationally restricted, and why, fifty years later, battles over the visual record persist.

Press censorship in post-war Japan applied to every facet of cultural production. Films, novels, children's books, musical recordings were all subject to careful scrutiny. So thorough were the censoring officials that anything thought to engender a threat to "public tranquility," anything that implied the bombings were a "crime against humanity," was eligible.[13] Writers were prohibited from even mentioning the censorship codes, leading one poet to comment, "we were not allowed to write about the atomic bomb during the Occupation. We were not even allowed to say that we were not allowed to write about the atomic bomb" (Braw 1991, 7). On more than one occasion, the publication ban was used as a basis for harassing and threatening artists into compliance. Well-known novelist and *hibakusha* Yoko Ota was interrogated by American officials about her novel-manuscript, *The Town of Corpses*, and *tanka* poet Shione Shoda was warned that if she defied the Code, and published her *tanka* collection, she would be sentenced to the death penalty.[14]

American and international journalists were also subject to interrogation. Among the first Americans to visit Nagasaki after the war was a documentary film crew. They recorded rare color images, which the U.S. military ordered locked away for thirty years. Their chief concern was that the film footage would rouse too much public opposition to the use of nuclear weapons. Wilfred Burchett, a noted left-wing journalist working for the *London Daily Press* and the first foreign journal-

ist to reach Hiroshima, faced a similar response when he attempted to
file a report from "ground zero." His efforts to draw international
attention to the plight of civilians who were dying of radiation effects
brought him into direct confrontation with the censors, who claimed
he had fallen victim to Japanese propaganda. After his visit, Allied
journalists were barred entry to Hiroshima for several years.[15] The journalists that arrived subsequently were members of *official* American
delegations.

    Postwar censorship codes operated to mute the voices of atomic
victims and conceal rudimentary information about the effects of
nuclear warfare and radiation. The consequences were manifold,
impairing treatment of the victims and distorting the postwar global
nuclear debate. As Monica Braw notes, "A full picture is difficult to
form of anything, but regarding the atomic bomb, there was one
aspect concerning which a reasonably accurate picture could have
been made but was not, because of American censorship. This was the
after-effects of the atomic bombings of Hiroshima and Nagasaki"
(1991, 155).

    The censorship period inflated the demand for narratives of the
bombings' effects. A history of prohibition added to the perception
that in retrieving representations from government and military store-
houses, the truth about history might be made accessible. The images
and texts that did reach audiences became replete with meaning, sad-
dled with the task of testifying to all that had been endured. But, here,
the idea that history (and consciousness) could be directly accessed
once the proper resources were found, and once writers and artists
were granted reprieve from censorship, assumed that these found and
liberated testimonies would generate self-evident meanings. What
could not be anticipated was how context and contingency would
influence encounters with these new narratives. In particular, whether
the new narratives would be, or not be, taken up so as to enable transformations in collective thought and action.

    While unfolding on the other side of the Pacific, the history of
John Hersey's article "Hiroshima" (1946) is revealing. Published in *The
New Yorker* one full year after the bombings, Hersey's chronicle from
ground zero crowded American newsstands with the stories of six
Hiroshiman civilians living through the bombing and its grim aftermath. "Hiroshima" employed a popular genre of human-interest jour-
nalism which relied heavily on naturalist description and individual
profiles. Numbers were replaced by names in an account that
attempted to individuate the effects of a decision made with a lump-
target in mind. This was a move toward countering a vast array of

allied war propaganda which portrayed the enemy as wholly inhuman. The most egregious examples of stereotyping were to be found in American pop culture. North American newspapers regularly featured bespectacled kamikaze-types and maniacal buck-toothed Japanese civilians who were portrayed as bearing a vicious disregard for human life. Under these circumstances, "Hiroshima" must be understood intially as an oppositional text. Released at a time when over three-quarters of the American population polled still approved of the bombings, it served to counter the reigning popular opinion. At the time Hersey first wrote, there was nothing banal about testimonies from ground zero. The survivors' experiences were emerging, quite literally, from the shadows.

Yet while initially breaking with dominant framings of the bombings, "Hiroshima" quickly became a "runaway bestseller" (Boyer 1985, 204). Controversy waned and "Hiroshima" soon settled comfortably among the folds of old knowledge and sentiment to become what Paul Boyer has called a "cathartic end-point" for many Americans (1985, 209). In providing an opportunity to vent emotion, in focusing on human anguish rather than on the political relations which had produced such suffering, Hersey's text "could be depoliticised at the very moment when—in a move subsequently characteristic of Cold War literary politics—it was being lauded for its humanity and aestheticised for its style" (Ruthven 1993, 39). "Hiroshima," thus, succeeded more in arousing the conditions necessary for a reaffirmation of American moral conscience and humanist sympathy than in inciting readers to critically question the political and ethical legitimacy of the Bomb's deployment and nuclearism more generally.[16] A public's will to know about the past conformed to what appeased its sense of identity at the time—an identity founded on grounds defined as democratic, just, and moral. "Hiroshima" entered the scene as an upstart testimony, but eventually a truce was worked out.

Acknowledging that testimonial forms may be transgressive at the moment of their introduction, the history of John Hersey's "Hiroshima" begs the question of how testimony can be made to endure in such ways as to prompt ongoing reflection. What possibilities do texts of public memory open up? What do they close off?

Scripting Events

Representational practices are critical in shaping and shifting our notions of what is worth perceiving. They produce a grammar for looking. In many instances they also produce the material basis for knowledge claims, thus determining precepts for social action and response.

The films, exhibitions, books, and monuments that largely mediate public consciousness of historical events have tended to adhere to realist conventions; they chase, you might say, a faith in objective representation. Yet as the 1995 Smithsonian Institute controversy indicated, no representational practice can ever be completely or positively realist. Here, an anniversary exhibition intended to commemorate the "Last Act: the Atomic Bomb and the End of World War II" was eventually abandoned after a Veteran's group successfully lobbied for the removal of ground zero artifacts and references. The controversy, which revealed an ongoing reluctance among certain Americans to confront human *evidence* of the bombings, flagged the limits of positivist commemoration: What are the details that count? What and why are people being asked to remember? The Smithsonian controversy, pivoting around issues of historic representation, raised compelling questions about the role visual culture plays in the formation of collective memory. How the atomic bombings of Hiroshima and Nagasaki would be remembered, and on what evidentiary terms, were the central issues up for debate.

The curators' original proposal was to "address the significance, necessity and morality of the atomic bombings of Hiroshima and Nagasaki."[17] Curators from the Smithsonian requested to borrow objects from the Hiroshima Peace Museum to provide a view from ground zero. Among the selected items were a boy's tricycle, a watch fixed at 8:15 AM, and a girl's incinerated lunchbox still containing carbonized food. The inclusion of these artifacts, photographs of bomb victims, and a text-piece that questioned the estimated number of American lives that were saved by the bomb, formed the center of the ensuing controversy. Conservative critics charged the Smithsonian curators with spin-doctoring history to secure a seamless portrait of Japanese victimization. In short, they stood accused of exploiting tendentious sympathies that were more attuned to "political correctness" than historical truth.

After intense pressure from veterans groups and several members of Congress, the exhibition was rescripted to emphasize Japanese expansionism and war atrocities. Any mention of the effects of the bombs on civilians, any reference connecting the bombings to postwar nuclear proliferation, was removed. Paul Tibbets Jr., former captain of the B-29 bomber that dropped the bomb on Hiroshima, was part of a veterans group protesting the initial exhibition proposal. In September 1994, the lobby had succeeded in getting the U.S. Senate to adopt a resolution stating that the "atomic bomb put a merciful end to the war."[18]

Prior to the last script-cut, six pictures of people injured by the bombings and one photo of a person killed were retained. When lobbying pressure continued unabated, even these images were cut. The final proposal essentially excluded any interpretive commentary. The exhibition was winnowed down to the *Enola Gay* fuselage, a plaque, and a video tape of the pilots recalling their flight. Republican House Speaker Newt Gingrich (a former history professor) proclaimed the final exhibition script to be a victory against "historical revisionism," and applauded the Smithsonian for recognizing that "the vast majority of Americans think that political correctness may be okay in some faculty lounge, but that the Smithsonian is a treasure that belongs to the American people and it should not become a plaything for left-wing ideologies."[19]

The decision to remove all discussion and analysis of the historical context of the bombings (on the basis that such analysis would be transgressive of a privileged commemorative narrative of the bombings), was met with criticism by several prominent U.S. historians, editors, and journalists. In response, Michael Heyman, Secretary of the Smithsonian, issued a public statement defending the institute's position:

> I have concluded that we made a basic error in attempting to couple an historical treatment of the use of atomic weapons with the 50th anniversary commemoration of the end of the war. In this important anniversary year, veterans and their families were expecting, and rightly so, that the nation would honour and commemorate their valour and sacrifice. They were not looking for analysis, and, frankly, we did not give enough thought to the intense feelings such an analysis would evoke.[20]

The controversy exposed how fraught publicly financed civic commemorations can become when they question patriotic assumptions about historical events. More importantly, it provided a critique of naive positivism. (An evidentiary display was devouring itself. How could it claim to represent the whole when parts were rapidly disappearing?)

The Smithsonian controversy showed that what is accepted as knowledge and evidence is constrained by the context of its presentation. Using an openly honorific discourse (valorizing U.S. veterans), the institute was able to name the character of those constraints, and thus, in turn, characterize what would be deemed as transgressive.

The Smithsonian curators, having been accused of impugning veterans, met to negotiate with the American Legion, then settled on a script that rubber-stamped a victory narrative of Hiroshima. The revised script, in other words, chiefly supported the idea that the use of atomic bombs on Japan had justly avoided a bloody invasion of the mainland and, in so doing, had saved a million American lives. This script, which spoke of the Bomb exclusively as a preserver rather than a destroyer of human life, mastered the tricky task of uniting the incompatible: a grisly military massacre with American ideals of decency and concern for life.

The remarkable fact is that carefully prepared press releases, penned two months *prior* to the actual bombings, have retained primacy in the recording of atomic-bomb history. This earlier history, conceived *before* the death of hundreds of thousands of civilians, could not of course register the *aftershock* of the bombs, the effects of radiation and the human fallout of nuclear weapons (then, at least, theoretically known). In stressing American humanity and achievement, it was a history that profoundly de-emphasized suffering.

Reporter William Laurence, recruited by the Truman administration and ranked among the more worshipful of bomb-witnesses, went so far as to embrace nuclearism as the ultimate symbol of human freedom. Describing the 1945 Trinity test explosion in New Mexico, he exclaimed increduously: "The mountain that grows above the clouds took the form for a fleeting instant of a gigantic Statue of Liberty, its arm raised to the sky, symbolizing the birth of a new freedom for man" (quoted in Lifton and Mitchell 1995, 16).[21] By invoking such hyperbolic terms as "destiny" and "divine justice," early reports of the Bomb were able to boast patriotic American feelings, while suppressing concern for the victims of the bombings. Truman's administration was well equipped to manage postatomic response: clichéd rationales were prepared to cascade over the American public even before the Enola Gay had left its hangar.

The battles over the Smithsonian script changes, which carried over to the editorial pages of major U.S. dailies, accented tensions that continue to shape memory-production about the bombings. More specifically, they showed that any effort to introduce a death-centered perspective was still apt to encounter obstinate opposition from conservative American lobbyists, politicians, and historians.

The tendency to whitewash atomic-bomb casualties (in prominent U.S. quarters) is dramatically—if expediently—challenged in Japan where Hiroshima and Nagasaki have been vaunted as symbols of Japanese suffering in the Pacific War. The contrast between American narratives of national triumph and the Japanese focus on national martyrdom is sharp and unremitting. Atomic bomb narratives continue to draw on two absolute (or "patriotically correct") themes: victory or victimization.

In Japan, the exclusive focus on Japanese suffering has only recently been called into question. The 1994 renovations at the Hiroshima Peace Memorial Museum marked a nascent, albeit overdue, commitment to challenge narratives that have neatly demarcated World War II victims and aggressors. In the new installation Japanese *hibakusha* and non-*hibakusha* are provocatively situated in relation to the tens of thousands of Korean laborers who died in the blast and suffered in its aftermath under conditions of systematic neglect. The renovated exhibition indicates that the place that has largely become known as a "City of Peace" had possessed, for many centuries, an unusually strong military identity. Originally the center of a feudal fiefdom, Hiroshima was known until the late nineteenth century as a castle town. The city was rapidly modernized during the Meiji Restoration, and by the outbreak of the Sino-Japanese War in 1894 it served as the main military base for invasions on the Asian mainland. It maintained this function until the early phases of World War II. For some, most notably President Truman, this history of Japanese aggression would serve as fertile ground upon which to elaborate claims of "retribution."[22] In the context of the Peace Museum, however, the renovated perspective reflects an important modulation of ground zero history. The Smithsonian controversy and the renovations at the Hiroshima Peace Memorial Museum lay bare ongoing contests over the meaning of the atomic bombings. These events have provided pedagogical openings by unraveling the seams of history. Through public battles waged in relation to the historical record, many people have been invited to become more conscious of the omissions that structure received evidence and information.

Categories of factual and neutral representation are not self-evident or natural criteria, but ways of buttressing a particular narrative, one that may come to assume the impossible and singular vantage point of objectivity. This is the essential dilemma facing all history writing. The facts we wish to verify are often bordered by those we may wish to obstruct. In the context of the Smithsonian, and, it can also be argued, in the context of the Peace Memorial Museum, notions of historical objectivity have been selectively deployed in such manner as to subordinate the memories of *others*.

While narrative closure cannot be assumed, given that a viewer's interpretive stance may open new meanings even in relation to the most ideologically hermetic texts, important questions remain about how dominant histories and institutional practices function to limit the range of possible meanings. What versions of the past are being made possible? What meanings and memories are vying to be heard?

Atomic Limits

The photographs that have circulated in relation to the atomic bombings have, in some respects, made these events more accessible. After the censorship codes were lifted, ground-zero images reached a considerable number of people who were unaware of the civilian casualties. But bringing the horrific human consequences of nuclear warfare before the public eye also promoted feelings of catharsis and resolution, bestowing a sense of closure and well-being on the part of some viewers.

Within a documentary frame, memory involves an appeal to the archives. Through catalogued traces of the past, we gain access to events and people now missing. But, as discussed in the example of *hibakusha* who were subjected to ABCC research examinations after the bombings, there can also be a forensic dimension to documentation. Looking at photographs of laboratory shelves lined with jars containing radiated body parts, for example, one wonders: Is this the kind of interaction that will facilitate ethical remembrance, a sense of living memory and responsibility?

The U.S.-sponsored Atomic Bomb Casualty Commission (ABCC) treated survivors in Hiroshima and Nagasaki as if they belonged to an anonymous species. The completion of a scientific record and census was seen to render all future commentary, intervention, and judgment superfluous. The documentary intention aspired to put every body, every artifact, in its proper place. And like other ordering systems since Linnaeus, this taxonomy of trauma constituted an act of power: invading the privacy of survivors, turning them into specimens for an inventory, whose purpose they had no role in defining. When human suffering becomes fodder for research, we have added cause to test the limits of evidential knowledge.

In the next chapter, I will expand this discussion of atomic limits by asking how norms of evidence may effectively diminish the myriad and nuanced ways that the traumas of Hiroshima and Nagasaki have been grappled with, and remembered, both by *hibakusha* and non-*hibakusha*. Even during times of intense suppression, many artists and writers practiced subterfuge by finding alternate ways of evoking their responses to the bombings. These works often escaped the purview of censorship officials precisely because they were less certain, less direct, and more allusive. These indirect challenges to blanket censorship need to be considered. We need to draw new criteria to encompass work that evokes the excesses of trauma memory, work that invades dominant frames of history with its own tellings.

Witness artists tell us that knowledge cannot be condemned to stasis. The flux and flow of memory contests the permanence accorded images of fleeting moments, taken only by the snap of a lens, from an airborne perspective.

Because There Were
and There Weren't
Cities Called Hiroshima and Nagasaki

After World War II, there was discussion about leaving Hiroshima's ruins untouched. Postwar development would be halted, and the city would stand as testimony to the terrifying proportions of nuclear violence. To have left the destruction intact might have cast Hiroshima as one of the most disturbing exhibits to modern warfare in the world. But these plans were quickly dismissed by a range of lobby groups. A variety of interests were linked to the ultimate decision to rebuild Hiroshima. Concerns about the shortage of space in highly populated Japan, and the importance of Hiroshima to commercial trade, were among the more pedestrian reasons. Other citizens of Hiroshima, including many *hibakusha*, felt that leaving the city scattered in ruins would render it impossible for people to overcome their painful memories and move toward healing and reintegration (Shono 1993, 267–68).

Fifty-odd years later, these debates seem remote. Today, Hiroshima is a postmodern metropolis, a major industrial and commercial center, home to one of Japan's most popular baseball teams, the 1994 sponsor of the Twelfth Asian Games, and the manufacturing center for Mitsubishi and Mazda Motor Corporations. In downtown Hiroshima, one can visit department stores, shopping malls, and office buildings. The normalcy is striking. One might be strolling in any First World city. The commerce of time has tracked *through*—and in some minds, *over*—the material ruins of the atomic bomb. More than half a century later, the only surviving atomic-bombed structure expressly marked for preservation is the *Genbaku* (Atomic) Dome. Formerly an Industrial Promotion Hall, the dome was designed by Czech architect Jan Letzel and built in 1915. The structure was one of Hiroshima's first modern buildings, and one of the few left standing at the epicenter after the explosion. Savaged by the fire which followed the bombing, it has been reduced to bare cage.

Naomi Shono, a *hibakusha* and physics scholar, laments the loss of concrete reminders of nuclear carnage. She connects memory to material preservation: "More and more victims of the bomb are leaving this earth, so that if the surviving structures disappear, there will be nothing left to remind future generations of the carnage of war and nuclear weapons. And what people cannot see, they eventually forget" (1993, 272).

Shono's comments reflect concerns that have been given added credence over time. With each passing year, the image memory relating to Hiroshima and Nagasaki seems to grow feebler; these events begin to merge into a background mutter of forgetfulness, a screen of clichés. Across the Pacific, an increasing number of North Americans have seen very little visual documentation of the bombings. When asked, many identify the mushroom cloud as the only image they can recall. For a book that relinquishes an emphasis on documentary image-matter, this lacunae in the collective image memory demands an ongoing sense of accountability.

The previous chapter was an attempt to challenge axioms pertaining to visual language, which, in positing that "seeing is believing," sever images from their viewing contexts, and consequently give primacy to pictures as conduits of evidentiary truth and knowledge. This positivist framing of visual culture, I suggest, has resulted in certain assumptions about the *kinds* of images that are seen to best work on collective memory. Residual notions of authenticity, in particular, have tended to foreground photo-based imagery.

In this regard, any foray into expressive visual culture must acknowledge the overwhelming power of photography as a primary testimonial form. Photography has been central to popular practices of commemoration in large part because photos are generally viewed as purer and less susceptible to bias than other sources of imagery. Regarded as the preeminent medium of fact and documentary reportage, photographs have been invested with central authority in the imaging of horror and the horrible.

In a text written to accompany battlefield images during the American Civil War, photographer Alexander Gardner assigned his own (sometimes posed, often stylized) photos the enormous task of informing a public and rousing it to refrain from future war: "Here are the dreadful details! Let them aid in preventing another such calamity falling upon the nation." Gardner's belief that photographs of horror could inspire public opposition has been widely shared. Over the course of the twentieth century we have been exposed to vivid depictions of death and violence. Decorum has been replaced by boldness as a means of compelling the attention of viewers increasingly familiar with images of suffering. The effect of such imagery, which may never be firmly established, concerns us less here than the overarching meanings attached to photography as a testimonial practice.

53

FIGURE P.1. Enlargements of original 35 mm negatives taken in Nagasaki on August 10, 1945. Photo by Yosuke Yamahata. Digital restoration: TX Unlimited, San Francisco. Copyright: Shogo Yamahata.

Photographs—seen to a lesser or greater extent as transhistorical images from the past—have advanced a genre of evidence-based commemoration; they condition certain expectations about the function of *all* visual forms of representation. Faced with positivist framings of the visual, art has been pressed under conditions of duress—warned against erasing the naturalism and technological facticity of photography itself.

While European painting since William Turner (1775–1851) has been governed by a suspicious attitude toward the idea of pure seeing, our concepts of photography have continued to endorse the cognitive claims of sight. Photographs, ostensibly, give us a prosaic, unembellished glimpse of the world around us. In this respect, photographic images, seen as the ultimate evidentiary form, serve as a point of reference to which art—and especially the art of witness—is necessarily in tension. In sorting through the prevailing images and dominant visual approaches associated with history—and the atomic bombings more specifically—we may gather some sense of what artists negotiate with and the struggles they face in testifying through art.

In discernible ways, distinctions between documentary and art, between truth and fiction, continue to condition our possible experiences of witness art. In the following chapter, I suggest that seeing the art of witness differently, beyond hit-and-run practices of looking or fact gathering, requires that we challenge the status of collective memory as an empirically transmissable, self-contained, and knowable object. By de-emphasizing the materiality of memory, we move away from visual approaches which conflate appearance with objectivity and essence, and turn our attention toward our own acts of looking. What we may witness in the changing historical face of art, its unique sensations, is a narrow pass: a straining between the seen and the unseen, a constant widening of what can be perceived and known.

And this work of witnessing, treading uneasily at the juncture between issues of representation and ethical responsibility, matters. All the more so, *Because there were and there weren't cities called Hiroshima and Nagasaki . . .*

2

Art from the Ashes

Life after 1945 for many *hibakusha* is perceived as an anomaly, a contradiction, a fluke. Creating when they should be silent, living when they should be dead, *hibakusha* artists and writers frequently express a sense of marvel *and* guilt. The specter of mass graves cheats survivors of any sense of triumph, and discloses their pain. Bound by duty to the dead, their art passes through durations of doubt and uncertainty, mounts to a pitch of horror. The questions they ask of themselves are definitive, if nothing short of impossible: How to represent the unprecedented? How not to? Thus, witness art, however explosive or anarchic its mode of expression, is always a plea for greater meaning.

The task of humanizing the consequences of the bombings befell artists and writers working amid the ruins of postatomic Japan. Waking from a technocratic nightmare, nothing seemed more pressing than to relocate vision on a plane connected to the positionings and possibilities of *human* observers. Nothing more urgent than to give form to the horror, place a finger to the pulse of shock.

Well into the early 1950s, Japan was still a country largely purloined of images and information. The U.S. censorship codes, discussed in some detail in the previous chapter, had led to a dispersal or deferral of artistic representations from ground zero. They had created a fast-fade effect. Witness art, spawned in a factual void, initially took on the role of dissemination. Survivors' testimonies and cultural works (poetry, novels, art, films, etc.) were used to lend material substance to otherwise undocumented consequences. Art, in this context, was seen as countermeasure: a way of peeling back the formerly impenetrable veils of techno-speak, press briefings, and codifications that had masked the bombs' effects, which included invisible radiation disease. Interviews with writers and artists who have worked thematically with the atomic bombings are filled with momentous comments about the responsibility they feel accrues to them, to provide "clear" and "honest" portrayals of the events. As word-smiths and image-makers, they are positioned, and position themselves, as renderers of trauma.

No matter how they had been accustomed to painting earlier, many artists adopted a realist style that might document the events as a camera would have done. Yet compiling observable proof that civilian suffering had indeed been massive was no small endeavor. Grief and pain had to be enumerated—and hence condensed—through objects and signs. Hewn and fragmented experiences had to be made visually coherent, irreparable and unreplenishable losses linked through hieroglyphs to the symbolic world.

Horror Beheld

The idea that the witness should not become more important than the testimony has been a recurrent theme in atomic-bomb representation. A stylistically extravagant painting is perceived to draw attention from the seen to the seer. Thus, many artists creating expressions from the ruins of nuclear violence have opted for documentary minimalism. Working under the mantle of evidence, they have sought to depict the events as convincingly as possible so that their experiences might be shared. Without doubt the desire to erase traces of the artist's subjective hand is sincere yet, paradoxically, the evidence of the work is often otherwise. In fact there can be very few works which have been so intensely felt or subjectively expressive as those made by survivors.

Tamiki Hara (1905–1951), a novelist who persisted against censorship restrictions and published several books, once described the forces and conditions that compelled him to write: "Amid the catastrophe of the atomic bombing, I was left alive. Since that time, both I and my writing have been violently dislocated by something. Even if I were to die, I still wanted to put down on paper all the graphic scenes I witnessed" (quoted in Treat 1988, 39). Hara's attention to graphic detail is evident in his short story, "Natsu no Hana"—a story which has been praised for its precise depiction of Hiroshima (Treat 1988, 40).[1] Sensitive to the excesses of trauma and the "dislocations" of language, Hara nonetheless persisted in his courageous struggle to render imaginable what had been systematically elided from public memory.

Hara's sense of ethical delegation dovetails with statements made by other *hibakusha* artists and writers. While many *hibakusha* continue to reveal doubts about the possibility of fully communicating what they have actually been through to anyone who has not themselves undergone the trauma, "convinced of its relevance to world problems, they return constantly to the principle of direct personal reconstruction of the event in a way that virtually puts others through it" (Lifton 1967, 302). Facts, they suggest, belong to the domain of necessity: a place where there is no drawing back before the blistering wound, the body becoming corpse.

The combined experiences of witnessing, survival, and death-guilt have, in essence, shaped tacit rules for representation. These rules have established a restricted frame for producing and interpreting witness art. Testifying before the grand tribunal of history frequently transforms the art of testimony into reportage, an enumeration of detail that lays bare the minutiae of an ordeal, in hopes that justice may be achieved. Voyaging into the truth comes to mean dispensing with "excess" considerations of form and style, and proceeding directly to the gateway of substance. These concise and directed efforts acquire an added sense of urgency when mortality haunts the artist witness. For example: Ota Yoko, author of the documentary-novel *City of Corpses*, described the feeling of struggling to finish her story as one of racing against the clock, while radiation sickness began to claim her own life (Treat 1988, 37).[2]

When art's efficacy is measured by its informational value, there are few options available to trauma artists and writers. At best, the sensuous and imaginative dimensions of art are considered accessory to content; at worst, they are seen to impede an objective view of the events. Thus, aspiring to remain faithful to the original subject matter, and true to the memory of the dead, creative artists tend to confine themselves to the memoir-novel, the documentary film, the realistic painting. As James Young writes in his book *The Texture of Memory*: "many survivors believe that the searing reality of their experiences demands as literal a memorial expression as possible" (1993, 9).

We hear, for example, that art may trivialize the experience of death and dying. Metaphor may dim or sweeten the nature of brutality. In short, the horrific nature of the event is seen to preclude imaginative response and demand testimonial realism. The risk that fiction or metaphor will diminish historical meaning has become a persistent theme. These concerns are not idiosyncratic, nor are they insignificant. In fact, they speak volumes about an issue that has been central to discussions of representation and trauma commemoration since Theodor Adorno wrote his notorious lines: "There can be no poetry after the Holocaust."

Adorno's words, penned in 1949, had ponderous resonances within the context of postwar Europe. At one level, Adorno was seen to propose that, however uncompromising and compassionate, there would always be something profane about turning mass suffering into art (Adorno 1985, 313). At another level, his remarks were taken as a cautionary note imploring thinkers to be wary of the fascist idealization of art, and the harnessing of beauty to reactionary politics.

Apprehensions about (the abomination of) creating "art from human ashes" thus converge with other equally important concerns, notably the role of culture in aestheticizing those politics which engage in subordination and murder. Adorno has not been alone in querying the blood-soaked connections between culture and genocide, between beauty and annihilation. Films such as *The Architecture of Doom*, and the installation work of Canadian artist Vera Frenkel, have also plumbed the duplicity of art in the context of fascist politics. Peter Cohen's *The Architecture of Doom*, for example, calls attention to aesthetic practices adopted by the Nazis, who used art and architecture to promote fascist ideals of purity and used codes of racially selective "beauty" to foster the patriotism of a nation singularly focused on exterminating its "degenerate" and "impure" others.

Vera Frenkel's *Body Missing* project (1994–1997) takes a more indirect approach in addressing the relationship between aesthetics and genocide under the Third Reich. At the center of Frenkel's mixed-media installation (1994) and website (1995–ongoing) are a series of short videotapes which look at Adolf Hitler's *Kunstraub* (art theft) policy and, specifically, *Sonderauftrag Linz* (Special Assignment Linz). Hitler's boyhood home, Linz, in Austria, was to be the location of his eventual retirement. It was also the proposed site for an art museum, which Hitler hoped to erect and manage following his projected world victory. Toward realizing his curatorial vision, Hitler amassed hundreds of stolen artworks from Nazi-occupied territories. Needless to say, much of the seized work belonged to Jewish families who had been sent to concentration camps.

Frenkel's videos address Hitler's obsession with the aesthetic and his fastidious program of listing, logging, registering, and transporting "great works." They focus on his "collecting fever." Hitler's program of genocide, which involved the pseudoscientific sorting, cataloguing, and extermination of European Jewry, stands as the implicit shadow-text. While the transportation and annihilation of European Jews is never represented or denoted on-screen, Frenkel's work repeatedly gestures towards Hitler's two parallel madnesses. Hitler had two lists, two sets of operating codes, two programs, which culminated in a vision defining both the destructible and the sanctifiable. In Vera Frenkel's video installation, these seemingly irreducible "projects" are set in dialogue.

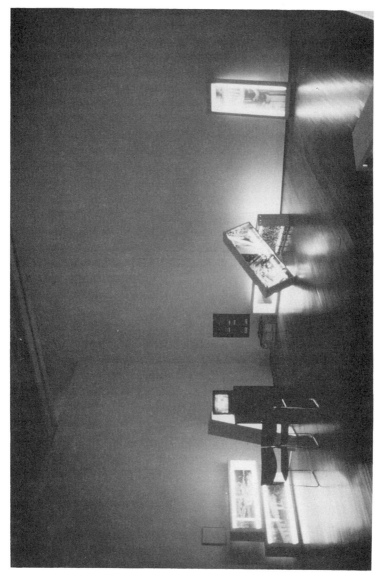

FIGURE 2.1. *Body Missing* (partial view). Vera Frenkel. Station 1 of 6 video stations dispersed about the Setagaya Museum, Tokyo, 1995. Photo: Setagaya Museum. Courtesy of the artist.

Leaders pursuing genocide—from Hitler to Franco to Stalin— have done so using a language of aesthetic refinement and cultural purity. Art has been suborned to military objectives. In reflecting on the fettered relation between beauty and horror, Peter Cohen and Vera Frenkel respectively consider how post-Holocaust art and literature might forge a way of setting these twinned sides in skeptical relation to one another. Art must keep paradox alive. It must contradict its own histories of violence. The hour of furnaces and mass graves is also the hour of poetry and art, notes John Berger (1993, 252).

Thus, while many have taken Theodor Adorno's words regarding the impossibility of poetry after the Shoah as an axiomatic demand for documentary minimalism, others have taken up Adorno for his summons to reconceive traditional orders of language and aesthetics. Adorno himself, in an essay entitled "Commitment" (written in 1962), which was originally intended as a response to Walter Benjamin, refers back to his earlier statement in an enduring effort to explore the transformational possibilities *and* limits of art. What becomes evident in the passage quoted below is Adorno's "commitment" to establishing a dialectical practice that might prolong the question of a work's social and historical relevance. For Adorno, the perils and potential of creative sublimity in the face of unsurpassed organized suffering and group hatred demand ongoing consideration:

> I have no wish to soften the saying that to write lyric poetry after Auschwitz is barbaric; it expresses in negative form the impulse which inspires committed literature. The question asked by a character in Sartre's play *Morts Sans Sepulture*, "Is there any meaning in life when men exist who beat people until the bones break in their bodies?" is also the question whether any art now has a right to exist; whether intellectual regression is not inherent in the concept of committed literature because of the regression of society. But Enzensberger's retort also remains true, that literature must resist this verdict, in other words, be such that its mere existence after Auschwitz is not a surrender to cynicism. Its own situation is one of paradox, not merely the problem of how to react to it. The abundance of real suffering tolerates no forgetting; Pascal's theological saying, *On ne doit plus dormir*, must be secularized. Yet this suffering, what Hegel called consciousness of adversity, also demands the continued existence of art while it prohibits it; it is now virtually in art alone that suffering can still find its own voice, consolation, without immediately being betrayed by it. (Adorno 1985, 312)

Forging new possibilities for art in the wake of mass murder confronts the question of how art has been used in governing operations, whereupon definitions of beauty and harmony become consonant with the "rationality" of state rule and violence. Atrocity has roots that are at once philosophical, political, and aesthetic. Over the course of this century, we have seen modern barbarism connected in deep, and even fundamental, ways, to the very core values of humanistic civilization.

The history of the atomic bombings is consistent with this. Here, an aesthetic language of nuclear sublimity contributed to shielding potential witnesses. Military advisors and strategists, who were gathered as onlookers, waxed poetic in their accounts of the explosions—effectively turning manmade tragedy into theater. In a Strangelove-ian twist, the bomb became lovelier and lovelier through description. Following the Trinity nuclear test on June 16, 1945, for example, Brigadier General Thomas Farrell stated that what he had witnessed was of the sort "of beauty that great poets dream about but describe most poorly and inadequately" (Ruthven 1993, 32). His own account was imbued with a sense of wonderment and awe reminscent of Wordsworth: "The whole country was lighted by a searing light with the intensity many times that of the midday sun. It was golden purple, violet grey and blue. It lighted every peak, crevasse and ridge of the nearby mountain range with a clarity and beauty that cannot be described but must be seen to be imagined" (Leo 1985).

The field of aesthetic response, as Theodor Adorno suggests, must be reconceived in view of a history that has seen art and beauty tragically misappropriated in such manner as to legitimize violence and suppression. Toward this, figures such as Emmanuel Levinas and Jean-Francois Lyotard have attempted to redefine "aesthetics" as *nonsynthesis*. That is, as a democratic dialogue that foregrounds the friction and conflicts intrinsic to any pool of "shared" emotions, thoughts, and sensations. The complementary tasks of art-making and theorizing involve elucidating social contradictions—contradictions that are smoothed over when notions of beauty and harmony are based on principles of symbolic unity and historical transcendence. In the work of Levinas and Lyotard, the aesthetic sublime, drawn from German idealist philosophy, and based on ideals of universal fusion and essence, is rejected. The sublime is reconceived to encompass the dislocations and disorderings of metaphysics. Experiencing art and the aesthetic, they propose, requires more on the part of the viewer than the vaunting of self-edifying knowledge or sentiment. For Lyotard, the sublime experience is not preexistent but rather comprises an interpretive "event" or encounter that may push us to a rethinking of the world "as we know it" (Lyotard 1990, 1988). The syntax of art is, thus, reenvisioned so that it can confront the violence of modern experience.

Testimonial art—showing sublimity of the sort described by Lyotard—is, herein, defended as both hopeless *and* absolutely crucial: invoking shreds of possibility that an audience may be affected in such ways as to react and reflect on suffering. At one level, art can testify to the impossibility of complete remembrance and mourning. At another, it can establish a network of witnesses, encouraging collective dialogue and action, which may contribute to preventing future losses based on domination.

It is perhaps in the paradoxical spirit of "impossible poetry" that poet Pablo Neruda once wrote of Chilean suffering under General Pinochet: "The blood of the children spilt through the streets like the blood of the children . . ." Here, Neruda, a poet renowned for his lush use of metaphor, evokes the limits of poetic language and analogy in testifying to material violence. Yet, using the syntactic structure of metaphor, Neruda *also* bears witness to the fissures in formerly enabling conventions of representation, and, thus, the disruption of a familiar moral and linguistic universe.

The Holocaust witness poetry of Paul Celan similarly insists through example that the language we speak in order to understand the experience of trauma is also irrevocably stricken by it. Both like and unlike Neruda, Paul Celan does not assume to represent the world directly. For Celan, metaphor becomes an irreducible and elliptical vehicle through which to express his experiences of the Nazi death camps—experiences lying neither in the realm of life nor death. In Celan's "Death Fugue" (*"Todesfugue"*), written in 1945 in a labor camp, we are introduced to a disordered universe, a terror-addled time, where night and day, fear and comfort, collapse into this impenetrable yet incantatory refrain: "Black milk of daybreak we drink you at night/we drink you at morning and midday we drink you at evening/ we drink and we drink . . ." German, for Celan, is a "death-bringing" language. Celan's poetry, scored with untranslated German words, comes to us with claims that have yet to be filled with meaning, hoping to mark us as they themselves have been marked.

With both Paul Celan and Pablo Neruda, poetry in itself becomes an event, a reckoning with trauma that can neither subsume nor be subsumed by the events to which it testifies. The art of witness is summoned to express the social antinomies, the cracks and crevices in its own formal language. The language of aesthetics is thus denatured, adopted codes are transformed, in hope of never leaving the order of things as they are.

Covenants

Pace Adorno the central question remains: how will we come to understand that which links the injustices of history to the gesture of art? This question is pivotal to artists and viewers involved with the art of witness. Thematically, these works challenge presumed universals in art and literature by foregrounding the historical encounter that comes with language-associated expression.

What becomes increasingly evident as we review witness discourse, the poetry of Neruda and Celan, is that choices and distinctions between realism and abstraction, between documentary and fiction, are never solely formal concerns. Struggles with the signifier announce more than the blurred confusion of an artistic vision. In bringing broader historical and discursive relations to the fore, in discussing the contours of survivor guilt, we may see that representational strategies cannot be reduced to, nor isolated as, unencumbered choices. The possibilities of representing Hiroshima and Nagasaki are complexly enmeshed with—and limited by—social, psychological, structural, and ethical relations. The definitional distance between *history* and *art*, *fact* and *fiction*, is saturated with questions of ethics and responsibility. As Lawrence Langer writes, "We are confronted by the perplexing challenge of the reversal of normal creative procedure: instead of Holocaust fictions liberating the facts and expanding the range of their implications, Holocaust facts enclose the fictions, drawing the reader into an ever-narrower area of association, where history and art stand guard over their respective territories, wary of the abuses that either may commit upon the other" (1995, 75–76). The tendency to sacralize traumatic events, in other words, creates an aura of taboo for artistic representation.[3]

If we turn to the specific history of postwar Japan, we may confront these representational dilemmas more directly. Here, cultural ideologies which supported binarisms—between the aesthetic and the political, the private and the public, imagination and reality—resulted in an array of creative decisions and responses. Artists' attempts to divine new covenants between art and trauma were far-reaching and conflicting. Indeed, the value of direct versus indirect depiction became a key source of dispute among postwar Japanese artistic movements. These debates centered on the appropriateness of abstract symbolism as contrasted with realist representation. They were, as such, not only aesthetic disputes between proponents of modernism and advocates of realism, they were charged political discussions that reflected much of the controversy surrounding history itself.

Thus, postwar artists living in the rubble of a defeated Japan, while sharing a certain preoccupation with apocalypse and social alienation, found different ways of expressing these themes. Some became publicly identified Marxists and by the early 1950s had moved towards social realism. The Tokyo-based Reportage artists, for example, directly incorporated symbolically charged figures into their work to personify various social evils. These artists, as their name suggests, saw no other alternative but to respond as directly as possible to the grotesque horrors of war. They devoted themselves to recording the violence of militarism, nuclear holocaust, and social oppression.

The Japanese Communist Party encouraged Reportage painting by sending artists to document instances of imperialism and class struggle in rural villages, industrial zones, and near military bases (Munroe 1994, 151). Yamashita Kikuji, one of the better known Reportage painters, dedicated his work to such subjects as atomic bomb suffering and the indignities endured by villagers at the hands of feudal-like landowners.

By the mid-1950s, however, the directness and alleged didacticism of leftist Social Realism and Reportage was being challenged by contemporaneous critics. Haryu Ichiro, one of the more vocal critics, publicly announced his affinities with the movement but nonetheless expressed concern that the choice of subject matter had superseded formal considerations (Munroe 1994, 154). Other artists chose to reject any realist conventions associated with prewar Imperial Japan and its traditional schools of art on the basis that such practices were irreparably tarnished by previous misuse. Social realism, while emblematically Left and politically progressive, was seen to employ a syntax too closely allied with that of propaganda art commissioned and coerced from artists by Japanese wartime leaders.

The overt ideology of Reportage was notably rejected by artist Yoshihara Jiro, who, in 1952, founded the renowned Zero Society (*Zero-kai*) with twelve other artists. Born of the premise that "every work of art begins from nothing," the Zero Society's forays into action and conceptual art appeared to be diametrically opposed to the works of the Social Realists (Munroe 1994, 87). Yet, in producing site-specific works designed to induce a sense of imbalance and fear, the Zero Society artists shared with Social Realists an interest in challenging norms of viewing. Their approaches may have been antithetical, but both major postwar movements were calling for an end to passive spectatorship.

In 1958, artist Shusaku Arakawa suggested that distinctions between abstract and realist art were rendered moot by nuclear warfare. For his debut at the Yomiuri Independent, Shusaku Arakawa created *Untitled Endurance I*, a series of wooden boxes resembling coffins. The boxes, when opened by viewers, were lined with satin quilting. Resting against the plush walls were amorphous masses of cement embedded with bits of fur and hair. For most viewers, these forms were disturbingly evocative of atomic radiation and the melting of flesh (Munroe 1994, 157). Arakawa had eloquently expressed a transgression of ordinary rites of mourning. The remains were leaking beyond accepted bounds.

The unassimilable dimensions of nuclear trauma and mass death had left artists, such as Arakawa, yearning for an artistic language "purified of the taint of normality" (Langer 1995, 93). Even those artists who had chosen to adhere to social realism found themselves overwhelmed by the surreal and excessive nature of the events. Their work was intercepted by uncertainty: Was it possible to express the dimensions of violence introduced by modern technologies of war? Without scaling things down, could trauma be made more symbolically accessible, palpable?

Witness art appears as a consequence of a need and a caring. It arises from a desire to communicate. It emanates from a belief that the future, left to itself, cannot be trusted. This distrust toward the future—based on real disappointments, perennial injustice—has led artists to underestimate the power and potential of their work's address. Thus, many suggest that if art is to remain accountable to the victims of atrocity, if it is not to diffuse historical agency, it must directly announce its allegiances. Art must be captioned, verbally explained.

In preparing this book for publication, I was again made aware that the viewing contexts created for witness art continue to be matters of prominent concern. I had approached a number of Japanese artists and photographers for copyright permission. Many promptly forwarded their images and letters of consent. I was bemused that among the earlier images I received was one from the U.S. Department of Defense. (Bureaucratic efficiency, I assumed.) Several artists, however, were more circumspect. Weeks passed. And finally, I began to receive letters—six in total—all variously asking: What is your purpose in publishing this book? Will my image be used to promote peace and nuclear disarmament?

There is always the incipient danger that witness art—no matter how hortatory or descriptive—will be mindlessly consumed. It is, thus, understandable that artists have attempted to diminish this risk by surrounding their work with an aura of responsibility and respect. Yet, the efforts of witness artists to circulate their images as widely as possible, and at the same time control the spirit in which people approach them, raises an issue that has been recurrent in contemporary culture. Walter Benjamin, in his reflection on photography, for example, observed the importance in some instances of captioning images through verbal narrative (Rabinowitz 1993, 121). Benjamin was chiefly concerned with historicizing image production, so as to ensure that images would not displace a sense of contingency, or be ruthlessly consumed. (His concerns, penned over half a century ago, take on added significance in our age of floating pictures and televisual gratuity.) Yet, what remains unique about Benjamin's notion of captioning is how it manages to retain sight of history without commanding interpretive closure. Benjamin would counsel in such essays as "The Storyteller" and "The Task of the Translator" against attaching a unitary message to art and story. While allowing a work to function as a declarative slogan, to attain its "revolutionary use-value," he felt that such expressions risked becoming normative in their didacticism, authoritarian in their logic.

Socially committed artists continue to waver over issues of direct versus indirect representation. The central challenge, as phrased by artists, involves making work more accessible, while promoting further thought on difficult themes. Enforcing a clear verbal message on an image may promote broad recognition, but may also curtail ongoing reflection on the part of viewers. Filmmaker John Akomfrah, questioning the nature of visual imperatives, which insist that cultural producers submit to predetermined political ends, has commented, "Because it is in a state of emergency its means always have to be guerrilla means, war means, signposts of urgency. When that begins to inhibit questions of reflection—doubt, scepticism, intimacy and so on—then the categorical imperative does exactly what it is supposed to do—it imprisons" (quoted in Coco Fusco 1988, 51).

Countering these representational imperatives has not led John Akomfrah, director of such docu-narrative films as *Handsworth Songs* (1986) and *The Last Angel of History* (1995), to naively embrace the alternative values of abstraction. The point, he suggests, is not to make images or narratives more complex for the sake of obscurity or confusion, but to allow for contradictions and questions to emerge. Artists like Akomfrah, whose work touches on themes of Black diasporic collective memory, push us to ask how established ideas—and, particularly, rigid delineations between fact and fiction, politics and aesthetics—may end up writing the limits of memorial activity, often moving us away from complexity.

Clearly, the desires that inform the conversion of art into historical artifact are deep rooted. To attend to the imaginative aspects of a
work means to cross that line in a dualistic logic that separates fact
from fiction, truth from falsehood, reality from distortion. The line has
constructed different rules for engagement. It has evoked suspicions
that the literary, the fictive, the imaginative, must in some way subvert
the truthfulness of narrative testimony. *Hibakusha* writer Yoko Ota conveyed the ethical paradox involved in writing disaster when she
asked, "Do I have the right to imagine? Can what I say about the dead
ever be authentic?" (quoted in Lifton 1967, 405).

What Words Now?

Artists have repeatedly remarked that past literary and artistic
methods are incapable of and inadequate in dealing with the atomic
bombings. The unique nature of the trauma and the absence of analo-
gous events brings experience beyond the measure of language and
comprehension. Attempts to represent the unimaginable have posed
paradoxical questions about what form, language, and narrative structure are best suited to the project. Addressing the impossibility of finding congruence, equivalence, or an explanation in systems of language, writer Takenishi Hiroko once asked: "What words can we now
use, and to what ends? Even: what *are* words?" (quoted in Treat 1994,
235–36).[4]

The atomic bombings signaled a near-total communication melt-
down. The death of grandiloquence, to be sure. War of such total
nature opposes the assumption on which all languages are based: the
assumption of mutual understanding across what differentiates. Peter
Schwenger notes, "*Ground zero* is itself a somewhat oxymoronic term.
Ground melts away at the point of a nuclear explosion, and the figurative ground of our conceptual systems disappears as well, swallowed by the yawning zero" (1992, 25).

The bomb that was dropped on Nagasaki exploded over the
largest Catholic cathedral in the Far East, missing its target by about
two miles. The cathedral was devasted: the roof collapsed, the rose
windows were shattered, the Virgin Mary was decapitated, and statues of saints were scorched. The photographs of Shomei Tomatsu
focus on the violent meeting of the sacred and the profane in the ruins
of Urakami cathedral. The comforts of religious tradition have been
stripped away. The floor of the symbolic world has bottomed out,
icons now decimated. The damage, he suggests, is irreparable. God
had betrayed the people of Nagasaki. God had been betrayed. His

68

FIGURE 2.2. *11:02 Nagasaki*, Deformed Statues of Angels from Urakami Cathedral, 0.6 kilometers from the Hypocenter. Shomei Tomatsu, 1961. Courtesy of the artist.

photos, collected under the title *11:02 Nagasaki*, depict objects baptized by the bomb. Stone angels have been toppled by the blast, sawn from the cathedral, wings shorn. They are flightless, lying scattered on the grass. Their open eyes are turned toward the heavens. As viewers, we behold the breaking down of a world that has defaced its own foundations. The angel, seen without God, is the very expression of meaninglessness.

Formerly enabling conventions and traditions of representation are compromised, if not obviated, in the wake of nuclear cataclysm. To capture "how things really were," in this ruptured context, is an act infused with inherent contradiction. The collapse of social order, both material and symbolic, heralded by the bombings made it more difficult to discern between the fantastic and the real. The line dividing the familiar from the unfamiliar was gone. Hence, many scenes were imaginable only in hell:

> Outlines of bodies were permanently etched as white shadows in black nimbus on streets or walls, but the bodies themselves had disappeared. . . . there were innumerable corpses without apparent injury. Parts of bodies held their ground, like two legs severed below the knees, still standing. Many of the dead were turned into statues, some solid and others waiting to crumble at a touch. (Dower 1993, 244–45)

Where do we draw the line between fact and fiction when in some work the use of detail reaches the point of hyperexactness, a kind of surrealism, that falsifies notions of assimilable reality?[5] How do we begin to separate the real from the imaginary when in other works the preponderance of similes and metaphors comes to expose the impossibility of obtaining recollection without elaboration? What do we call "evidence," when in many instances struggles for signification are perhaps all that is left to be, or not be, represented? While these questions are clearly rhetorical, they push us toward the limits of positivist looking. How are we constrained by a rigid, and arguably untenable, preoccupation with evidence?

Artists ranging from Shusaku Arakawa to Alain Resnais have asked us to consider if direct representation is the sole or even the best means for ensuring responsible recollection of the atomic bombings. Through counterexample, their works have asked us to ponder whether documentary realism is the only measure of art's political value and use. Even the most "literal" and minimally descriptive accounts of the bombings, they suggest, are evocative in figural, liter-

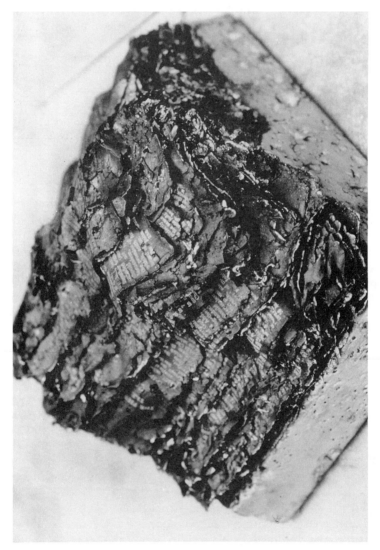

FIGURE 2.3. *Testimony of Atomic Bomb* (ceramic). Takako Araki, 1983. Courtesy of the artist.

ary, and imaginative terms. Does realist depiction simply become a matter of degree—the degree to which a representation observes social conventions promoting sparsity, clarity, and directness?

Metaphor is often read as extrafactual, as nontruth. Imagination becomes synonymous with falsehood. Fiction frequently means lies. The distinction, which bypasses the richness of the intermediate zone, sows the first refusal. It creates a galactic distance between languages that are deeply connected. I believe it precludes the very possibility of witnessing, rejecting as it does memories that might be prefigurative and tentative in their expression.

What would it take then to see the fictional and the factual, the metaphoric and the referential, as mutually imbricated, rather than mutually exclusive? Carrying out artistic responsibility would extend beyond simple description and naïve realism. It would mean residing in that space of approximation, a dialectical space between art as frank recollection *and* art as unfettered imagination. It would require recognizing the impossible reconciliation between art dealing with events and the reality of those events.

We might find, as with Takako Araki's *Testimony of Atomic Bomb* (1983), that it is precisely the presence of the connotative, the extrafactual, and not its absence that haunts these expressions—conveying a restless, yet incomplete, search for meaning. For ultimately Araki has created an unreadable testimony. Her tome, its pages melted into an irradiated mass, is beyond evidentiary use or disclosure. One can imagine that it contains some inscrutable alphabet, the runes of a vanished people bearing testimony to a vanished world. But this kiln-destroyed ceramic book has no analogue: neither sculpture nor historical record, it aspires to be both.

If there can be no poetry after the Holocaust, perhaps there can be no art after Hiroshima and Nagasaki . . . Or put another way, perhaps Adorno's caveat to post-Holocaust poets and writers about the need to consider the relation of language and culture to historical trauma is apposite. Language is itself evidentiary: changed and marred. The language may not convey crisp information or be "about something" immediately discernible or political, but still testify, as with Araki's work, to the wreckage introduced by modern violence.

3

The Art of Witnessing

In 1938, Marc Chagall painted "White Crucifixion" in hopes of drawing attention to the anti-Jewish Nazi pogroms taking place in Germany at the time. In hindsight, the painting, with its central Christ figure, is undeniably tragic; prophetic in its warning of the dangers impending for European Jewry. We now know that bystanders failed to answer when called. Yet, having been unmet once, Chagall's testimony endures. Its call to witness has not been used up. Such is its power that the questions it raised about the role of Christian theology in legitimatizing the Nazi program, its open consideration of Church complicity, still resonate over half a century later.

Antonio Frasconi's woodcut series, bearing the euphemistic title *The Involvement*, appeared in 1967. It disseminated, in large print editions, a nightmarish vision of the war in Vietnam at a time of American military escalation. Beyond their value as protest documents, however, the prints introduced another objective. For Frasconi, each print represented an effort to change the channels through which the war was being seen. He wanted to slow the flux of viewer attention, but in order to do so, he felt that familiar visual elements from pop art and front-line newscasts needed to be combined. Thus, he presented American viewers with a dual optic through which to view the war, setting large graphic portraits of Vietnamese civilians against a background blunted with carpet bombs.

Nancy Spero is a printmaker whose work has extensively addressed the consequences of U.S. intervention in Central and South America. In 1995, she turned to the subject of atomic warfare when she joined a group of artists commemorating the fiftieth anniversary of Hiroshima and Nagasaki. Her memorial collage, "Atomic Ash," depicts blanched humans squatting and curled in fetal positions against a foggy, and ultimately unreadable, landscape. Because the figures are so overexposed, so beyond immediate recognition, they seem to imply a world that cannot be taken at face value.

74

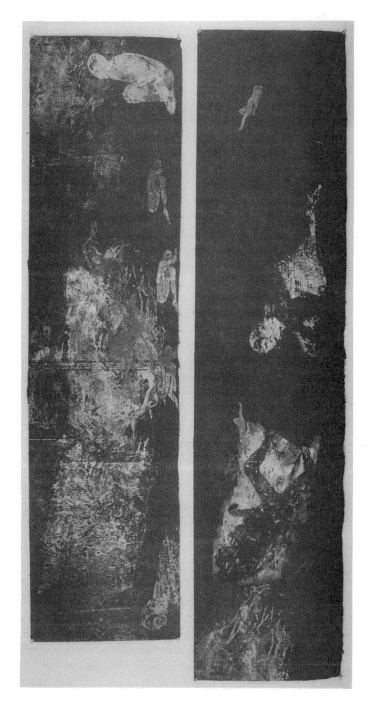

FIGURE 3.1. *Atomic Ash* (handprinting and printed collage). Nancy Spero, 1995. Photo credit: David Reynolds. Courtesy of Nancy Spero Studio.

There is a span of thirty years separating these works. Taken together, their pained and contorted figures speak of a century rife with examples of group hatred, defamation, and assault. Playing the role of seers, these artists have created images filled with haunting insights into the dehumanizing terrors of war. The work, while diverse in form and scope, has shared the potential to traffic into the lives and imaginations of viewers who might otherwise have considered these events peripheral to their own affairs.

War experiences that might have passed unobserved—passed in the absence of outside witnesses—have found, in testimonial art, a (posthumous) means of rousing viewer awareness. Francisco de Goya's intaglio series, *Los Desastres de la Guerra* (1810–1820), which testifies to the Napoleonic invasions of Spain, serves as one notable example. Another more recent example can be found in the Chilean *arpilleras* (small hand-sewn story quilts), made by women testifying to daily suppression under the Pinochet regime during the 1970s.

To say that viewers have been roused by these creative testaments, however, does not necessarily bring us closer to understanding *how* we have responded as "witnesses." It remains an open question as to whether or not a space has been created for viewers to explore their own subjective and social passages through art and the events to which this work refers. We know that art has the power to peel our eyes open, but what is it that art makes us see? How can art teach us to witness?

In this chapter, I argue that witnessing is the will to push at the limits of our looking. Finding where the visible cheats us of knowledge and memory is intrinsic to the act of meeting absent worlds. We are surrounded by the vapor of the unseen, the outstanding claims of the dead, the ghosts of histories that have been excluded from contemporary society. Thus, witnessing involves endless imagination. It takes time and foresight; it requires an insistent gaze that can both refuse finality and exceed evidentiary necessity.

Art, I suggest, has the potential to introduce a new pace for eyes used to scanning newspapers and television monitors. Amid the onrush of media and commerce, witness art asks that we slow down, that we disengage from hasty chaperones of history.

Only in our patience, our openness before the unknown, can we keep testimony company. There are few other ways of protecting testimony against the ambush of historical progress, few other ways of judging history's judges. Only by encouraging faith in the reality of the invisible—as art does when its language opens—can we develop an inner eye which retains a sense of what, and who, is missing. The power of art, its unique force, derives from a wordless acknowledgment of that which remains absent, or *other*, to our known worlds.

However intensely and empirically observed at the moment, an impression gathered through art often becomes, like a memory, impossible to verify. We are compelled to remember what is no longer—who has never been—available to us as physical presence. Yet because of this, the frame or edges of the visible world, its alcoves of evidence, no longer act as a barrier. Though we cannot see clearly, we proceed. We are in some ways witnesses traveling through a dense fog, learning to overcome our poor vision. Thus, we accept a strain, a pressure on the eyes that reminds us: perfect sight—while certain memories remain unmet and inequality persists—cannot be accorded.

Passive Witness

In an age of atrocity, witnessing becomes both an imperative and a problem: how does one bear witness to suffering and before what tribunal? If history were best surmised, justice best served, through the compiling of lists and accounts, we might rest assured knowing that virtually every major twentieth-century encounter has undergone a fair reckoning. In due course, we have racked up endless timelines, chronologies, body counts, and assorted numerical tallies to better measure and understand events that are ultimately enumerable in consequence. From high-school history drills to nightly newscasts to courtroom trials, we have learned to be judiciously fact-conscious in our accounting of world events.

Yet, there is defeat and despair in information's numbing cadence, its flatness of tone. Facts may define the broad parameters of the news and the law, not the singular experiences of the traumatized and besieged. It is a sense of humility before the unknown, and perhaps unknowable, that has brought many artists to testify where judicial witnessing has floundered, thus bringing us to a place where we can negotiate with the ethical sublimities and cesspits introduced by mass atrocity. In art we gain a vital personal supplement to impersonal documentary accounts.

Whereas court tribunals have provided evidentiary forii for witnessing—entrusted with prosecuting mass crimes and violence according to absolute standards of truth, justice, and collective good—art has provided different clearings and criteria for witnessing. Less Manichean, more suspicious of closure, art has the power to respect claims of difference and otherness inherent to trauma commemoration. While the act of respecting the gap between self and other (between the time of witnessing and the time of trauma), has opened up the problem of relativism—introducing the prospect of infinite regress into a past beyond determination, beyond accountability—the testimonial dimensions of art have suggested the need for different criteria of judgment. These testimonies, most significantly, have asked that they be judged by their consequences, not by our ability to verify their truth. The witness artist, to paraphrase poet Carlos Fuentes, entreats *us* (who are outsiders to the original event), to "imagine the past" so that we may "remember the future." Art's nonempirical testimony, its unfulfilled pledge to the future, requires that we participate more actively in its construction—joining the ongoing tide of memory and response.

Thus, to apply girdings of accuracy and authenticity to art's "voicing" of trauma may neglect its unique, extrafactual clamour, its expressed frailties. Predisposed as these evidentiary terms are to prevailing models of information-based knowledge, they may quickly exhaust art of its possibility to test framings of the past, its power of appeal and transformation. As Walter Benjamin notes, "The value of information does not survive the moment in which it was new. It lives only at that moment; is has to surrender to it completely and explain itself to it without losing any time" (Benjamin 1968, 90).

Within this tight economy of meaning, art is parsed of its potential as a *nonjudicial* testimonial form, its special ability to transverse accepted knowledge by stirring new responses and sentiments. There can be no after-life, no *sur-vivre*, for the work once the relevant facts and information have been extracted. Rather than allowing us to consider how *we* might be variously called forth to witness these memorial forms in order to examine our own ethical and political responses, the framing of art as information, evidence, or confession reverses the task of witnessing—displaces the work of explanation, reflection, and feeling onto the artist and work. The notion of transparency as applied to memory production, in this sense, is a troubled one, not so much because it depends on a truthful artist or narrator, but because it promotes the illusion of clarity and access on the part of the spectator and reader. Far from requiring a vigilant mindset, this model of witnessing is intrinsically passive and forgetful.

Memory is fragile, and we are subject to forget those things we have not intimately and actively experienced. The art of witness can provide either catalyst or buffer for our grief and guilt—grief that comes from knowing too little, guilt that comes from responding too late. We may turn to these images to foster open ethical connections with people and events wavering in the slipstream of time and con-

78

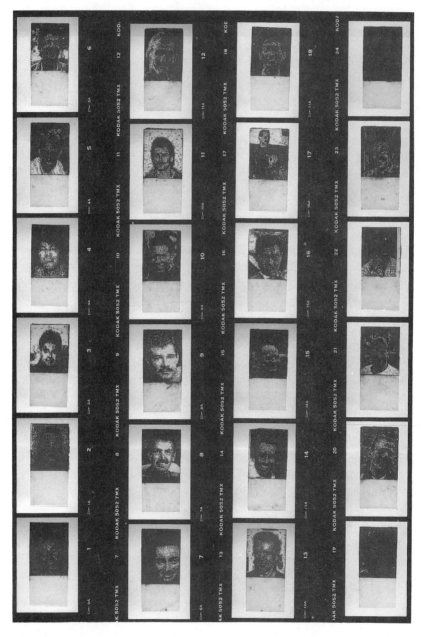

FIGURE 3.2. *Facsimile, Part 4* (graphite on beeswax). Stephen Andrews, 1993.
Photo courtesy of the artist.

sciousness. Or, we may rely on these images to fulfill our desire for facsimile, for portraits that can fill in the blanks in our collective memory,
mollifying our need for temporal continuity and a sense of communal
significance.

Artist Stephen Andrews presents us with images that have been
remorselessly cross-examined by death. The sense of elegy that per-
vades his work takes root in an awareness that grief, in these plague
years, is always close by. His portrait series, *Facsimile* (1993), was generated to commemorate those who have died of AIDS-related illness.
It is a sparse and unadorned installation. Row upon row of faces are
presented on bleached beeswax boards across a wall. Despite their
mannered presentation, one gathers the disturbing impression that
these death portraits could stretch on to infinity. Hence, the crisis.

The faces, originally appearing as journalistic photographs in the
obituary section of a Toronto newspaper, were sent to the artist via
transatlantic fax. They are copies of copies of copies, and thus several
generations removed from the original subject. Mimetic detail and imi-
tative likeness have been eroded through the graphic distortions and
pixel marks of a laser printer. Several portraits are blotted into shad-
owy silhouettes, anonymous dark smudges. Here the gap between the
portrait and its *inimitable* subject becomes most apparent. The layers of
distance and artifice involved in memory reconstruction are exposed.
We glimpse, only glimpse, at the pixelated faces that were once friends
or lovers. We sense, only sense, the presence of those now absent to
touch.

Yet even as the facsimile burns the idiosyncrasies of personality
away, a singular sense of loss migrates into each frame. Those who
knew the deceased intimately are given a subjective space in which to
imagine their loved ones, while those arriving as strangers are given a
fleeting view of the many individual lives sacrificed to an epidemic of
disease and neglect. There is no attempt to deny or compensate for the
photographic origin of the image. What we see, however, is the photographic image openly pulled into the space of art and integrated into
the present experience of the viewer. The facsimile, instead of being
simply an object of perception with one face, provides a locus for many
memories. It is a movement toward raising the dead from oblivion.

Memory's Sightlines

Photography, as Stephen Andrews acknowledges in *Facsimile*,
has the dubious reputation of being the most realistic, and therefore

straightforward, of the mimetic arts. We approach reality through the photograph, hoping to grasp the finest details of a subject: the pores on a dead man's face, the dirt on a child's torso, the welts on a woman's shoulder. Many of us approach these pictures with the hope of being touched by a stranger. We strive to effect an empathy with those who have suffered to resist their disappearance from the momentum of history. The image of horror can be both sobering and comforting: a cold compress on the brow of grief. In the case of Hiroshima and Nagasaki, images of atomic-bomb destruction represent a line of defense against the force of oblivion that the bomb almost succeeded in establishing. The image is a barrier against the very loss of human existence.

Regardless of how chaotic things become, the picture suggests that in the longue durée of history, balance and reason can be restored. An overwhelming event can be contained and miniaturized within the bordered frame of a photograph. The demoralized viewer can achieve a state of knowledge, revelation, and, therefore, power by converting an otherwise confounding experience into a mental object. As Susan Sontag notes, "the most grandiose result of the photographic enterprise is to give us the sense that we can hold the whole world in our heads—as an anthology of images" (1989).

The image is most reassuring when it appears to give us incontrovertible proof that a given event occurred, and, more significantly, that it is now over. Our moral imaginations seem to rely on such assurances. The desire to have seen (the ruins, the graves) has a deep ontological basis. Our identities are beleaguered, even jeopardized, without a stable sense of history and memory. It is hard to let go of feelings of sure-footedness and historical certitude, to risk the fall into ontological vertigo, the headlong plunge into grief without reprieve. Slipping into the depths of uncertainty and not-knowing—those moments of transformation between cognition and confusion—forces the articulate self to become less locquacious, less sure.

By contrast, confirming the truth or accuracy of an image or testimony allows us to proclaim a secure relationship to the history under investigation. If the window is transparent, the viewer has a socially and morally credible perspective. So long as a picture is viably realistic and accessible in its portrayal of history, we, as viewers, will never be bereft of meaning and purpose. Like the dead friends and family preserved in the family album, whose presence in photographs removes some of the sorrow and remorse prompted by their disappearance, so photographs of cities destroyed, people disfigured into corpses, provide our token relation to the past. They conjure up the appearance of people and places that are now absent. They bestow coherence upon events, however fragmented and horrible.

While a photograph can be treated as a narrowly selective fac-simile of the world, a painting or poetic description can never be other than a subjective interpretation. Even when a particular theme seems impatient, artists reveal the act of their own looking, the gradual process of their own making, more obviously. Thus, art's unique con-tribution to witnessing rests in its explicit overflow, its ability to spill out beyond the empirical, so enlarging the arena of witnessing beyond available historical sightlines.

The dead, as artist Stephen Andrews suggests, reside in the imag-ination of the living. In the spirit of broadening our imagination and, by extension, our social vision, art lends form to the missing *and* to the missed encounter. In so doing, it speaks to a century of banishment—a century of people witnessing others, who were friends or strangers, disappear over the horizon.

Witness artists have inserted themselves into their work in vari-ous guises: as narrators reciting chased-down facts, as researchers treading through public and private archives, as archaeologists con-fronting missing remains, as healers tending to memory lapses and inexpressible burdens, as survivors bearing personal and transper-sonal witness to violence. There are elemental contradictions sown into these many roles and guises, each alone proving inadequate. Artists wanting hard knowledge and disclosure have also sought to honor residual silences. So paying due respect to the haunting power and subtlety of the unspeakable, art has ventured to find ways of cut-ting through to the soft parts untried in the pursuit of hard-edged knowledge; art takes us to places beyond the smooth everyday capac-ities of speech.

As many artists have come to recognize, a single testimony is composed of many scatterings and fragments. By dint of violence and displacement, testimony cannot travel across the chasm of time and space intact or unscathed. In a paradoxical manner, the histories these artists hope to clarify seem to lose rather than gain precision as they proceed. Time has skewed memory and obliterated its markers. The headstone of a grave is gone, an old picture is fading, a village has dis-appeared. All that is left are wisps of evidence, often less tangible than the materials of prehistory. Historical reality, they find, can only be approached through constant re-creation; memory is only given shape through imaginations, at once embellishing and denuding.

The implicit demands we place on testimonial formations reveal these inherent paradoxes: Do we desire a memoir, diary, or film to meticulously chronicle every detail of a remembered experience? Or do we want a synopsized, gestural dramatization that can furnish us with history's armature, trauma's bare bones?

For reasons both material and symbolic, trauma's bare bones may be all we have to guide memory. The Middle Passage, the Shoah, the Cambodian killing fields, the Argentine Dirty War, have turned the earth's vast lands and oceans into mass graves. The sundry corpses of history's wreckage are all that is left to remind us: we have come too late. There is an abyss between the time of an event and the present moment of participating in its memorialization. This gap is both a sign and symptom of human mortality. This gap is also a powerful stimulant for cultural and ethical activity. Yet, it is too easily collapsed when we ardently confine ourselves to detecting signs and details decodable under the rubric of knowledge. To satisfy our "mirror of history" longings, our relentless search for tangible evidence and chronology, art must deny the gap of difference, and forfeit itself to the familiar. And if familiarity means something we no longer question, something we no longer see, then testimonial art is rendered incapable of transformation. The winding and living movement of testimony as it flows out of the past into a yet-to-be-determined future requires more of us than this. Art does not reflect memory, it anticipates it.

The demand for certain forms of testimony—for example, testimonies that can convey vivid descriptions of horror, a generalized overview of events, evidence of harrowing possession by the past—creates a memory barrier. Victims and survivors are confined to making certain statements that may symbolically routinize the experience of traumatic violence. The testimony that allows us to procure a sense of immersion may inadvertently turn trauma experiences into liturgy. Yet, because a survivor's decision to adhere to facts or familiar phrases may be an emotional or cognitive requirement, and because there is always something still to be learned, we cannot afford to bypass any act of testimony. We can, however, consider how our own situated desires for completion, our need to close and fill gaps in our comprehension of these events, may interfere with the testimonial process.

Testimony is an unceasing labor, vulnerable and exposed. It seeks to bring together what life has separated or violence has torn apart. Testimony can mend no loss, but it can defy the forces which separate. It can improvise a shelter for memories. It does this by its patient work of reconstructing what has been scattered. The labor is continual and disorderly. Our efforts to extract colorful disclosures, so as to connect with survivors, so as to violate our own innocence, may close us off from exploring the significance of ineloquent, fragmented, even mundane, testimonies.

At the same time, the desire to develop a palpable and sensuous connection to these events and their direct sufferers cannot be over-looked—especially if the alternative is detachment or disinterest. It is morally disquieting to stand outside the frame of an event. So the questions we ask must incriminate passivity and direct us toward a place of responsible assembly: How can we encounter the sensuous aspects of testimony while respecting our distance from the experience? How can we bridge contact with trauma survivors without incorporating their otherness?

Ultimately, as I will be arguing in the next chapter, witnessing demands that we forgo the compulsion to render the experiences of others in terms recognizable and imaginable as our own. The time the testimony is attempting to evoke must be maintained in its differences.

Foregrounding these differences allows us to appreciate the poignant, yet elastic, gap between then and now; or between the past and the present. At times, this gap may pose a communicative impasse. Always, it presents an ethical reminder that events always recede in time. Lateness is a condition of all visual representation, forever announcing our belated arrival.

Unfinished Matters

Pierre Nora has cautioned that in our attempts to *enshrine* the past through material forms of representation (i.e., monuments and pictures), we may truncate memory, creating, ultimately, the conditions for forgetfulness. He warns against "venerating traces" (1989, 13). When memorial forms are taken as surrogates for an epic collective memory, we are disempowered. The ethical gap between present and past becomes a chasm, cleaving us beyond possible connection. History becomes a separate precinct: an archive or atrium of a *distant* and *remote* time.

Constituted as the lump sum of its essential parts, Mikhail Bakhtin describes the epic past as both temporally absolute and spatially surveyable. The view onto this domain can only be construed at a remove. To know the whole past and nothing but the past is to know "it" as preconstituted in its distance from ourselves, in the now:

> The epic world is an utterly finished thing, not only as an authentic event of the distant past but also on its own terms and by its own standards; it is impossible to change, to re-think, to reevaluate anything in it. It is completed, conclusive and immutable, as a fact, an idea and a value. This defines absolute epic distance.

One can only accept the epic world with reverence; it is impossible to really touch it, for it is beyond the realm of human activity,
the realm in which everything humans touch is altered and re-
thought. (1981, 17)

In quoting Bakhtin, my point is not to suggest that we adopt the
embodied pains and agonies occasioned by twentieth-century atrocity
as our own. Some sense of distance and humility is required if we are
ever to address our own histories of complicity. But the distance,
evoked here by Bakhtin, resonates more as a chapter closing, locating
the past as a *fait accompli*: a time-locked and inevitable "fact." Without
recognition of contradiction and indeterminacy, there can be little
negotiation of concepts, no movement or shifts in bearing witness to
the ongoing significance of an event.

In reflecting on the perils of putting a *finish* on the past, thus
extruding memory from everyday life, both Pierre Nora and Mikhail
Bakhtin have encouraged us to redefine the relation between representational practices and the historicity of events. Rather than viewing
commemorative artifacts as devices that can bring us closer to the original meaning of an event—an omniscient way of seeing that presupposes a stable referent called "the past"—we are beckoned to shift our
perspective. For both philosophers, history comes to be defined less as
a wellspring of finite events and permanencies, and more as an open
resource, which, in the Benjaminian sense, may be replenished
through our own acts of translation and transformation.

Having adopted the standpoint of a translator in relation to the
past, it becomes more difficult to presume that we stand apart from
that which we see. (Here, looking cannot become a process completely
"other" to me.) Witnessing invokes this experience of participatory
viewing: it restates our connection to matters of history and memory,
broadens consideration of whose responsibility it is to bear witness to
a historical trauma, and questions how this can be justly achieved. For
example, the more oblique the representation, the less synthesized the
testimony, the greater the need for responsible and reflexive participation on the part of viewers and witnesses.

Witnessing, thus, does not imply a re-collecting of an epic "past"
through a sweeping vision, but, rather, a translation of many pasts
within a vision that, while necessarily located, cannot be arrested. The
demands of witnessing, as such, surpass any finite act of transmission.
The viewer is complicit in the creation of knowledge generated
through representational practices. Yet to understand the scope of our
complicity requires that we also be witness to our own located desires

and longings for closure, always alert to disjunctures in meaning, and the power to mean, that may confound attempts at resolution. As Shoshana Felman writes, "[W]hat the translator has to give up is the temptation to translate history by making sense of it, that is, by using an apologetic or apocalyptic discourse" (Felman and Laub 1992, 158).

The transfer of meaning and memory in this world can be utterly ruthless, so much the outcome of omissions, muggings, murders, and betrayals. Translation involves keeping watch for the vestiges of violence and exclusion accenting every historical utterence.

Seeing Double

There is a powerful scene in Marcel Ophuls's documentary film, *The Memory of Justice* (1975), in which U.S. prosecutors at the Nuremberg Trial are listening to the testimony of a Holocaust survivor. The testimony is lagging because every word spoken is being meticulously translated and transcribed. The rat-a-tat-tat of a court stenographer hammering for days on end lends a metronomic, numbing soundtrack to the court proceedings. The sense of fatigue and boredom presiding in the room is visibly expressed on the faces of those gathered there. In the spirit of expediting justice and the mass processing of victim claims, one prosecutor brashly interrupts the testifying survivor. The testimony has become unwieldly and repetitive. It has departed from laconic summary. Much of what is being said, the prosecutor suggests, has been heard before.

Protocols of justice, as Ophuls opines, have a tendency to grow impatient where memory is concerned; they sometimes collide violently with the ethical requirements of trauma remembrance. For Ophuls, it is precisely the "memory" of justice that must be restored as a phantom critic of contemporary protocols and standards. This "memory" of yet-to-be-fulfilled justice is crucial in a world increasingly worn down by atrocity; a world too inclined to standardize trauma through judicial procedure.

If the ideal of Justice is at the same time necessary and unattainable, Ophuls's "memory" of justice reminds us that no society can proclaim to be totally or forever free of the threat of injustice. The ability of modern societies to put an end to war crimes and human-rights abuses on the basis of a clear definition and application of the ideal of Justice has been called into question since the Nuremberg Trials. The prosecution of several dozen individuals for the institutionalized murder of millions created judicial norms for legal procedure that have become tragically paradigmatic over the past fifty years—

exported, in part, to Argentina, Rwanda, South Africa and the Hague.

Art cannot supplant courtroom witnessing and judicial procedure, nor should it. It can, however, provide a powerful reminder of lapses in justice; it can remind us that justice, like memory, can only be partially and imperfectly conceived. Where words tire and slip into routine, when memory-work becomes a closed turf, expressive culture may open up new sites of possibility by providing opportunities to see and hear what has become familiar differently; it may provoke memories that could not be generated elsewhere.

In marking passersby and bystanders as potential witnesses, these expressions may summon us to test the limits of what we have seen and known. They may invite us to admit messages whose meanings have yet to be completed. For these possibilities to emerge, however, requires that we go beyond seeing art solely in evidentiary terms. When the visual is seen exclusively as a terrain to confirm what we know, to spot resemblances, to find exact replications of reality, then art will only be able to reproduce received understandings and assumptions. For visual art to testify differently, to different realities and knowings, we need to be open to looking as a process of defamiliarization and dehabituation. "Certainty may be instantaneous; doubt requires duration," writes John Berger; "meaning is born of the two" (1982, 89).

The process of witnessing commemorative art thus encompasses a double gesture: a parallax vision. At one level it is *corrective*—encouraging us to ask what counts as evidence, how testimony is socially enframed; at another level it is *contemplative*—affording us passages through which we may revisit our own perceptual and epistemic assumptions.

Seeing "double" encourages an encounter with the connotative surpluses of verbal and visual languages. In exceeding the names that we give to "what is" represented and representable, these surpluses may allow us to better critique the stifling and choking effect that norms of witnessing and justice have on our ability to think and imagine otherwise. This is not a call for unnecessary memory acrostics, nor is it a pitch for aesthetic trancendentalism. Upsetting norms of viewing becomes an ethical task if we can provoke enabling crises of witnessing. As Trinh T. Minh-ha writes: "Knowledge (a certain knowledge) cannot merely be rejected (in a contaminated world where every gesture reverberates endlessly on others). But it has to be exceeded" (Minh-ha 1991a, 189). When we tend to what remains after meaning has been declared completed, after verdicts have been delivered, we begin to illuminate the unrest and the excesses which underwrite desires for interpretive closure and social equilibrium. We begin to create conditions whereupon we might heed the call of meanings and memories that have been marginalized as disruptions or intrusions: cast beyond the pale of the acceptable.

These questions of viewing are always more significant than disciplinarist disputes about the best or most effective ways to relate to visual art. These questions are deeply imbricated in fundamental considerations of how we will comprise our ethical relation to the worlds in which we live. As Theodor Adorno writes: "Perspectives must be fashioned that displace and estrange the world, reveal it to be with its rights and crevices, as indigent and distorted as it will appear one day in the messianic light. To gain such perspectives without vulgarity or violence entirely from fleeting contact with its objects—this is the task of thought" (Adorno as quoted in Cornell 1992, 35–36).

To participate as a witness involves entering the fold of trauma testimony, while bearing a commitment beyond the immediate moment of encounter. The "task of thought" evoked by Adorno allows for the potential realization of political and ethical responsibility; it invites us to awaken from nostalgia, to act in the "memory" of justice.

4

Strange Gaze

In 1965, Andy Warhol became one of the first North American visual artists to make specific reference to the atomic bombings. Warhol's silkscreened painting *Atomic Bomb* presented viewers with an image of the mushroom cloud patterned into pop symbol through rote repetition. Like his famous Brillo boxes and Campbell's soup cans, the painting evoked the serial nature of consumer images, the assembly-line product. Far from being a glossy celebration of mass culture, however, *Atomic Bomb* appeared as an anxious reminder of technology's lull and the media's disastrous boredom. In quoting a pictorial motif that had become commonplace, even ornamental, in its familiarity, the painting evoked a paradox that remains central to visual culture. This paradox, which at its essence relates to the ways we grow accustomed to images of horror, is captured by John Berger when he writes, "Without a pictorial language nobody can render what they see. With one, they may stop seeing" (Berger 1988, 16).

What does it mean to "stop seeing"? This seems a pertinent question to be asking in this age of rapid image-flow, with nightly newscasts beaming scenes of mass death *live* from so many perennial, regional wars. More pertinent still: What does it mean to become accustomed or inured to images of mass violence and persecution? How does this happen? An initial approach to these questions might address the media as a key culprit in routinely purveying mind-numbing images of violence. Visual fatigue overwhelms denizens of television, who are bombarded regularly with feckless montages of catastrophe. We hear repeated warnings that those who live under the sway of televisual images are likely to become deadened to them. With earthquakes, car crashes, and genocide passing into near blur, media critics have suggested a need to explore how viewers are left to respond to fast-edited news features, which inform only by inundating us with broad-sweeping images of horror (Sontag 1977).

The central concern, here, is that images and events—however jolting initially—may leave us emotionally inert through repetition

FIGURE 4.1. *Atomic Bomb* (silkscreen, acrylic on canvas). Andy Warhol, 1965. Photo courtesy of Alesco AG, Zurich.

and familiarization.[1] In the context of this general thesis, the Bikini atoll tests in the Pacific in July 1946 have provided a striking illustration. Although the tests incited opposition from those fearing global ecological disaster and from those objecting to the forcible displacement of Bikinians from their homes, several critics have suggested that these tests also had the strange effect of pacifying general attitudes toward atomic weapons (Lifton and Mitchell 1995, 85). The catastrophic dimensions of the atomic bomb could be scaled down and standardized with repeated deployment. After four explosions, the bomb could be regarded by some as "just another weapon." The mushroom cloud could become an iconic fixture—more or less commonplace, more or less meaningless.

While it is impossible to fully gauge the effect that strategies of representation have on viewing practices, these issues are significant enough to warrant ongoing discussion. Concerns that visual repetition may do more to normalize historic events than make them memorable are clearly as relevant today as they were in 1965 when Warhol painted his *Atomic Bomb*. Perhaps more so. With the connected worlds of media (and even fashion) continuing to adopt "retro" textures and pictures, the content of archival images is easily reduced to style and stereotype. In this sense, the decorative impulse behind Warhol's silkscreen image guards against semantic shock. It highlights the apparent ordinariness of these events today, the way in which images of atrocity have been rendered anodyne, fit for casual consumption. Clearly, this attrition of meaning and emotion has ethical as well as perceptual consequences.

While it could be argued that visual literacy is cultivated through such mainstream abbreviations of past events—because these images are readily understandable to those with minimal knowledge of the subject—it may not be of the kind to encourage a depth of memory. With the unceasing appropriation of collage and pastiche techniques for corporate marketing, even the most inventive visual installations and rebellious image-montages risk slipping into background visual patter. Noise is everywhere. Even with media vectors breaking out of their provincial orbits to loop around the globe, the possibilities for responsible witnessing seem to recede rather than expand.

The need for new ways of seeing cannot be dismissed if we are to create a different kind of onlooker, a less innocent witness, less in league with the camera, less susceptible to the mainstream media's numb course. If through sheer ubiquity these images risk instilling a sense of boredom and breezy familiarity then it is up to us—as artists, critics, and educators—to contribute more rigorously to analyzing how images get construed and circulated in ways that prompt this ten-

FIGURE 4.2. Soviet Jeans Ad. Photo by the author.

dency. The concept of viewer habituation reinvigorates the thesis of *Beclouded Visions* that we have to continually reinflect our relationships to history if we are to invite ongoing reflection and action. As the news camera searches for snapshots of wreckage, indiscriminately documenting, the viewer—as witness—becomes its ethical aperture.

Mythic Memory

When struck by the apparent meaninglessness of mass civilian death, it is natural to crave explanations, to seek out familiar moorings—however inappropriate or inadequate. Establishing historical analogy, turning to documentary witness, can help ease the pain of mind experienced when encountering the errant and the overwhelming.

In relation to Hiroshima and Nagasaki, the temptation to look for familiar motifs and archetypal symbols by which to enter these events has been—in all respects—promethean. Nuclear destruction augurs a terrible sense of finality. Everything becomes loss. Our very notions of progress and continuity are up for grabs when children are stolen away suddenly, when scientific invention is turned into murderous weapon, when artists become scribes of death.

In an effort to reinstate meaning, popular history has tended to gravitate toward a quasi-religious language of apocalypse and sacrifice. Victims have been cast as messengers of eschatological doom. The figure of death has been translated into terms of the Final Judgment. I do not intend to belittle the persistent trend toward imagining and understanding the atomic bomb in relation to older paradigms (of science, myth, and war). I am, however, interested in how collective attempts to confront and represent these cataclysms have been inhibited by anxieties and fears riveted to the prospect of losing foothold in a familiar social, symbolic, and moral order.

Nuclear anxiety took on palpable dimensions with the escalation of the nuclear arms race throughout the 1970s and early 1980s. As nuclear stockpiles increased, many Americans felt overcome by a pervasive sense of doom and destruction. The provisional security offered by the simplistic 1950s "duck and cover" public-service announcements and do-it-yourself bomb shelters was rapidly eroding. Opinion polls surveying a youth generation revealed that Cold War paranoia and nuclear brinkmanship were seriously infecting their sense of future possibility. By 1983 when *The Day After* aired on ABC television and antinuclear attitudes were spreading, many felt that human extinction posed a real threat to be averted.

During this time, apocalyptic chimings and fear-jerkers warning "it could happen to us" tended to encapsulate a mythic memory of Hiroshima-Nagasaki and displace the singularity of these events under an all-pervasive and universalizing notion of nuclear threat. *The Day After*, for example, removed survivors of Hiroshima and Nagasaki from their specific history to treat them as symbolic harbingers of an end-time to be avoided at all costs.

While honoring this rhetorical strategy for its contribution to nuclear prevention, some critics have expressed wariness about the mythic characterization of historical events and agents. In his book *Letter Bomb*, for example, Peter Schwenger reminds us that human death and suffering must always be treated as more than symbol:

> In its future orientation, the mythic version of Hiroshima is one of the most responsible of its fictions. Yet, we should proceed with caution here. For Derrida's memory of the dead, he says, *seems* greater and older than us. This may be so, or seem so, only because we have assigned those qualities retrospectively. Apprehending Hiroshima in this way, we are in danger of forgetting what Hersey reminded us of: that these are human beings, even though caught in an incomprehensible nuclear sublime—which was conceived, constructed, and exploded by human beings. In memory, in mythic memory, the figures of Hiroshima move, looming in shadowy grandeur; and their larger-than-life size provides a kind of comfort. More than human, they are heroes, perhaps, or archetypes of suffering, of innocence violated, of death's other kingdom. (1994, 244–45)

The mythic effect described by Schwenger, and based on Jacques Derrida's notion of a memory which seems "greater and older than us," allows us to consider how archetypes, initially intended to guide us toward better remembering the future, may effectively place commemorated events and their protagonists in a trans-historical realm. Images which idealize the victims, Schwenger suggests, make a virtue of depoliticizing suffering. Their notion of fate implies the abnegation of choice, agency, and responsibility. It is the sense of universality intrinsic to mythic narratives which should be disputed. Memories aroused by archetypes are, and will remain, abstract: they accuse everybody and nobody.

In the West, to be sure, the survivors of Hiroshima and Nagasaki have been caught collectively in the halo of a mythic memory. Over the decades, they and their benumbed cities have receded into amorphous symbolism. They reflect the tragedy of the modern world, the dangers that reside in the unbridled use of technology. From time to time, we have been informed that the survivors suffer still from radiation sickness into the second generation, but while worldwide movements have arisen to ban the bomb, they themselves seem to have been eclipsed by a peace culture forged in the name of *all* humanity.

The mythic narrative, as Schwenger observes, is essentially a finite story (martyrs triumph over historical vicissitudes, victims retain their dignity and nobility amid the ruins). Like all morality plays, it erodes the need for further reflection and further caring. Most importantly: by reducing the world to blunt forces of "good" and "evil," mythic memory sidesteps the gray-zone of violence.

What is preempted from broader consideration is the question of complicity. What, for example, can archetypes tell us about bystanders—those who neither openly endorsed nor opposed the use of science for killing and destruction? (The question of complicity is essential because the majority of those who supported the development and detonation of the bombs were neither sadists, nor incarnations of pure evil.) Because mythic memory shuts down recognition of ambiguity, because it can only seize upon absolutes, it moves toward ethical and political closure.

Of course, there are many authentic pressures—not least of which involve the ongoing risk of nuclear disaster—which may drive us to want to find ways of boldly characterizing the unfamiliar dimensions of events, both past and present. Insofar as we can, we *do* need to know what happened at Hiroshima-Nagasaki, or the Bikini islands, Three Mile Island, Chernobyl. The value of knowledge cannot be underestimated, linked as this knowledge may be to significant ethical, political, and emotional requirements. I am, however, interested in understanding how our struggles to find coherence and clarity in our encounters with trauma may be linked to our need to reconfirm our own (ethical, social, political) identities, and by extension, a stable symbolic order. Eschatological fears associated with worries about sudden death, violent annihilation, and tragic technological errors (of the red-button variety) may, in this sense, conceal a more revealing and consequential fear—that is, fear of the unknown.

Visual culture has played a tremendous role in giving popular countenance to the unknown, to horrors exceeding our everyday imaginations. Films and paintings, as Akira Kurosawa once noted, have supported important viewing needs: they help us "put a face to our fears so that we may overcome them." Many North Americans first encountered the atomic unknown, for example, through a glut of science-fiction films that proliferated in B-grade cinemas in the 1950s and 1960s. The mutant monsters featured in these films, created through a mad alchemy of test-tube science, were frequently depicted terrorizing hapless pedestrians in Tokyo. Outcrops of uncertain times, these monsters embodied a contradictory presence, displaying traits ranging from the vulnerable to the invincible.

The postapocalyptic imagery employed by these films has been widely interpreted as a pop-reckoning with Hiroshima and Nagasaki. As Susan Sontag declared in her remarkable 1965 essay "The Imagination of Disaster": "a mass trauma exists over the use of nuclear weapons and the possibility of future nuclear wars." Most science-fiction films "bear witness to this trauma and, in a way, attempt to exorcise it." Indeed, tapping into a vague but vast sense of foreboding, sci-fi atomic thrillers helped audiences characterize and imagine the strange and unfathomable effects of radiation and biological mutation at a time when basic atomic research was still classified by the U.S. government. The innately evil Godzilla—spawned in the toxic rain of a nuclear catastrophe by Director Inoshiro Honda in 1954—provided a metaphorical specter for fears, both proclaimed and unconscious. While low-budget effects lent these films a caricaturish quality, their enormous popularity suggests that they filled a social vacuum, putting "a face"—however improbable, however tame—to otherwise inexpressible fears.

Facing Chaos

The chaos that arises when our world view is disrupted can make everything seem precarious and threatening. The need to latch onto a familiar, mythic, sci-fi (and arguably commercialized) memory of Hiroshima and Nagasaki arises from this sense of chaos—chaos as ruin, as metaphysical maelstrom. We are conditioned (through a knowledge of "order") to pull away from chaos, to avert the unknown, even if this means forestalling a process of admitting events and experiences on their own unique and often incomprehensible terms.

In this chapter, I propose a need to look for ways of passing into the chaos of nonknowing; without succumbing to helplessness, to enter into the throes of events whose meaning cannot be possessed through direct denotation alone. This is not about rejecting the necessary search for knowledge. Rather, in the spirit of filmmaker Claude Lanzmann, it is about advancing a search for a different order—one that may recognize the clutter and waywardness of events as producing new obligations.

Lanzmann, renowned for his epic documentary *Shoah* (1985), has written and spoken extensively about the impossibility of precisely or seamlessly capturing the Holocaust. Addressing the "obscenity of understanding," he insists that the destruction of six million European Jews cannot be fully reasoned or explained (in Caruth 1995, 206). To understand what happened is almost to justify. Thus, Lanzmann resists psychological and historical explanations that have pursued definitive answers for the Shoah in German *volkisch* (folk) ideology, in Hitler's childhood, or in the social-economy of Weimar Germany. The obscenity, for Lanzmann, arises when trauma—of the scope and scale visited upon European Jewry—is submitted to forms of simplification. At the heart of Lanzmann's project is an appeal to ethics not based on straightforward understanding; ethics that may address the indelible gaps, disjunctures, and disappearances inscribed by catastrophic events into our collective historical ledger.[2] Beyond the buried corpses, the metaphorical zeros, beneath the rubble, the static monuments, Lanzmann urges us to uncover the commotion of death and survival.

Sometimes brash and frequently confrontational, Claude Lanzmann embodies a certain kind of witness in *Shoah*. The task he sets himself as an interviewer involves prolonging questions that may resist the reduction of collective memory. He admits the outrage of his own confusion throughout the interviewing process. This has led some critics to accuse him of being too present, too aggressively centered, as the individual subject of a film that purports to be about a collective event. For others, however, his insistent presence as interlocutor is vital. As an ardent animateur of testimony, Lanzmann reminds us of the role we might all play in relation to those testimonies that still patiently await an active listening.

The history of Nazi genocide becomes more rather than less dense through Lanzmann's questioning. Near the beginning of *Shoah*, for example, he puzzles over an interviewee's seemingly cheerful disposition: *Why does Mordechai Podchiebnik, one of two survivors of the Chelmo massacre, smile all the time?* Responses to the event seem incongruous with what one might expect. In Treblinka, the incongruity is placed in a different light, when Lanzmann interrogates eyewitness Czeslaw Borowi about the villagers who farmed the fields surrounding the camps: "While all this was happening before their eyes, normal life went on?" Later, the mundane and the horrific collide yet again. This time Lanzmann ushers us into a Munich beer hall where he confronts former SS officer Joseph Oberhauser. Now a bartender, Oberhauser is asked how many quarts of beer he sells a day, then—without missing a beat—Lanzmann asks him of his memories of Belzec and its overflowing graves. The questions are as thick and unpredictable as their answers. As witnesses to Lanzmann's film we are faced with on-screen responses and reactions that defy easy categorization. This film isn't concerned with chronology or with simple cause and effect. Rather, its cinematic quest focuses on the actual reliving or acting out of the past, particularly its traumatic effects, in the present.

Through the layering of witness perspectives and experiences we are brought to the brink of chaos. Lanzmann suggests that we must face this sense of chaos, insofar as it may serve as the only basis for establishing new significations and insights that can challenge the adequacy of existing historical frames. Constantly invading the given and the familiar, this chaos may allow us to brush up against "the death dwelling in every life, the non-sense bordering on and penetrating all sense" (Robbins 1996, 27). That which is unfamiliar and uncanny, that which confounds, reminds us that witnessing is born of the impossible.

This is a paradoxical standpoint, but one that heeds the danger of reductive viewing. Open to memories that cannot yet be represented or judged, it is more importantly a standpoint that acknowledges the importance of bereaved thinking in a world in which dominant narratives of history continue to support exclusion and subordination; a world in which the taxed engine of judicial procedure expedites justice only by policing boundaries between admissible and inadmissible evidence. In such a world, Lanzmann's call to witness at the borders of evidential understanding entreats us to heed the unresolved claims of trauma, to recognize the discrepancies between political and judicial logic and the erratic logic of mourning and ethics. Ultimately, it is a call to ask, What *remains* after trials, transcripts, and hard evidence have brought rationality and control to the chaos (or perverse order) of the past? What lasts a lifetime?

Lanzmann provides a critique of historical empiricism to show us that trauma memory is never totally accessible: a correspondence between representations and events can never be fully attained. Testimonies can never fully retrieve their sundered bodies, corpses, histories, and meanings. Significantly, Lanzmann insists that the impossibility of complete correspondence is more than a psychic and emotional limit. A collapse of comprehension was, in effect, written into the actual event of Nazi genocide. Knowledge was segmented among the train conductor, the concentration camp guard and the local farmer. Thus, *Shoah* bids us to bear witness to an occurrence abetted through the dispersal of cognitive and ethical perspectives. What is crucially important for Lanzmann is that viewers bring the question "how?" through the diverging testimonies of the film's participants.

Lanzmann establishes through nine hours of interviews that the Holocaust, while intransigent before linear understanding, demands of us
an encounter with the ethical significance of *not-knowing*.

Introducing an ethics of "not-knowing" challenges certain ideas
about the roles of understanding and familiarization in memory-work.
The fact is that *familiarization* in commonsense terms is more closely
aligned with the act of remembering, while *not-knowing* is more often
equated with neglect and forgetfulness. But, as Lanzmann repeatedly
suggests in *Shoah*, the extreme nature of certain events raises provoca-
tive questions about the efficacy and possibility of mobilizing a sense
of familiarity in viewers. Under certain conditions, familiarity may
ease us away from disaster, eliminating the possibility of cognitive and
affective transformation, thus perpetuating the basis for historical res-
ignation.

Picturing Paradox

> To what extent do all the current versions of apocalypse now
> merely feed the vice of the hypocritical reader, the deep-seated
> boredom of an alienated public that dreams of debris, of swal-
> lowing the world with a yawn? To what degree do the stereo-
> types of nuclear destruction, like the proliferative figure of the
> mushroom cloud, aim to make us forget by their mechanical rep-
> etition the reality they are supposed to designate? (Treat 1984, 3)

Artists have worked tirelessly to prevent the brutal excesses of
history from becoming visually acceptable, clichéd, or mythic. The
paradox that a pictorial language, in attempting to render events and
things "visible" (and familiar), may promote viewer complacency has
rested at the heart of many representational and ethical dilemmas. In
Shoah, so as not to facilitate this risk, Claude Lanzmann refrained from
screening any archival or newsreel footage of the Nazi extermination
camps. In his nine-hour film, the only access we have to this world of
death is through the words of surviving inmates and through the
assorted memorial ruins and monuments strewn on the former concentration camp sites. Utimately, Lanzmann's approach is to challenge
the immediacy of these events, the illusion of transparency and direct
access provided by historical documentation. He rejects the possibility
of photo fascimile. Instead, he wants us to look through other, more
human and thus less certain viewfinders—to see these events in a way
that may honor the impenetrability and separateness of this death-
filled universe.

Visual artists, while sharing Lanzmann's concerns that visual access may lead to viewer complacency, are generally less apt to forsake pictorial reference. Despite the admitted dangers, many artists have continued to look for new visual passages into events. In pursuit of openness, they struggle with representational clichés, which condense history only by imposing a flat veto on ambiguity. Often, they find their symbolic language swaddled with prior aesthetic and historical associations. (To give a linear outline to an image, to employ the color red, is already to make use of a symbolic convention.) The point is not that artists can achieve a pure language, rather it is to stress that any groping beyond the threshold of present knowledge must work—however tentatively—against symbolic compression.

The issue of symbolic compression is particularly acute in the static arts. Painting and photography, for example, have a penchant for making the momentary look momentous by unifying events through framing and iconography. Events that can only be approached by cobbling together cryptic scraps and bits of visual evidence come across as seamless, caught within a frozen order of language. It is difficult to visualize these events—strewn bodies, unstoppable fires—in repose, and yet this is what the static image seems to demand.

If we are to ever understand how representational gestures become compacted in meaning and affect, we need to ask how such icons *get made*, how history and art get incorporated within a canonical (and increasingly, digital) ordering of people, places, events, and things. (From the point of view of ethics, the iconic image—while demonstrating a *general idea*—functions as a road block in the way of thought and imagination.) Practically speaking, then, we might trace a particular image in the process of its solidification: looking, for example, at how a painting like Francisco José de Goya's *The Third of May (1808)*, once porous with meaning, an example of powerful and unflinching seeing, becomes dense—even decorous—through the mutating forces of museum endorsement, artistic fame, and temporal distance.

What is most relevant to this discussion is how the slide toward an iconic memory may act to conceal a contradiction integral to the art of witness. The contradiction is this: for many artists, giving form to the unknown requires nothing short of translating *nothingness* into *somethingness*. Imaginations bereft of language have looked for appropriate analogy and comparison. The premise here is that the unfamiliar might become more tangible in its similiarity to something known. Hence, metaphors, such as those describing survivors wandering the streets and wading in rivers *like* walking ghosts, have scored literary and artistic works over the past fifty years.

FIGURE 4.3. *Hiroshima* (oil on canvas). Keisuke Yamamoto, 1948. Courtesy of Keizo Yamamoto. Collection: Hyogo Prefectural Museum of Modern Art.

Recognizing the power of shared symbols, it has not been uncommon for artists to cite earlier examples of protest art as an evidential reference. In a notable example, postwar Japanese artist, Keisuke Yamamoto, painted a mural simply titled *Hiroshima* (1948) that bore a striking and studied resemblance to Picasso's *Guernica* (1937). In directly citing Picasso's famous cubist mural depicting Franco's reign of terror in Spain, Yamamoto hoped to forge links between human suffering and to draw attention to the perennial role of the artist as witness. *Hiroshima* is a painting that depends on an iconic prototype for its meaning and point of reference.

These associative references and visual metaphors have provided important cues and entry points for viewers, especially for those concerned about their visual "literacy." They have the potential to resound powerfully with viewers because they are based on an extremely readable symbolism that employs familiar images with accepted meanings. But there is a random and incomplete dimension to every pictorial metaphor that must be remembered if we are to evoke a sense of representational limits in conjuring the unknown. This sense of randomness is wonderfully illustrated by Spencer Weart in his book *Nuclear Fear: A History of Images* (1988). Here, Weart cites various metaphors used to picture the atomic cloud—"a geyser, a cauliflower, a raspberry, a convoluting brain"—concluding a discussion of why the nodal metaphor of the "mushroom cloud" came to prevail (in Schwenger 1992, 24). Weart's study shows how nature-bound metaphors have slowly bloomed and clustered around this decidedly technological and unnatural event. The effect, he suggests, has been one of transporting our terrors into our raptures—turning by way of hypnotic grandeur what should be loathsome into something magnificent.

Weart invites us to see visual metaphor less literally, that is, as a provisional and indirect means of giving form to still-forming memories and knowledge. Metaphor suggests the overflow of a trauma that cannot be spoken otherwise. To see metaphor in evidentiary terms, he suggests, is perhaps to believe in our own figures of speech too rigorously: to make plain that which is attempting to invoke the extra-ordinary. The central task, if we are to allow metaphor to continue moving on the processual grain of memory, involves destabilizing the fixed conjunction between symbolic codes and their material referents—between "mushroom clouds" and atomic explosions, between "walking ghosts" and bomb survivors. These metaphors, in giving a shape to shapelessness, a face to a faceless world, may, in some ways, be treated as a sensuous paradox.

To approach this paradox responsibly brings us to the realization that defamiliarization is never simply a formal gesture. Representational practices which render objects "unfamiliar" often coincide with historical experiences of displacement and alienation. To put it plainly, the trauma of war tends to defamiliarize one's everyday surroundings. The atomic bombings, more specifically, rendered objects and people "unfamiliar." The conditions which give rise to trauma metaphor disrupt commonplace understandings of direct and indirect language. Grim technology and mass dying allow the unnatural, the unfamiliar, to attain a sense of quasi-normalcy through ubiquity. The near-dead walk. Skin crawls. Plato's cave shadows get etched on buildings through a blinding flash. Trauma's vision, as distinct from its pathology, is that of reality consuming itself like a phoenix.[3]

The Limits of Empathy

Both Victor Shklovsky and Bertolt Brecht developed theories that highlighted the role of art as one of de-habituation and defamiliarization. For Shklovsky, the art of "making-strange" was primarily a formal aesthetic concept. He saw in art a means of renewing perception, a way of prolonging the perceiving process. For Brecht, however, the art of estrangement and defamiliarization had clear social implications. As a Marxist playright, Brecht was interested in provoking the consciousness of his spectators. Creating theater without grand finales or conclusions, Brecht hoped to encourage his audiences to actively work through intrinsically unfinished works (Arato and Gebhardt 1985, 210).

Brecht's theory of "alienation" was, to state it simply, put forward as a critique of European industrial capitalism: "making-strange is one of the many devices used by artists and theorists to take a 'crack' at the 'objectivity' of capitalist society and consciousness," thereby challenging taken-for-granted conditions of existence (Mitchell 1994, 75). For Brecht, more than Shklovsky, formal alienation had a targeted focus: namely, the alienation of consciousness and labor in capitalist society. Conceived as a means of shocking people from what he perceived to be an inert state of complacency and teleological acceptance, the role of art in Brecht's world was to alienate the alienation, make it strange and unacceptable. If the epic world of theater could challenge the idea that oppression and social division were inevitable, then perhaps the world could be imagined—and remade—differently.[4]

A standpoint of estrangement was taken to promote the possibility of active and critical thought. Bertolt Brecht felt that empathy and character identification were modes of response that led to political and esthetic passivity on the part of the viewer. The closer the viewer came to closing the distance between the perceiving self and the representational other (by drawing on parallel or substitutable experiences), the greater the chance of emotional *frisson*. Having had an emotional response, the viewer could leave a performance feeling sated and relieved. Brecht felt that to seek identification in order to achieve catharsis and resolution was, at best, socially and politically ineffectual, and at worst, ideologically stilting and counterrevolutionary.

Brecht has not been alone in questioning the limits of empathy. In fact, as will become clear over the next few pages, empathy has been a recurrent theme and problem in work on trauma witnessing. How should identification be achieved? Based on what assumptions and to what effect? Flagging the danger of empathic catharsis and habituation, theorist Cathy Caruth has written, "The difficulty of listening and responding to traumatic stories in a way that does not lose their impact, that does not reduce them to clichés or turn them into versions of the same story, is a problem that remains central" (1995, vii).

Empathy, as Caruth has noted in her work on trauma, is extended most easily to individuals whose conditions and experiences are readily recognized and assimilated on the basis of likeness. Yet, because social transformation cannot be exclusively located on an individualistic-moral plane, empathy has inherent limits. Displays of kindness and understanding on a one-to-one basis of the self-same are insufficient means of rectifying political inequalities based on structural violence and subordination.

In recent years, the construction of "innocent" AIDS victims has provided added reason to consider the limits of empathy. By the late 1980s, as the AIDS epidemic reached crisis proportions in North America and could no longer be symbolically contained as a disease solely affecting designated "carrier" groups (namely, gay men, prostitutes, Africans, and other marked "others"), politicians and journalists began to profile victims who could serve as composite representatives of the "general public." Those featured for public sympathy tended to be heterosexual, white, and were generally described as having contracted the virus through "low-risk" activity. One prototypical AIDS "innocent," Kimberly Bergalis, made national headlines in the United States after contracting the virus from a dentist. The overwhelmingly sympathetic public response to the Bergalis story—a story that even "touched" such hardened arch-conservatives as Republican Senator Jesse Helms—stood in sharp contrast to the reactions faced by those deemed "less innocent." While Bergalis was "humanizing" AIDS, a majority of people diagnosed with the virus were still being socially quarantined, many blamed by an AIDS-phobic media for willing the disease upon themseves through sexual promiscuity, drug use, and general transgression.

Fashioned in relation to perceived sameness, empathy could only be extended to those people who might be seen to fit into a mainstreamed "us," applied to those experiences that could be likened to "our own." Counted among those who could elicit strong public sympathy were newborn children, cheated lovers, and blood-product users. The plight of countless others would remain strange and untouchable. Cultural-critic and AIDS-activist Douglas Crimp, who followed the Bergalis phenomenom closely, has observed how public empathy, in failing to account for (and in stigmatizing) social difference, had the unfortunate effect of reaffirming the basis for discrimination and exclusion (in Caruth 1995, 263). As the mainstream media castigated AIDS activists for their alleged rancor and militancy, empathy was directed at those model victims, who, gracious in their suffering, expressed silent forbearance.

Further illustrative of how social trauma requires model victims as ciphers for public sympathy and reconciliation are the "Hiroshima maidens" who were elected to play this role in postatomic America. In 1955, the Hiroshima maidens, a group of young women severely disfigured by the bomb, were brought to the United States to undergo plastic surgery—to restore their stolen beauty. The initiative, organized by writer Norman Cousins, captured national attention when several of the maidens appeared on a televised episode of *This Is Your Life* (May 11, 1955):

> [T]he gracious demeanour of the Maidens suggested that *hibakusha* did not blame anyone for their misfortune and considered the atomic bombings unavoidable. . . . one historian has observed that "the curing of the Maidens symbolized the healing of wartime hatreds and projected an image of American compassion, benevolence, and generosity toward a former foe." (Lifton and Mitchell 1995, 255)

The campaign, which during its most humane moments sought to undo some of the physical effects of the bombing, met with controversy. The predominant criticism was that this symbolic "face-lift" was just that: little more than an epidermal, and hence superficial, undoing of the ravages of war. Cosmetic surgery could not begin to repair the deeper scars left by the bombings.

106

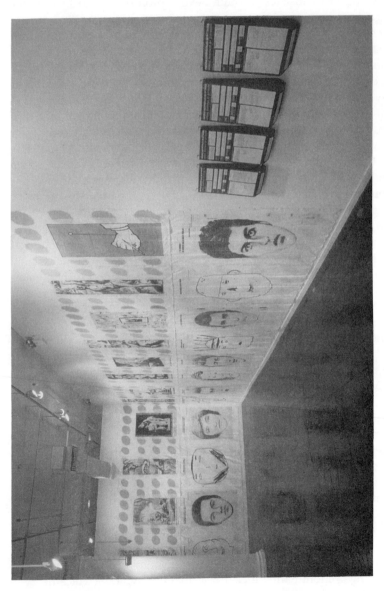

FIGURE 4.4. *La Cuisine et La Guerre—Airmail Painting No. 112* (detail, paint, stitching, and photo-silkscreen). Eugenio Dittborn, 1994. Photo courtesy of The Museum of Contemporary Art, New York.

The campaign, critics still argue, was used as a form of reprieve, as a way of resolving extant ethical and political tensions. Once the "maidens" were subsumed under an order of looking based on ideals of gendered beauty, they could be integrated into a familiar world of "women"—integrated as if this world had not already been defaced by their emotional and spiritual disfiguration.

The danger is that empathy based on common ideals and likenesses negates those differences that may reveal any given community's exclusions. We can see this danger addressed, if not rectified, in the work of Chilean artist Eugenio Dittborn. In a series that began as a means of addressing Chile's sense of geographical and cultural isolation under the Pinochet military dictatorship (1973–1989), artist Eugenio Dittborn created large-scale "Airmail paintings" which he folded and sent to galleries worldwide. On sections of unprimed canvas, Dittborn printed and collaged faces taken from diverse Chilean sources—mug shots of petty criminals, ethnographic photos of indigenous peoples, drawings by children and schizophrenics, and a newspaper photo of a political dissident murdered in cold blood. Through these collaged paintings Dittborn hoped to draw international attention to those erased from the memory of official Chilean culture.

As viewers, we look at Dittborn's assembled faces and the faces appear to be looking at us. On the one hand, as critic Guy Brett has noted, the intimacy assumes the comfortable habit of centuries of looking at others—in portraits, in the movies, on television.[5] On the other it completely disperses this convention and any certainties we might hold about the meeting of faces. Looking is no longer pedestrian or predictable. We are coming from dissociated times and different lived realities.

Wall texts equip us with the knowledge that the faces that look out at us do so from a space that is radically divided—by death—from our own here and now. Gazed at posthumously, the ultimate vulnerability and loneliness of each face resides in the way they seem to separately anticipate this death. Still present before the camera, each face is imminently disappearing. We are too late to stop these particular disappearances, but Dittborn still wants to make us witnesses to the acts of force which turned life into unnatural death. His faces of the dead and disappeared signal an erasure that is no less determinant for our present and future in having happened in a different time and postal zone.

To be meeting face-to-face like this requires an enormous journey, a vast spanning of distance. How will we attend to those strangers who have suffered if not through proximity? Through Dittborn's "Airmail paintings" we are sent in search of connections that may undo the promise of closeness offered by shared location and identity. We are decentered in our looking. From this perspective, philosopher Alphonso Lingis suggests, we begin to establish an ethical relationship between the living and the dead:

> To catch sight, beyond kinship, of this *community in death*, we should have to find ourselves, or put ourselves through imagination, in a situation at the farthest limits of kinship—in a situation in which one finds oneself in a country with which one's own is at war, among foreigners bound in a religion that one cannot believe or which excludes one, with whom one is engaged in no kind of productive or commercial dealings, who owe one nothing, who do not understand a word of one's language, who are far from one in age [for even being of the same age-group is a commitment]. (1994, 157)

Like Eugenio Dittborn, theorist Kaja Silverman has asked how we might introduce memories and experiences that are not our own, images that are "not us," into an active ethical reserve. *How can we become responsive to those others with whom we appear to share nothing in common?* Silverman's notion of productive looking challenges us to face those who are strangers to us, while recognizing "our involuntary acts of incorporation and repudiation." She asks how we might be brought to accept as our own that which we might otherwise "throw violently away." How we might "acknowledge as other" what we conveniently claim as an extension or mirror of the self (1996, 184). The danger, she admits, is always two-pronged: that we will create too little or too much distance. Too little distance may lead to narcissism. Far worse is too much distance: it may lead to murder.

Thwarting intersubjective identification is not only impossible, but undesirable. Unlike models of empathy fashioned around the figures of Kimberly Bergalis and the Hiroshima maidens, however, Silverman insists on linkages that are nonassimilative, connections that defy the principle of "corporeal sameness upon which the normative ego is predicated" (1996, 85). Like Bertolt Brecht, both Dittborn and Silverman search for forms of identification that may recognize intervals of difference. In so doing, they call us to reach beyond local networks of community, to consider the commotion of "far-flung" lives and deaths as they traffic into our otherwise self-preserving worlds.

More than Meets the Eye

There are undoubtedly images and portraits whose ostensible meanings appear quite obviously—even strikingly—familiar. Yet even in these instances, the visual economy of art may produce excess associations and stirrings, provoking a fresh response to the subject and new requirements of the viewer. But the overflow of art, the open claims of trauma, are vulnerable to our looking, our tenderness, and our patience. The following extended passage, excerpted from Ineko Sata's atomic bomb story "The Colorless Paintings," draws this into focus. Sata shows that the ethical and social possibilities of art are jointly created by artist and viewer.

> I go on standing in front of K's colorless paintings and look at his photograph with the black ribbon, painfully holding back the thoughts that well up in me, I want to say something to the people viewing the pictures. I want to say something to the visitors who look at K's paintings and display a polite attitude of sorrow before his photograph and then pass on. . . . The disease that killed him, after inflicting rapidly increasing pain, was cancer of the liver.
>
> The natural result of physical emaciation was expressed here in the paintings—is that the right conclusion? The inevitable relation between the artistic production and the physical power of the artist is verified by the black ribbon. No, that's not true, I would still insist. I want to say something, because the paintings devoid of color and the photograph with the mourning band tell us that and nothing more. And yet I cannot express it clearly. I myself am afraid to probe into the matter. The name of the disease is liver cancer. But what is the name of the thing that deprived this man of all color? What could it be called? It seems that the ideas suggested by these paintings preclude anything that is commonplace. They appear to belong to another realm. They rather seem to be produced by the will to defy, but that defiance had to be painted, even though colors escaped the artist, and that's why they display an unnameable grief. But this will probably not be apparent to the visitors passing from gallery to gallery. People seem to trust to the impression they get from the black ribbon as they stand in front of the paintings that have lost all color. (Sata 1985, 124–25)

I have been suggesting, as Ineko Sata's protagonist does, that there is comfort and consolation in certain modes of recognition. Through associative links we may establish precedent. For example, we may look upon the black ribbon as a common memorial emblem for funeral ceremonies in Japan and conclude blithely that mortality is universal, that "others have died before." We may view the painting Sata describes as a closed circle of meaning, much like a wreath or lifecycle, and declare that "this grief, like all grief, will pass."

To recognize something is to be able to track it back and read it against what is already known (and hence, already processed through language and consciousness). To recognize something, in short, is to find an analogy or parallel through which to name the unknown, to find a means of making a potentially discomfiting painting "readable" on a continuum of history and narrative. In sorting through common trauma signifiers—a dead body, a distraught child, a bombed building—and what they *mean*, we develop a collective vocabulary through which to name the dimensions of a disaster. In this sense, realist signifiers and details encourage viewer identification, allowing for a sense of pathos, a flash of sympathy. But as Bertolt Brecht might ask: what is it that the viewer is seen to be identifying with?[6] (The warm glow of identification with the point of view of victims is so easily made, yet so presumptuous. It is less easy to identify, however critically, with the cultures that nurture aggression.)

Ineko Sata invites us to encounter the unfamiliar, the remains which slip unmanageably beyond our symbolic worlds, even if they scramble and upset our initial terms of reference. What was stressed and implied in order for empathy and identification to be realized? What dangers, what destabilizing encounters, averted? Sata's protagonist suggests that by submitting an event to a unified explanation (based on epistemic or empathic identification) something of its singularity—or otherness—may be foresaken. To respect this otherness, to aspire toward becoming accountable to it, means to contemplate that which may exceed and disrupt historical understanding and conventions of viewing.

Opening oneself up to trauma's excesses is a profound undertaking. Death is tragic, but less so when it can be instilled with deep significance. The prospect that hundreds of thousands, even millions, of people were murdered for nothing is unbearable. The impulse is to invent meaning by engaging in symbolic or ritual identification. In this way we fill the spiritual vacuum.

Yet the "colorless paintings" bequeathed to us cannot be reduced to the symbols necessary for closure to occur. Those traditions of looking that sustained us before may be improper when we apply them to commemorations of mass death. For Sata's protagonist "K," the muses have been silenced. All the former metaphors, the harmonies, the lyrics, the colors, they mean nothing. The colorless paintings wrestle, it seems, for an attention that might yield the meaning that lies in their incoherence, their impasse, their nonsequitur.

The violence of nuclear destruction is ultimately incalculable and uncontainable. As such, it consistently threatens to unstitch the fabric of representational narrative. Terminology is rendered impotent, weak, in evoking these events. In February 1946, General Thomas Farrell, commander of the first U.S. army research team to enter Hiroshima, revealingly remarked: "This isn't a bomb at all. The use of the word 'bomb' carries with it a completely inaccurate picture of what this thing really does" (Boyer 1985, 66).

The inevitable gap between what happened and its representation is powerfully explored in the works of Yamashita Sohoh. Sohoh is an artist whose own "colorless paintings" drifted into my life during a meeting with Hiroshima survivor and activist Setsuko Thurlow. Although I had already selected the works I proposed to discuss in this book, his ink paintings continued to haunt me, pressing their way into my life.[7]

Consciously or not, Sohoh's work highlights the importance of memory (by which to communicate and encourage solidarity), while acknowledging the impossibility of its direct access. Because his paintings call attention to the unreliability of cultural referents after the atomic bombings, we are pushed to reconsider how we delineate narratives of trauma. While Sohoh's titles frequently provide strong associative cues, his pictures also suggest the need to demarcate new and more nuanced ways of relating to these experiences. Verbal captions are insistently surpassed. We cannot see this if we concentrate solely on what the work is "about," or aspects that are recognizably descriptive. These paintings, falling out of grief, provide an absorbing meditation on the elegiac in art—and its agonizing limitations. Sohoh summons a vision marooned in a world of fragments and ruins. One senses, quite literally, that Hiroshima is the past that refuses to go away, the dark blot on the psyche of a survivor. Death seeps across the paper like an unwashable stain. Truly this is what is meant by haunted.

An image, entitled *What I Saw in the Ruins*, in bearing no indexical relation to anything I have seen or known, presents me with a challenge to symbolization. What cannot be seen—the invisible movement of atomic radiation, the vaporized subject—imposes itself on the painted surface and consumes it. The image depicts a moment that in reality is utterly discontinuous with my own "now." It conveys the unsettling effect of a decentered reality, the void left behind by a people's mass murder.

The severed relationship between Sohoh's images and their titles implicates me in a motion of translation that may or may not generate a memory for the nameable and unnameable dimensions of

112

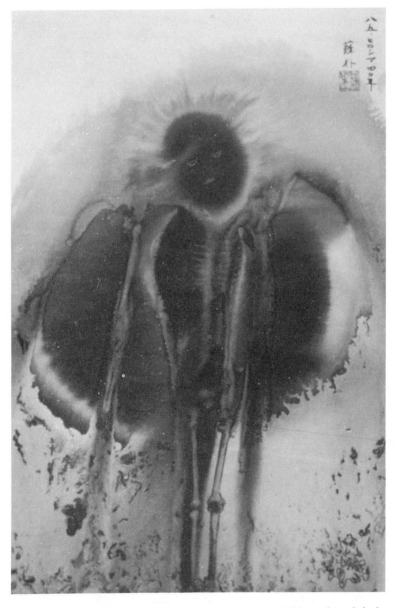

FIGURE 4.5. *What I Saw in the Ruins* (ink on paper). Yamashita Sohoh, 1985/1986. Photo courtesy of the Yonemata family.

the bombings. In threading my way through his work, in running along the edges, I can sense memory as it yearns at the barricades of language. Sohoh hasn't given up on art, despite a subject that continues to stray past the limits of what can be said and shown. Still tremulous with energy, the image vibrates along my social nerves, communicates its vital stimulus.

Beyond the Looking Glass . . .

Yamashita Sohoh's paintings are Rorschach blots for viewers to test their historical and emotional reactions. They are offered up as an absence made tangible, a space onto which viewers can project their own feelings about what was lost as a consequence of the bombings. At the same time, Sohoh shows us that abstraction is not necessarily the antithesis of reality. Abstraction, figured here as the irreducible stain of disaster, carries its own demands. The painful withdrawal of reference asks that we become translators—connecting the language of the work to the events whose traces it bears. In the moment of translation, art asks something of the viewer: How do you experience these events?

The process of ethical translation requires that we collaborate with efforts to represent historical trauma, even as we confront the difficulty of entering into meaningful dialogue. Through the multilayered dimensions of art, we may be ushered to the limits of comprehension and narrative sense. Rather than attempt to resolve the dissonance we experience—or project it back on the work through a language of pathology—we need to find ways of tending to the excessive dimensions of a testimony. How do these unassimilable aspects testify to the limits of what we know and understand? What do these borders tell us about conventional frames and certainties of history? In asking such questions, we redefine our role and relation to the testimony *throughout* our encounters. As Alphonso Lingis writes, "One exposes oneself to the other—the stranger, the destitute one, the judge—not only with one's insights and ideas, that they may be contested, but one also exposes the nakedness of one's eyes, one's voice, one's silences, one's empty hands" (1994, 11).

It is up to commemorative practices and pedagogies to find ways of enframing what might be considered a crisis of significance—whereupon a person's historical, cultural, and social assumptions, values, and memories are disrupted—in ways that promote continued thoughtfulness and action. We are often third-order witnesses, removed by geography, even by generations, from an event. The truth is that any response to testimony is bound to feel insufficient. Those who were there in the situation, those who held the hand of the dying or bandaged a wound, are not experiencing the moment as we do and their responses are of an altogether different order.

In light of this experience of discontinuity, we need to find ways of enticing historical inquiry and ethical translation rather than encouraging retreat. The decision to turn away, to say nothing at all, rather than to say something that might be seen as inappropriate or inadequate to the occasion becomes what Ken Ruthven has termed a "meta-response" (1993, 23). Such "meta-responses" should be considered unhelpful and dangerous by those of us who believe that modern warfare is not simply a textual effect but a reality which introduces new risks and ethical questions.

For commemorative educators, the challenge is one of providing a supportive environment without encouraging coping mechanisms that would invite students to shelve away (nuclear) aggression and modern violence as impenetrable existential and moral quandaries. Students need to be creatively pushed to think about the dire (ethical, political) consequences of militarism and domination. The impulse to close-off and shut-down in the face of this challenge has been discussed in depth by Robert Jay Lifton. "Psychic numbing" is Lifton's shorthand term for a complex response to anxiety and guilt which results in a "cessation of feeling" (Lifton 1968). Lifton remarks sensitively on how forms of dissociation (often therapeutically necessary for trauma victims to function in daily life) are conditions of "enormous collective and historical significance" because they expose a widespread reluctance to imagine, and act against, the relations which produce genocide and oppression (Lifton and Markusen 1991).

In a broader North American context, our search for ways of coping with environmental and social upheavals has given rise, in recent years, to flourishing millennial movements—both religious and secular—all joined by a need to instate systems of explanation. End-time fear mongering, in the forms of apocalyptic forecasts, and gloom-merchandizing, have helped fill an anxiety vacuum by tapping into nonspecific fears. At the same time, definitions of social crisis are being increasingly relativized by the media, such that the O. J. Simpson Trial, the death of Princess Diana, and the genocide in Bosnia-Herzogovina can be placed on a par. All pervading worries are being detached from real causes and crises. Anxiety becomes free-floating, stripped of particular referents, ending in a state that Freud called "angst." When anxiety is this aimless and nonspecific, our sense of apathy, helplessness, and cynicism is increased. As a result, there is a tendency for many to indulge in a rejection of hope that borders on nihilism. Need-less to say, despair, of this sort, takes on the world's suffering to no purpose.

The temptation to evade disturbing and difficult experiences can-not be diminished here, especially if the encounter begs for some accommodation or transformation on the part of the witness. There are many defense strategies that the self uses to escape feelings of inade-quacy and uncertainty. When overwhelmed by the immediacy of a tes-timonial encounter, for example, I have found myself retreating into the abstract solace of an atlas, into the merciful particulars of historical facts and figures. The necessary context and momentary respite that ascertainable knowledge provides should be recognized.

At the same time, the search for ethical ways of remembering those who have suffered and continue to suffer in unspeakable ways continues. As witnesses, we look to return a sense of humanity to media-ized events, so that we will not become insensitive to images of human pain. We look for a moral language that can yield to the incomprehensible, while providing guidance for future action.

It is my belief that expressive culture provides a space for such encounters to occur: it helps to deliteralize yet not dematerialize trauma, to entice rather than shock spectators into contemplation. Given that it is impossible to react indefinitely to these events at full emotional pitch, the capacity of art to reach beyond our barriers is worth stressing. In its potential to disarm reluctant witnesses of the immediate impulse to turn away from trauma issues, art has a crucial role to play. Art encourages us to acknowledge and reflect on our uncertainties. It allows us to transcend dichotomies between hope and dread.

5

Mourning the Remains

1995 was the year of memory. Whether watching television or venturing into the somber space of the Museum, one was apt to see numerous reminders of World War II. The zeitgeist—emphatically commemorative in Berlin, Tokyo, and Washington—seemed to spread with each passing milestone, to be recharged with each new day of reckoning. Wreath layings, anniversary tributes, diplomatic apologies, monument raisings, exhibitions, and kitsch souvenirs were heaped together (sometimes uncomfortably), through stringed themes of guilt-honor-victory-repentance. Kick-started by the fiftieth anniversary of the war's end, commemorations took on vast, if controversial, communal significance.

For former Axis nations Germany and Japan, fifty years appeared to provide a safe distance from which to eulogize and simplify events, an arm's length from their use of arms. For former Allied nations, the fifty-year mark lent occasion to honor past deeds and triumphs, to erect memory walls between then and now. For nations increasingly nostalgic for a sense of positive and unified collective identity, these ceremonies, ranging from the austere to the ebullient, provided an important outlet for group sentiment and catharsis.

Watching the televised commemorations—the live coverage of V.E. and V.J. Days—one could gather a pervasive ethos of closure, a sense that now was the time to wrap-up past traumas and patch up diplomatic travesties so that "we" (the G7, the First World) might herald in the new millennium with a greater sense of normalcy and stability. Linked to the whirlwind of reflection and remorse, there seemed an impetus to move on to the year 2000 unencumbered, scraped clean of the tarnished past, free of the agitations of the aggrieved. As spectators, we were being invited to work toward this millennarian deadline, to create for each nation a zero hour, a fresh beginning.

By August 1995, most of North America's major dailies, networks, and news magazines were winding down their anniversary coverage.[1] Commemorative features on the final days of World War II tended to blur into reportorial synopses of dates and major figures. Photographs were reproduced as scrapbook pastiche, providing a skimmed view of major Allied battles and victories. Coming at the tail end of a year taxed by media-led war retrospectives, the anniversaries of Hiroshima-Nagasaki passed as final denouement: signifying, perhaps, a much-awaited "period mark" for war-weary commentators.

In Japan, public discussions leading up to official commemorations of World War II were initially overshadowed by the Kobe earthquake and the *Aum Shinrikyo* poisonous gas attacks in Tokyo subways. When August 6th and 9th did eventually arrive, ceremonies were mutedly routine. As in previous years, doves were released in Hiroshima Peace Memorial Park while the local mayor declared the city's pledge for peace. Other Japanese cities marked the anniversaries by folding origami cranes, painting atomic shadows on sidewalks, and floating paper lanterns in nearby rivers. While these familiar peace rituals were made to feel slightly more urgent and relevant by the French Government's controversial decision to test nuclear weapons in the South Pacific Atolls, commemorations tended to feel more nostalgic than critical. Debates surrounding Japan's war-time aggression, including criticisms of Prime Minister Murayama's tepid expression of "remorse" to former victims of the Japanese Imperial Army, which might have complicated official attempts to commemorate Japan's relationship to the war, made only fleeting appearance in the Japanese media. Unlike Germany, a country for which postwar memory has been an area of ongoing public debate since the early 1960s, Japan has only recently—in large part due to growing pressure from former victims—witnessed the reluctant emergence of a public discourse relating to its militaristic past.[2]

In the absence of a critical public discourse on postwar memory, commemorations of Hiroshima-Nagasaki in Japan have tended to *appear* nonconflictual. Ironically, even the theme of "peace" has tended to inhibit reflective remembrance of its constitutive opposites: violence and war. In many quarters, "peace" has become shorthand for healing and revival. Hiroshima's phoenixlike recovery from the ashes of the atomic bombings has similarly become a metaphor for postwar hope and development: urban renewal has been the preferred means for overcoming the devastation of the past.

These by now commonplace visions of postatomic "peace" were, in fact, projected onto the imagined city of Hiroshima from the outset. Within weeks of the bombings, news cameras zoomed in on flowers that were starting to sprout amid the debris. By 1947, tourist brochures (carefully edited by American Occupation officials) were insisting on an astonishingly complete recovery. Toppled neighborhoods were carefully rebuilt, block by block. The blood-soaked earth was tilled so parks and gardens could grow. The immediate postwar reconstruction of Hiroshima and Nagasaki, intended to restore a social infrastructure as quickly as possible, hurtled survivors—both literally and symbolically—into the dizzying space of a brand-new city. These reborn cities would become, in many ways, the symbolic focus of all the aspirations of a country eager to start afresh, a country yearning to finally emerge from the long shadow of its imperialist past and defeat.

Forever anxious to establish a distance from the war, the Japanese government and mainstream media continue to make a point of turning urban development and public occasions into positive showcases of the postwar era. In fact, since the late 1940s, themes of "bright and jovial peace" *(akarui heiwa)* have been so closely tied to commemorations of postatomic Japan that to remember any other way is to invite heated controversy, even assault. Former mayor of Nagasaki Motoshima Hitoshi found this out the hard way. In 1988, hoping to retexture the concept of "peace" and deepen postwar reflection, Mayor Motoshima made public reference to the war responsibilities of the late Showa Emperor Hirohito. Shortly thereafter he was shot by right-wing terrorists for his statements.

Many survivors of the bombings have challenged the commemorative emphasis on *akarui heiwa* (Yoneyama 1994). Living on a landscape once penetrated with sorrow, they resist modes of remembrance geared toward resolution and shallow recovery. Some worry that other times of memory are in danger of being swallowed up by the time of so-called "progress" and technological advancement. Economic prosperity, they remark, has made Hiroshima seem unremarkable in many ways. Sunny portraits of peace and regeneration have glossed over persistent divisions and differences among Japanese and Korean atomic-bomb survivors.

Hibakusha (atomic-bomb survivors) continue to raise vital questions about the ethical limitations of commemorative discourses of hope and renewal that are enacted in lieu of confrontations with loss and displacement. Robert Jay Lifton's observations of Hiroshima, made thirty years ago, describe a city scarred by its inability to accommodate those still living with loss:

> [M]ention of the city's prosperity or of its other accomplishments brings an immediate cautionary statistic about unemployment and economic hardship among day labourers, and about the high percentage of *hibakusha* in this group: "Hiroshima is well known as the 'Peace City,' but that Hiroshima is also the 'unemployed city' is not well known." And with a similar sense of contrasting

imagery, it is pointed out that people with keloids are no longer
frequently observed because "they seem to feel hesitant to go out
and be seen on the clean and bright-looking streets of the city."
(Lifton 1967, 264)

Increasingly, the aphoristic idea that saying "yes" to life and a
peaceable future is the equivalent of saying "no" to atrocity and history's carnage, has been revealed as facile and even proscriptive.
While we must undoubtedly say "no" to acts of dehumanization and
destruction, and affirm life if we are to struggle against immobilizing
despair and cynicism, this in itself may be insufficient if we are to
interrupt relations of memory/forgetting that continue to structure
collective experiences of disaffection and oppression. (Postwar Japan,
while unified to a large extent by a collective peace culture, is nevertheless crowded with separate solitudes and lingering inequalities.)
The often frustrated plight of trauma survivors for social support and
restitution provides a sobering reminder of links between past and
present expressions of group hatred and neglect. The presence of these
"others," who have been left stranded on the borders of collective
memory and power, entreat us to revisit traditions of recovery based
on restoring calm and order, that is, to consider how commemoration
might involve a durational practice of *mourning* trauma's ethical ruins
and remains.

In contrast to official State commemorations of World War II, this
work of durational mourning would aspire to remember 1945 not as
the ending of another conventional war, but as the onset of a different
stage in the history of mass death and trauma. Fifty years have not
cauterized the ethical, social, and psychological wounds wrought by
World War II—a war that saw the eruption of new technologies of
mass extermination and degradation. Efforts to pace or measure these
traumatic events through chronological remembrance have tended to
move us less toward a rethinking of the past's significance and more
toward smoothing over lingering conflicts and questions.
    Guided by the rote obligations of chronological remembrance,
for instance, it is hardly surprising that after a brief moment in the
early 1990s of "coming to terms with the past," public discussion in
Japan seems once again gripped within the narrow spectrum of economic concern. In 1996, only *one year* after the fiftieth anniversary of
the war's end, Japanese newspaper editorials were commenting on a
changed commemorative climate. A disturbing aspect of post-fiftieth
anniversaries, these editorials suggest, has been the diminished focus

on Japan's brutal wartime record. In place of 1995's outpouring of apologies and expressions of atonement, the Japanese newspaper *Asahi Shimbun* remarked, in a commentary published in August 1996, that, "The atmosphere within (Prime Minister Ryotaro Hashimoto's) Liberal Democratic Party is that there is no need to pay for the past any more because it is no longer the 50th year after the war." Hashimoto's 1995 promise that the nation would bear "future responsibility" for its wartime aggression seems to have evaporated. Much to the chagrin of Japanese activists, article 9 of the postwar Japanese constitution, which, imposed by the United States in 1945, renounces war and forbids Japan to participate in the threat or use of force, is slowly being reinterpreted. The events of World War II are being placed in the aspic of history.

During a bilateral U.S.-Japan summit in April 1996, Prime Minister Hashimoto announced that Japan's long journey to exorcize the ghosts of the war was almost complete, and, notwithstanding article 9, he hoped that Japan would soon be able to take a more active role in international security. Separating the commemoration of the past from the climate of the present, Hashimoto proclaimed: "Last year in Japan we commemorated the 50th anniversary of the end of the war. This year we are taking the first steps toward a new era."[3]

Moving on Memory

During the research phase of this book, which coincided with the fiftieth anniversary of the atomic bombings (or "V.J. Day"), I was made doubly aware of how acts of commemoration and mourning are extruded from our everyday lives. From acid-rain-soaked bronze monuments in parks to one-shot anniversary specials on CNN, there is a tendency to see the "past" as containable and unremittingly separate—as something that can be tidily hedged off in green-spaces and marked via satellite TV-time.[4] What and how we remember World War II—its tragic cluster of events—is socially organized and sanitized through conventions which tend to lend the past a mythic, even majestic, quality. As if it were all so clear, so symbolically mappable, we are told to "look back" on history, to pay tribute to the past, to erect plaques and place wreaths in honor of the dead and fallen. While comprised of complex and unresolved relations of violence and oppression, the events of the war tend to be regarded as objectifiable, iconic, even inevitable. Through this looking glass, World War II becomes a series of episodes more distant and remote than anything we might consider within our field of present concern.

Yet, from the Shoah to Nanjing to Hiroshima-Nagasaki, from Bhopal to Vietnam to the Gulf War, this century has seen mass death and industrialized violence take on unprecedented dimensions. These events—produced through old and new racisms, nationalisms, and hatreds—make demands on our ability to remember justly. These events require of us a steady commitment to test the boundaries of socially sanctioned remembrance and commemoration: What do commemorations desire? What and how might they seek to forget?

Public ceremonies and rituals are clearly crucial to the work of communal mourning, helping lend common structure to collective losses. These rituals can provide comfort and guidance when we are in states of shock, assist us in our grieving. But commemorations also perform an exclusionary function. By recognizing certain forms of loss, and ignoring or marginalizing others, these rituals reflect power structures operating in society. Even in common burial practices, we can see, in microcosm, how a hierarchy persists. The poor are still buried in unmarked graves. Churches are still used to decide who will be buried where and how. Jewish cemeteries continue to be desecrated—a form of double death, a second extermination. Mass graves used to inter the eternal regiment of the nameless and unknown. And in North America, battles continue to be waged over the archaeological excavation of sacred native burial sites.

It is distressing, but perhaps illustrative, that memorial spaces tend to mirror the distortions of power that abide for those who have lived, and died, on society's fringes. The power to influence the shape of mourning—the girth of collective memory—persists as a matter of selection and devaluation: Who, after all, has the power to decide what we commemorate, when we mourn, and in what manner? And perhaps more importantly, what are the penalties for those who defy this?

The thrust of these questions assumes that there are socially acceptable times and outlets for invoking memories rooted to expressions of grief, lament, reflection, and mourning. And further, that expressions transgressing these boundaries may be derided and pathologized as *griev*ance, com*plaint*, or quite simply, a failure to *move on*. These proper and improper ways of coping with trauma are drawn by a *cordon sanitaire*. For example, mourning the AIDS crisis in funeral parlors may be deemed acceptable, whereas taking to the streets in vigils for government AIDS action may be seen as politically opportunistic, aggressive behavior. While the former interiorized expression of grief over trauma is contained within the "private" sphere, the latter communal expression understands mourning as necessarily social and political, and is, hence, resignified as disruptive.[5] Projects ranging from the Vietnam Veteran's Memorial to the AIDS quilt have gone a long way in testing this separation of mourning from activism. But even with these popular efforts to politicize bereavement, there is still a marked tendency to separate mourning from routine spheres of social and political life. Rather than garnering public compassion and support, for example, social mourners are frequently disparaged as angry, weak, even destructive.[6]

By contrast, ritual forms of mourning associated with national commemorations and funereal or anniversary events are seen to serve a healing or redemptive function. These ritualistic events, which operate on the basis of social consensus rather than social conflict, provide a means of reaffirming a sense of "normal" communal life *as it was previously lived*—thus restoring the promise of a *new* social equilibrium on the basis of status quo values and social relationships. Memorial Day weekend in the United States, for example, is a public holiday that is as apt to be associated with summertime celebration and leisure as it is with remembrance and contemplation.

Ritual approaches to mourning—borrowing, as we will see, from Sigmund Freud—appeal to a basic human longing for recovery and life-affirmation. If we are to gradually heal rather than harbor residual griefs and pains, the place of ritual and communal ceremony is clearly important. What is less clear is how, and why, ritual mourning and social transformation have come to be seen as antithetical, and how, and on whose terms, social consensus and "normal" life are being defined.

Durational Loss

For many people, national commemorations are associated with the yearly staging of remembrance in public plazas and institutions. Commemorations provide a special time to honor, to pay tribute, and in some cases to reflect on past wrongdoings and sacrifices. A time for sentimental and collective gatherings, national commemorations are performative: they allow for otherwise dispersed groups of people to attain a sense of their present communal significance. Frequently cathartic, commemorations can also provide a ritually confined means of moderating anxieties over losses, converting collective dread into collective hope. Remembering within the bounds of sanctioned definitions of commemoration is considered healthy, even obligatory. It is assumed that a well-adjusted society can only be enhanced by its ability to reflect on its progressive passage from a perhaps less illustrious past.

Yet to suggest that there are befitting ways for a society to remember might also be to suggest that there are other, less appropriate means of invoking our relationships to a nation's past. Remembering out of bounds, at the borders of commemorative protocol and governance, is *unsettling*. Hence, definitions of social equilibrium and individual healing are sometimes used against those who do not adhere to the proper place and time for commemoration and communal mourning. There is a cautionary note here warning us of a potential loss of ontological perspective and identity. But this cautionary note, as we will see, presumes a homogeneity, a simultaneity, among the members of a commemorating community predicated on the erasure of differently timed memories.

Insofar as we embody different social biographies and have experienced different traumas, it is important to remember that we *do* live in different "nows." The hauntings, the injustices, which bring us to inhabit and inherit the meanings of trauma differently are not easily settled or lain to rest—notwithstanding prevalent healing programs or protocols of legal justice. For example, while the 1988 Redress Settlement represented a significant political victory for Japanese Canadians and Japanese Americans seeking an official apology and reparations for their forcible internment, a brief glimpse at recent writing and art by Japanese North Americans would suggest that the discord and upheaval spawned by the internment and postwar relocation continue to infuse questions of community and identity.[7] A similar but more sustained history of government-sponsored relocation has had lasting effects on aboriginal communities in Canada. An earlier history of colonial violence and conquest was compounded throughout this century by a Church-run residential school system that forcibly removed Native youth from their homes. Now grown, many former students continue to testify to their traumatic childhood experiences of sexual, physical, and emotional abuse.

Many first-generation survivors of violence and displacement insist that they need to forget the horrors of their experience so as to "get on with everyday living." Appealing to a metaphor of vision, for example, Nobel Prize laureate Kenzaburo Oe once wrote: "If a person is so clear-eyed to see a crisis in its totality, he cannot avoid falling into despair. Only the person with duller vision, who sees a crisis as part of ongoing life, can possibly cope with it" (1995, 125). While recognizing that survivors of brutality face, to varying degrees, the real psychic danger of being resubmerged in trauma or deep memory, the question remains as to whether or not the desire for commemorative closure on the part of those who were not directly immersed in, or subjugated by, trauma actually advances the interests and divergent claims of the victims. Depending on how we are located, efforts to resolve personal and social trauma may enforce a strategy of containment. Ideologies of pacifism and harmony, for example, may support the social management of conflict. In mapping trauma out of the socius, we block out difficult questions—for example, questions about how today's social "order" is constituted through commemorations that marginalize testimonies bearing witness to *ongoing* social crises and violence.

Crypts of Memory

National commemorations can both engender and, at the same time, neuter the uneven memories and divergent trauma experiences of its citizenry. Contrary to common perception, dominant practices of remembrance may seek to *encrypt* rather than *openly suppress* lingering experiences of loss and trauma. The special preservation of atomic ruins in Japan, the processing of victim-claims through war crimes tribunals in Argentina and truth commissions in South Africa, the perennial unveiling of new monuments in North America, while invested with commemorative intentions, have all, to varying extents, also served the dual purpose of reinstating social order and reinvigorating the possibility of national unity and pride.

In the case of Hiroshima and Nagasaki, humanist narratives about the war and nuclear holocaust more generally have prevailed in structuring encounters with the meanings of the bombings. Lisa Yoneyama is among a handful of scholars who have, in recent years, focused on how these narratives—lent form through popular representations and monuments—have tended to universalize the experience of the bombings. Yoneyama, in particular, has looked at how Korean minority memories of the atomic bombings, which factor in histories of Japanese colonialism and subjugation, have destabilized dominant commemorative approaches (which position Japan uniformly as a "victim-nation"). Yet, as these memories have been articulated more vocally over the past few years, Yoneyama has observed parallel attempts on the part of Japanese nationalists to domesticate them:

> [T]he hegemonic process within the production of Japan's national history is moving beyond what we currently see as reprehensible—that is, beyond amnesia—to a point where those in power are contriving to "come to terms with the past" (Adorno 1986), through at least partially acknowledging the nation's past misconduct and inscribing it onto the official memoryscape. Yet as Theodor Adorno wrote, the coming to terms with the past

(*Aufarbeitung Vergangenheit*) "does not imply a serious working through of the past, the breaking of its spell through an act of clear consciousness. It suggests, rather, wishing to turn the page and, if possible, wiping it from memory." (Yoneyama 1995, 115)

The demands of economic and political relations in the Asian Pacific region and international pressures accompanying Japan's rise to "superpower" status have forced the government of Japan to relinquish its past strategy of silence and denial in relation to Japanese colonial and military atrocities. Instead, a language of "remorse" has facilitated the absorption of difficult and potentially disruptive memories into the fold of "national history" without undermining longstanding power imbalances (Yoneyama 1995, 513). This new trend toward "coming to terms with the past" has had inauspicious effects in Japan. That is to say, Korean minority memories, formerly relegated to junk-heaps of history, have been co-opted into a framework of reconciliation, thus hampering their potential contribution to an enduring critique of contemporary Japanese social relations. Yoneyama suggests that practical concessions made by the Japanese government have been a matter of political expediency—a gesture of ritualized penance. Japanese officials could be exonerated of their war crimes once they became protective guardians of minority memories. She believes, in effect, that the initial impulse to commemorate events like the Korean atomic bomb experience may actually derive from an equal desire to forget them.

How does a nation remember events it would much rather forget? In the wake of ever-shifting practices of remembering and forgetting, Yoneyama addresses how important it is for us to remember and *mourn* vestigial legacies of amnesia in national histories (505).[8] Those in positions of dominance cannot be given exclusive title to the past when definitions of history are used to decide the social terms and material grounds on which everyday lives and possibilities are to be realized. If the assimilative spirit and ideal of national commemoration encrypts otherness, then a politics of *mourning* is required that can unravel this tendency. The dream of collective nostalgia, the aura of national recovery, may, thus, be vexed by the insistent return of yet-to-be confronted losses and injustices. The act of remembering changes in this way: instead of anguish and glory it becomes work and continuity.

Hauntings and Specters

In Hiroshima's Peace Park, under a mound of grass (about ten feet tall and fifty feet wide), there is a hollowed-out space containing a collection of porcelain cans. Each can, among the thousand lining the shelves, holds the ashes of a single victim of the atomic bombing; each victim's name has been carefully marked on the side. Fifty-some years after the bombing, these ashes remain unclaimed by families. Under the mound, stacked behind curtains, rest several dozen wooden boxes. These simple boxes are said to contain the ashes of seventy thousand unidentified victims of the atomic bomb (Lifton and Mitchell 1995, 358). Beyond the toponyms written on each wood crate, which generally register where the remains were found (a kind of desperate poetry), the ashes are anonymous. These human remains, returned to the shores of the River Ota without names, have compatriots in such places as Poland, Cambodia, Argentina, and Bosnia.

Wherever there exist mass graves, humanity has been desecrated. According to Jacques Derrida, the hauntings arising from these unmourned deaths and unnamed remains continue to stake claims on the present. As if to reject the unsettling specter of these hauntings and ghosts, however, commemorative rituals have generally aspired to lay the past to rest: to certify that the "dead" are in fact uniformly "dead"; that bygones are bygones. If it is unnerving to be stalked by ghosts, the guiding mission of commemorative work, Derrida suggests, has been to stave off the revenant of the past, to ward off the unknown and unnamed:

> Nothing could be worse, for the work of mourning than confusion or doubt: one *has to know* who is buried where—and *it is necessary* (to know—to make certain) that, in what remains of him, *he remains there*. Let him stay there and move no more! (Derrida 1994, 9)

Mourning, in the absence of ghosts, carries the promise of its own termination. Once the (material and symbolic) "remains" have been sifted through and *grounded,* the meaning of violence and its resultant human loss can be localized. Yet, as Derrida suggests, the moment the significance of an event or trauma has been fully named, it enters the final throes of death, only to be forever interred. This mode of remembrance, which enacts a final incorporation of loss, has a parallel in Sigmund Freud's triumphalist phase of mourning. Here, mourning's completion is attained only through prohibition: that is, by embracing life while attempting to eliminate irreducible *difference.*

Deaths and remains which cannot be fully materialized and consecrated through factual liturgy, linear chronology, or common burial practice must, according to this conventional model, go unmourned.

Those trauma experiences that cannot be entombed through an appeal to reconciliation ("it is over now") or precedent ("it has happened before"), must similarly pass unmarked. Rites of mourning which refuse the spectral presence of ghosts (i.e., those unnamed others, that which is still unfamiliar) obliterate the remains of trauma at various levels: they close themselves off to those bereft of the social and symbolic power necessary to erect monuments or preserve spaces of memory, and shutter themselves to that which remains unknown and thus outside a community's memorial boundaries.

In view of such restrictive and expulsive rites of mourning, Derrida proposes another meaning for mourning which will be central to the development of this and the following chapter. Describing mourning as "in fact and by right interminable, without possible normality, without reliable limit," Derrida proffers that mourning "responds to the injunction of a justice which, beyond right or law, rises up in the very respect owed to whoever *is not*, no longer or not yet, living, presently living" (1994, 97). Derrida's notion of mourning, in other words, aspires to heed the claims of the dead and the as-yet-unborn, to grieve for what is no longer, for what never was, for what could have been. He invites these liminal presences to be admitted into a contemporary ethical community of concern and reflection.

Derrida provides an impetus to reconceive traditional understandings of mourning. While Freud suggested that mourning is terminated when there is a return to "normalcy," Derrida takes mourning to be by necessity ceaseless. To locate the extended significance of Derrida's departure from conventions of mourning and remembrance founded on the incorporation and resolution of loss, it is necessary to revisit Sigmund Freud's oft-cited essay "Mourning and Melancholia." One cannot travel far in the landscape of grief without acknowledging his preeminent influence. Thus, I take up Freud here, issuing one caveat: while Freud does not purport to offer a general theory of mourning, explicitly limiting his purview to a discussion of melancholia (that is, "pathological mourning"), his work continues to be cited as a key reference and resource.

According to Freud, the shift in mourning from ritual to routine marks the mourner as pathological. Mourning, in the Freudian sense, is thus governed by distinctions between a normal and abnormal disposition. What is of interest here are some of the distinguishing features that Freud cites in his attempt to ascertain the slide from good (healthy) to bad (unhealthy) forms of mourning. Freud argues near the beginning of his essay that the difference relates less to the empirical conditions which give rise to expressions of grief (the actual instances of trauma, which might involve the experienced loss of a person, thing, or ideal) than to the subject's *self*-perception and disposition within this economy of pain. While mourning frequently involves "grave departures from the normal attitude to life," Freud argues that over time, the healthy subject will eventually overcome or exteriorize the pain and find a means of reintegrating themselves into normal society (Freud 1984, 252). Freud ventures so far as to suggest that attempts to intervene in the process of mourning's completion may be dangerous and harmful. Melancholia, or pathological mourning, by contrast, is characterized by a profound "disturbance of self-regard," such that the melancholic's ego is threatened and debased by an over-whelming loss of self-worth and identity. Freud writes:

> In mourning it is the world which has become poor and empty; in melancholia it is the ego itself. The patient represents his ego to us as worthless, incapable of any achievement and morally despicable; he reproaches himself, villifies himself and expects to be cast out and punished. (1984, 254)

The melancholic's interiorization of pain, guilt, and self-abjection is so all-encompassing and immobilizing that little energy or interest is invested in anything or anyone else. All thought of remorse and shame is angled inward, leaving the prospect of consolation remote. While the state of melancholia Freud discusses here might be usefully (albeit *carefully*) compared to forms of self-denigration that accompany what in popular parlance is known as "survivor guilt," I am more interested in returning to Freud's foundationalist description of pathological mourning. To help us along a little, I will quickly summarize some of the main features of "healthy" mourning, as suggested by Freud.

According to Freud, reality-testing is a key component con-tributing to the cessation of mourning. Through a process of recon-necting with one's "normal" surroundings, one may attenuate or fix the disjuncture experienced as loss. Immersed in a healthy and non-hurtful socius, the trauma may be scaled down to size. Freud's tri-umphalist phase of mourning, thus, gauges success by assessing the extent to which the ego/libido has been divested or severed from the "object-loss" or "lost object," which "no longer exists," "is dead" (1984, 265). The work of Freudian mourning, thus, constitutes a double movement: it both produces a historical object (through historical chronology) and situates that object on the periphery of a temporally and spatially bounded socius. The verification of a dead corpse, in senses both material and symbolic, becomes the condition of possibil-

ity for those commemorative rituals which enact and establish a separation betwen the past and present, life and death, presence and
absence. This rite of passage, as Eric Santer has noted, requires "something on the order of a funerary ritual or elegiac procedure lest the
spirits of the revenant, vampiric object haunt us eternally from that
space of the unmourned, the unconscious" (1990, 68).

It is immensely significant that Freud, writing in the early twentieth century, refrained from addressing the collective experience of
war and extermination. His initial silence before the traumas of the
First World War was resounding. The earth had recently opened up to
receive the bodies of eight million young men. Putrefied corpses and
stunned survivors haunted Europe. Freud's early "death-instinct" theory could scarcely encompass violence of this scope. And yet, it is to
this theory that he turned in an attempt to explain the deadly combat
and mass destruction he had witnessed. As Robert Jay Lifton notes:
"The war's traumas to the movement must have been perceived as a
struggle for survival. . . . The problem for Freud was to assimilate these
experiences into his already well-developed theoretical system" (1979,
64). Events which shaped the body politic were granted no significant
place or consequence in the origin and development of Freud's theories. It was, in fact, only by assimilating the vast and reverberating horrors of the "Great War" that grief could be isolated and mourning sundered from its social and political surroundings.

Freud's central characterization of mourning as a solitary and
interior activity is incomprehensible once we invite consideration of
historical trauma. While these collectively incurred losses are
undoubtedly experienced intimately and personally, the conditions
which give rise to mass trauma cannot be isolated in the psychic lives
of individuals. The experience of loss, in the case of Hiroshima-
Nagasaki, for example, cannot be separated from complex practices of
militarism, racism, and imperialism. What is the "object-cathexis" of
(collective) mourning in this instance? What if the conditions which
give rise to mourning are structured conditions of everyday life for
certain communities? Can we conclude, as Freud does, that mourning
signals a "grave departure from the normal attitude to life"? What constitutes a "normal attitude"?

The closed shutter that Freud hoped to introduce between the
time of trauma and trauma's aftermath was clearly ineffective for
renowned *hibakusha* writer Tamiki Hara, who saw such a shutter as
enforcing a blinding of memory. Hara committed suicide in 1951 upon
hearing rumor that the U.S. was considering use of tactical nuclear
weapons after China's entry into the Korean War. He took his own life

rather than bear the burden of witness to a trauma repeated. Through his final actions, we can see that Hara took the renewed threat of nuclear warfare *personally*, experiencing the events surrounding the Korean War as part of ongoing relations of military trauma from which he could not extricate himself.

Guided by Freud, we might look upon Hara's suicide as a manifest expression of pathological mourning. But where does pathology begin and end? One might argue, as noted Canadian engineer and pacifist Ursula Franklin has, that industrial militarism and technocratic warfare are fundamentally and infectiously dysfunctional. If the very idea of rational mourning presumes an objectively healthy and stable social order, Franklin would question whether such mourning is possible: Are we not all somehow contaminated by the pathological death-driven world in which we live?

Tamiki Hara's "pathology," I would submit, emerged from his desire to participate in transforming the terms of war so that another Hiroshima would be unthinkable. This transformation could not occur amid the unreflective war mongering and military momentum of the 1950s. For Hara, the very threat of nuclear warfare, the U.S. bid to secure democracy *at any cost*, suggested a radical severing of any connection to the legacy of atomic suffering. Nuclear weapons had been accepted as part of postwar civilization, somehow becoming ordinary weapons of war. This, for Hara, was unconscionable. Was it possible to lament the suffering of irradiated victims and contemplate further use of such weapons?[9]

Ultimately, Tamiki Hara's death had nothing and everything to do with the trauma of Hiroshima. Hara's decision to end his own life, exceeding any one single explanation, was at once intensely personal and profoundly public. Perhaps he wished to avoid being counted as one more impersonal figure in the growing toll of atomic victims— saved, thus, from the pyre of one vast collective cremation. Perhaps he was too fatigued by the challenge of resuming life after the bombing. Perhaps he never overcame the loss of his wife to radiation sickness. We will never know everything about his death. Through his writing, we can only gather that from the time of the atomic bombing of Hiroshima in August 1945, to the time of his death in March 1951, the countless farewells and griefs Hara experienced resounded like a "dirge" in his heart.

Through the story of Tamiki Hara, we approach the troubled core of Freudian mourning, essentially understood as a process of termination, whereby trauma is materialized and ritually guided into the past tense of our lives. Hara's "madness," his durational grief, interrupts the "rational" process of recovery to confront the social forces which block such recovery from taking place. In his wake, in his unresolved indictment of military aggression and postatomic memory, we are left to ask about our own reactions to other possible catastrophes. We are challenged to consider our connection to the social traumas we have witnessed: What "irrational" forces infect *our* thinking and actions in the present? What will be the basis for *our* survival?

In contrast to Sigmund Freud, Jacques Derrida proposes an ethical discourse of interminability as central to considered approaches to trauma memory. Given the grim legacies of twentieth-century violence and domination, the inequalities and forced displacements that continue to be produced in the service of liberal democracies, Derrida invites the possibility and necessity of establishing a postmelancholic framework of "perpetual mourning."[10] Mourning, thus, may make us more attendant to the discordant losses of life and possibility—which continue to haunt the everyday global order.

Mourning at the Limits

At the beginning of this chapter, I questioned what it meant to *move on* with memory. Taken in another register, "moving on with memory" might be heard differently, more descriptively. As more and more communities are being displaced by military and political upheavals, uprooted by dint of global economic restructuring, millions of people are *moving on* with memory in the most literal sense. They have become global refugees—looking for asylum, for status and citizenship in the heartlands of the economic North and the urban centers. Today, as I write, for example, Roma refugees from Czechoslovakia are waiting in a detention center in Toronto. They are being held while Canadian immigration authorities process their claims and check for evidence of past criminal records. Meanwhile, a crowd of neo-Nazi demonstrators that gathered several days ago to picket for their deportation have gone unquestioned by the police.

The Roma (or "Gypsies") are among a growing population of political refugees who are lugging their legacies across borders, from place to place, across mountains and oceans. Dispossessed and displaced, they remain ambivalently within the histories, cultures, and memories of their homelands. They are exiles, marooned between the bonds of the past and the promise of renewal. It is difficult to imagine that some of them must live among us now as ordinary women and men, employed in North American factories, offices, and homes. For they have been marked as outsiders, foreigners, outcasts. They are welcomed only reluctantly by

nations caught in a paroxysm of contradiction: nations wavering
between racism and liberal ideology; between xenophobia and a commitment to human rights; between the need for a cheap labor force and
the limits of the welfare state. They come to nations still loathe to recognize the land claims of aboriginal communities, the shaping force slavery
has had on African American communities, and, thus, the inaugural
losses that laid the foundations of "New World" existence.

The flight from the Old World to the New World is generally seen
to be a flight from memory—memory of oppression and limited free-
doms—to a limitless future. The attraction is one of rebirth into a kind
of clean-slate historylessness. Yet, in truth, the passage is rarely so simple or amnesiac. A large number of refugees continue to harbor
wrenching memories of partings and losses. Others embody a violence
writ too deep. Hunger. Rape. Torture. Deportation. These short words
seem horribly inadequate: engraphing little more than the paucity of
headlines in rendering living biographies.

These memories in transit, formed and forming, cannot be
named, spoken, let alone absorbed, by North America's mythic sagas
of settlement. Nor can they be assimilated by anthemic stories of "harmony" and "New World beginnings," in which freedom and security
can be seen to flourish in the soil of free-market egalitarianism. *Remembrance Day* with all its settled imagery of wind-blown poppies and
crosses row-on-row cannot testify to memories of violence still
wrought by ongoing power imbalances. Many of the brutal, no-quar-
ters battles of modern urban war with civilians as victims, cannot be
named let alone remembered within these symbolic enclosures.

It becomes harder to mark trauma monumentally or chronologi-
cally when it is the legacy of *cumulative* confrontations and struggles
against class, race, and gender-based domination. Harder to seize a
monolithic moment to grandstand or demarcate as the Official Event.
Harder to pinpoint an appropriate time or venue for commemoration
when trauma is the shuddering result of a barrage of dehumanizing
encounters and slow but constant acts of force. Civilian memories of
social upheaval, which course through the interstices between private
grief and public discourse, cannot be called forth through simple symbolism, cannot be arrested through commemorative sites or memorializing conventions—however solemn.

These memories are still happening. They cannot be assigned
dates or limits, which are not their own. These memories mark an
excess. They test the alienating slumber of tradition, the exclusions of
national communities, and call us to remember at life's boundaries—
to *rethink* the boundaries. Heeding these unfolding testimonies from

our multiple standpoints would require nothing short of a radical transformation in the way we see, think, and feel our relationship to the past and otherness. It would mean rigorously scrutinizing our collective ideals of order, peace, tranquility, redemption, and justice in order to examine how these concepts may hamper, and even pathologize, the remembering of historical suffering and those enacting memory. It would mean finding *trans*-memorative passages that may link unnamed losses, undocumented deaths, unspoken sorrows, to expressions of collective grief.

Experiences of trauma, whether spawned by sustained exposure to abuse or violence, or borne of a sudden assault or loss, need to be listened to carefully. As Kai Erikson has observed: "Trauma is normally understood as a somewhat lonely and isolated business because the persons who experience it so often drift away from the everyday moods and understandings that govern social life" (in Caruth 1995, 198). Erikson asks us to consider how trauma testimonies might convey "a wisdom" about the world, suggestively inviting us to consider what it would mean to give public voice to mourning that might otherwise be marginalized.

This nascent wisdom may enter our worlds only when we heed the power of and need for bereaved thinking. Without such thinking, we learn to painlessly separate from everything—to see everything as passing and fleeting. In renouncing a connection to the dead and lost, we lose the ability to mourn. Teaching us daily lessons of disposability, media culture and consumer capitalism encourage us to disavow the importance of reflection, to resist the "dirge" in our hearts. In the flickering world of television, things and people pass by rapidly, disappearing as soon as they extend beyond the reach of our sensory perception. Faced with a culture saturated with distractions, the introduction of secular thinking about trauma and death becomes a pledge to forbearance and responsibility. Determined not to let the specter of past and present injustices fade, we become patient before latent wisdom, mournful of memories murmuring just below the surface of everyday life.

We are, in the end, all mourners on this fragile earth, making daily choices about our participation (or lack thereof) in the fate of others who live, die, and grieve around us.

The work of artist Felix Gonzalez-Torres (1957–1996) employs commonplace objects to entice his viewers into everyday practices of mourning. The seduction occurs at the level of the work's formal beauty. The subtle elegance of his art bids contemplation, reinvesting beauty and simplicity with new purpose. His printed billboard series, for exam-

FIGURE 5.1. *Untitled—Beds* (detail, printed billboards). Felix Gonzalez-Torres, 1991. As installed for The Museum of Modern Art, New York "Projects 34: Felix Gonzalez-Torres," May 16–June 30, 1992 in twenty-four locations throughout New York City. Courtesy of Andrea Rosen Gallery, New York. The Werner and Elaine Dannheisser Collection, on long-term loan to The Museum of Modern Art, New York. Photo credit: Peter Muscato.

ple, interfacing with a pedestrian public, infused the most ordinary sights and objects with elegy. Normally associated with outdoor advertising, the billboards had the strange effect of drowning out the surrounding visual clamour with images of tranquil quietude and calm.

In 1992, Gonzalez-Torres mounted a collection of billboards in the busy core of downtown Manhattan as an intimate tribute to a life-long lover lost to AIDS. A black-and-white photograph of an abandoned double-bed—sheets still ruffled, pillows still impressed—brought the domestic sphere in direct contact with a commercial environment. By rezoning the "private" into the "public," Gonzalez-Torres hoped to unite these seemingly incompatible and inviolable spaces. Mimicking the informational strategy of advertising, he aspired to insert AIDS awareness into the collective social memory of New York City.

In another installation, the very act of consumption, so tied in with our retail culture, is reinflected with memorial significance. Cutting across market values, Gonzalez-Torres's signature candy-spills reflect a generosity of spirit, a willingness to openly collaborate with the public. A vast candy spill called *Untitled (Portrait of Ross in L.A.),* *1991,* is comprised of individually foil-wrapped candies, hundreds piled together, which approximate the weight of a lover lost to AIDS (175 lbs). The actual candies, intended to be shared and distributed among viewers, are gifts of art, or giveaways, intended to incite thought about, and possible reaction to, the social issues buried amid the sweetness. The sheer number of candies, countlessly consumable, register something important about AIDS mourning—conveying the catastrophic accumulation of near-identical disasters.

Using an intentionally edible and carnal metaphor, Gonzalez-Torres encourages us to partake in the aftertaste of eros and death. Inscribed at the core of this poetic creation, however, is a friction between dispersal and dissipation. We watch with a sense of pathos as the memorial slowly disintegrates. A body of grief is shown to coexist with a memory of sweet love, and we are asked to carry these contradictory remains away with us. This is not a liturgical rendering of death. We are asked to be more than reverential observers. In binding his viewers to this bittersweet ritual of AIDS mourning, in making us carriers of its legacy, Gonzalez-Torres insists on our role in shaping collective memory. The candy spills, unlike permanent memorials, decentralize the task of remembering, as if to remind us: people are not meant to endure grief alone; we are all witnesses to this social tragedy.

Appealing to a lyric sensibility through his billboard series and candy piles, Gonzalez-Torres suggests that "our erotic spaces are filled with ghosts."[11] Where there is eros, there is the body, and where there is the body, there is decay and death. As soon as we engage the organic world of pleasure and the senses, we engage the mortal, vulnerable body. Although death is our natural and destined end, AIDS reminds us that many deaths occur as unnatural intrusions rendered more grotesque by their presentation as merely spectacular images. For Gonzalez-Torres, eros captures the melancholy and loneliness of surviving with death, but also the impulse to reinvest in life and the memory of love. His candy piles remind us that we can become gluttons for pathos. (We await the sorrowful experience because it allows us to feel *deeply*.) He warns that we can idealize death, just as we can become mourners without cause. This is the danger of separating mourning from its social and political contingencies—a danger we must work against.

Until his own untimely death in 1996 of AIDS-related illness, Felix Gonzalez-Torres devoted himself to the work of mourning. With poignant effects, he explored how scopophilia and desire were stricken by loss. The work he left behind, employing metaphoric allusion and faint traces of absent life, presses us to keep asking: What lies outside of art and history which can nevertheless be felt as the shadow of some life or thought realized long ago, passing and settling in the hollow of empty arms? What can be missed or measured that does not reside in a physical presence?[12]

Bereaved Witness

Relating art to matters of historical witnessing, this book opened with two questions: What are the limits and possibilities of art in challenging traditional ways of seeing the past? What philosophical shifts might be necessary in order for "spectators" to engage art toward "witnessing" a disruption of conventions of thought? To these questions, I now add a third: How might the art of witnessing, in allowing us to test the limits of remembrance, engender a social practice of mourning? Now that half a century has passed, what we see before us in places like Hiroshima and Nagasaki is a daily life from which most traces of trauma have been erased. Are there images that might be capable of piercing through our "well-adjusted present"? Are there changes we can make to contemporary commemorative rites that would facilitate a respectful death for the dying, as well as social grieving for the survivors? Are there ways to construct memorial spaces that would allow us to remain open to inexpressible and ongoing losses?

Amplifying the possibilities of art in evoking the remains and residue of trauma memory has been a central aspiration of this book from the beginning. In preceeding chapters, I have attempted to develop a conceptual terrain that might allow us to understand how our acts of looking at witness art are constitutive of an ethical vision. In the last chapter, for instance, I explored the potential of art to defamiliarize assumptions about what we have seen and known, thereby creating conditions in which divergent and unexpected understandings about the past might be generated. In inviting us to acknowledge the limits of what can be concretely or descriptively represented, I have suggested that art may testify to the excesses created by discursively organized knowledge and narratives. These memorial excesses demand an attentiveness on the part of the viewer-witness that I have proposed is akin to a process of vigilant and reflexive translation.

Translation, in this sense, becomes an ethical practice of mourning trauma's remains: a gradual process of coming to a trauma's significance. Enacted as a means of keeping impassioned thought and reflection alive, ethical translation carries with it a recognition of its own impossibility. Moving where evidential meaning collapses and bodies go missing, stumbling through experiences of catastrophe that cannot be contained by any patterned response or schematic interpretation, translation cannot be completed. There is no closure. The world survivors inhabit now can never be connected to their lives before. Is it possible to resume an "ordinary" life having experienced the prospect of an extra-ordinary death? If you survive *in spite of* your historically designated "fate," *whose* life do you step into?

Sigmund Freud sought to assist his patients in enacting a termination of trauma memories. He hoped to provide them with new raiments of self. In images, dreams, rituals, he saw a restorative function: the possibility that a traumatic event could be integrated into an individual's psychic economy and symbolic order. Taken as a compensatory measure, art has been generally placed within the reassuring terms of therapy. Through art, it is thought that patients will find the means to lend shape and coherence to their otherwise overpowering pasts. Following a Freudian model of trauma recovery, art has been seen to act as a redemptive force, moving to cure the afflicted of memory, breaking links to the past. Like a moulting process, recovery represents the shedding of death, the overcoming of mortality, the renewal of the (personal and social) body.

But if trauma is the spectral return of a past injustice, it is also a gradual reckoning with that emptiness that remains afterward—*after* bodies have been buried, cities rebuilt, history books closed. Defying chronological time, trauma's legacy wades into the present in unpredictable and unremitting ways. The unofficial graffiti of death appears unexpectedly. Faults and cracks on a building submitted to an atomic blast are discovered decades after the city of Hiroshima has been redeveloped. Personal effects and artwork seized by the Nazis from Austrian Jews are retrieved a half century later—only to testify to their owner's absence.[13] Were it not for the sudden obliteration of Hiroshima, the steady persecution and annihilation of Jews in Europe, these buildings and artifacts would still be fulfilling their normal functions in everyday life.

We are surrounded, Eric Santer notes, by the stranded objects of a "cultural inheritance fragmented and poisoned by an unspeakable horror" (1990, xiii). These stranded objects crop up periodically in places like Berlin, Buenos Aires, Santiago, Phnom Penh, to recall the void left by a people's mass murder. Installed in museums, they ask to be reinvested with the fates of their former owners and inhabitants, to be reconnected to vanished, even discarded, worlds. Frozen in a state of expectant unrest, they wait for a person who has never returned. A history of violence insinuates itself into artifacts as benign as a child's jumper, a crocheted wall-hanging, an antique wristwatch. There is pathos in the ordinary. The portent of death.

These concrete remains of war and genocide have irretrievable counterparts in those experiences for which no records whatsoever exist, those losses precluded from thought or direct remembrance. Together, they express the very obstacles to social recovery. They reveal injuries and abrasions that have not yet healed. By evoking a sense of normalcy that cannot be repossessed, the traces of violence etched into everyday things and expressions, these remains suggest that justice and reconcilation are bereft if we cannot mourn their limits.

6

The Limits of Vision

In 1957, following the international success of *Nuit et Brouillard* (*Night and Fog*, 1955), a fact-driven journey into the Nazi concentration camps, Director Alain Resnais was approached to make a documentary surveying Hiroshima twelve years after the atomic bombing. He agreed to take on the project and set off for the atomic city. After months spent filming on location, however, Resnais decided to abandon a documentary genre, opting instead for a fictional film which would devote its first fifteen minutes to footage from his aborted documentary. Acclaimed French writer Marguerite Duras was approached to write the revised dramatic screenplay and the film became a joint French-Japanese venture. Resnais's decision, motivated in large part by what he understood to be the limitations and inappropriateness of realist cinema in relation to the atomic bombings, has had a long-lasting impact.

Today, *Hiroshima Mon Amour* (1959) is one of the best-known works of the French New Wave—an "avant-garde classic" that has continued to circulate in repertory theaters, film courses, and festivals. Variously remembered as a haunting love story, an antiwar picture, a tale of remembrance and forgetting, *Hiroshima Mon Amour* has persisted in evoking a range of interpretive responses. The paradox in all this might be that despite Resnais's conscious efforts to subvert assurances about docu-mimetic representation, the film has arguably become the source of many people's imagery of the city of Hiroshima and the atomic-bomb experience.

Yet, the paradox manifested in viewer desires to "fill in" memory and meaning within the context of a film that so deliberately seems to "empty out" perceptual and epistemic certainties should not be lost or minimized. Indeed, it is precisely this tension between the desire to "know" something about the subject being represented (in this case, Hiroshima) and recognition of the limits of that knowing that, I submit, may comprise an ethical vision connected to a social practice of mourning trauma's *remains*.

As a hybrid film, *Hiroshima Mon Amour* is comprised of many layers and forms of narrative. In the course of the first twenty minutes, for example, we move from an entwined lovemaking scene, to what appears to be a straightforward newsreel documentary, to a breezy on-screen conversation between two new lovers. Taken together, these contradictory plotlines—threading through fact and fiction—highlight the different ways memory inscriptions and film genres shape our understanding of historical trauma. As a "false" documentary, for example, the film calls forth our own atomic-image arsenal—unsealing any simple faith we might have in photo-realism so as to move us beyond evidentiary remembrance. But this deconstructionist move is always accompanied by another narrative gesture—a passionate, poetic reflection on memory which addresses the high stakes involved in forgetting and remembering loss. In this sense, Resnais offers what might be called a *parallax* approach to visual commemoration: he attends to the impossible task of representation *and* to the persistent struggle to express something about the subject, however incomplete and inadequate that "something" might be.[1]

Resnais's approach, in other words, recognizes the incommensurable gap between perception and reality, while encouraging us to explore the theme of what one sees and doesn't see in epistemological and ethical terms. *Hiroshima Mon Amour* thus introduces the possibility and necessity of elaborating a critical framework that might allow us to take up this gap (or aporia) as constitutive of the limits of knowledge. *How do we open a space in which to signal that which cannot be seen or shown? How might we encourage reflection about the relation of vision to knowledge and ethical action?*

These last questions resonate with concerns that have been recurrent in critiques of postmodern and deconstructionist approaches to historical representation. Cathy Caruth and other scholars have argued that deconstruction has been wrongly identified with the claim that historical reference is inherently fictive, and "accordingly been dismissed as denying memory, history, and all notions of truth" (Caruth and Esch 1994, 2). These misleading charges have led many scholars and critics to distance themselves from deconstruction as a philosophical discipline; to malign it as a destructive, nay-saying, even nihilist practice. What is generally missed, or willfully ignored, is the central contribution deconstruction *can make* in opening up fields of historical and ethical inquiry. In testing the criteria by which we compile and adjudge history, for example, deconstruction opens itself up to the unknown—inviting an awareness that historical reference and knowledge may not always occur, or present itself, in ways we immediately recognize. This recognition of indirect or unfamiliar reference is crucial to the study of historical trauma. Turning to such examples as the "gaps and breaks in survivor narratives," Caruth reminds us that trauma history and memory are seldom experienced in seamless or concrete ways.

Ultimately, the potential value of deconstruction rests in its application. Recognizing the limits of vision, to be sure, can either foreclose access to historical reality altogether, or stress the provisional and fragile nature of its representation. Central to the development of this chapter is a view that a deconstructionist aesthetic requires a context that can foreground the underlying philosophical and ethical implications of problems of representation. The question of context is paramount—perhaps more so for works which openly play with cultural and historical references. Aestheticist approaches that broach the dismemberment of the past, the limits of trauma testimony, solely as a matter of formal interest invariably rationalize the violence.

Since the late 1960s, there has been a growing emphasis on conceptual minimalism in North American contemporary art practice, a bias toward postmodern abstraction and installation-based work. The gradual break from modernist representation—in a challenging of canonical notions of authorship, artistic value, realism, originality—has given rise to a range of contradictory practices. There is no unifying agenda tying these manifold expressions and artists together. While often sharing nonfigurative stylistic features (such as sparseness, simplicity, openness), each work demands a separate and situated response. In valorizing creative minimalism and aestheticizing memory "gaps," we may bypass the particular responsibilities involved in negotiating with the limits—the remains—of any given commemorative practice. To conclude, for example, that "less says more" is perhaps to skirt problems of representation and memory reconstruction entirely.

In this chapter I will be looking at *Hiroshima Mon Amour* with an eye to elaborating what Drucilla Cornell has called a "philosophy of the limit" that can call forth the ethical aspirations of deconstruction. A philosophy of the limit, as suggested by Alain Resnais, might make us more humble about what we claim to have seen and allow us to move away from conflating seeing and understanding. But Cornell's philosophy of the limit pushes us further. Because *all* description and narrative constitute limits of remembrance, because the atomic-bomb experience conjures an excess that cannot be fully incorporated, we are pressed to explore the ethical implications of partial memory. In this sense, "like the Angel of History," we are asked to witness trauma's

144

FIGURE 6.1. Still from *Hiroshima Mon Amour*. Director Alain Resnais, 1959. Photo courtesy of Photofest, New York.

ruins and remains while becoming "complicit in a process of making meanings and making history" (Rabinowitz 1993, 136).

Remembering at the limits is what I have chosen to call a practice of *trans*memoration. It is a practice that ushers us to the borders of perception, thought, and possibility. When it comes to memory, the border is more important than any temple, shrine, or monument. It is a place of remembering that a death, as unique as a life, is always in excess of any representational system, always more than a symbol or a slogan. Even as we enlist artifacts and images to "name" and "picture" the dead, the *limits* bid us to keep our minds and hearts open to the people, losses, and sufferings which cannot be captured. As Derrida suggests, these excesses, these remains, these "ghosts," call forth infinite responsibility and an aspiration to live "more justly" (1994, xviii).

Hiroshima Mon Amour

Hiroshima Mon Amour follows a twenty-four-hour affair between a French actress and a married Japanese architect. The one-night lovers are anonymous, unnamed throughout the film. *He*, the architect (Eiji Okada), is involved in a project of swift development, rebuilding over Hiroshima's charred cityscape. *She*, a French film actress (Emmanuelle Riva), is finishing up a peace film set in the atomic city. The two strangers meet in August 1957. *He*, originally from Hiroshima, has lost most of his family in the bombing. *She*, originally from Nevers, France, where she was punished as a collaborator following an affair with a German soldier, has a less obvious relationship to the city of Hiroshima.

The film begins with a sequence of grasping limbs and torsos. Cascading into camera-dissolves, these sweat-soaked bodies can be seen moving into the clutches of love *or* death. They enter into the visual ruins of a film which will repeatedly intersperse images of sexuality and annihilation. The off-screen voice-over is flat, formal, repetitive: a metronomic exchange droned in counterpoint to the images of fluid passion that fill the screen.

The spectacle of their lovemaking in a hotel room slips into newsreel footage of postbomb Hiroshima. The dialogue continues. Set against a realist memoryscape, an "official parade of already well-known horrors from Hiroshima" (Duras 1961, 9), the female voice claims a total vision. The male voice refutes and inverts every statement.

He: You saw nothing in Hiroshima. Nothing.
She: I saw *everything. Everything.*

She continues to insist that she has seen *everything*.

She: Four times at the museum in Hiroshima. I looked at the people. I myself looked thoughtfully at the iron. The burned iron. The broken iron, the iron made vulnerable as flesh. I saw the bouquet of bottle caps: who would have suspected that? Human skin floating, surviving, still in the bloom of its agony. Stones. Burned stones. Shattered stones. Anonymous heads of hair that the woman of Hiroshima, when they awoke in the morning, discovered had fallen out . . .

He: You saw nothing in Hiroshima. Nothing.

She: . . . I've always wept over the fate of Hiroshima. Always.

He: No. What would you have cried about?

She: I saw the newsreels. On the second day, History tells, I'm not making it up, on the second day certain species of animals rose again from the depths of the earth and from the ashes. Dogs were photographed. For all eternity. I saw them. I *saw* the newsreels. I *saw* them. On the first day. On the second day. On the third day.

He: *(interrupting her)* You saw nothing. Nothing.

As he repeats his incantation, his impersonal voice coldly denying her every claim, we see images of the Peace Park, the Survivor's Hospital, panoramic newsreels, the Hiroshima Peace Museum. What she describes, insists on having seen, is an archival history of Hiroshima. These well-ordered images, catalogued for museum-goers and memory-tourists, sweep by the screen. *He* suggests that what is being "seen" is a swift memorial that can offer little more than a design of the past: an architectonic view that pinches the vast horror between four walls for all to see. Arranged within the four walls are mementos, safeguarded memory-objects. Their presence offers a kind of solace, a sort of companionship. The four walls provide a centre, a focal point, for envisioning meaning. Four walls so that we might know where to look to see *everything* (that counts, can be counted, accounted for); four walls so that we may be freed from looking *beyond* to bordering longings and miseries for which no records whatsoever exist.

As the narrative unfolds, we are forced to relinquish the provisional security of a single or unitary vision, the desire for omniscience, to see it all. The flickering film-frames accord with the experience of a glance: the random movement of a viewing process that cannot possibly ascertain everything. This is a way of seeing that highlights discontinuities. It is impossible to sustain a prolonged gaze. Resnais, thus, declines from projecting or asserting an absolute vision of Hiroshima.

He offers no final moral ground, no steady harbor, from which to apprise the event of the atomic bombing. Instead, the film adopts a strategic mode of address, constantly subverting narrative authority, casting doubt on the reliability of perceptual claims. The film not only accentuates the limits of its own narrative construction, but also calls into question received sightings and knowledges. Always in excess of any name, image, or meaning, Hiroshima is never "given" as pure, uninterrupted memory. Instead of the reduction of memory to a site, Resnais invokes complex and even banal spaces of remembering where we confront the presence of loss through everyday living and chance encounters.

Hiroshima Mon Amour is, in this sense, a narrative that folds itself *into* and *away from* a commemoration of the bombings. It is a film of endless lamentation that is dramatically suspended between the acting out of a traumatic past and the difficult effort to work through it. The vexed impossibility of memory, the fleeting salve of amnesia, the unstitched terror of remembering and witnessing beyond bounded stories and sites: these are themes that reel through *Hiroshima Mon Amour.*

While Shoshana Felman suggests that *Hiroshima Mon Amour* instructs us "in the ways in which testimony has become a crucial mode of our relation to events of our times—our relation to traumas of contemporary history," it does so by consistently breaking with referential narration (1992, 5). The film evocatively gestures toward the unknowable, toward sites and sights that exceed our immediate frames of reference. These are events that dash efforts to gain hold, grasp, and enclose understanding. Unfathomable are the words: *enemy, atrocity, destruction.* They exist only in the larger perception of History's recording. "You have seen nothing" if you imagine this trauma self-transparent, or so the narrative seems to insist.[2]

Seeing Everything

For the French actress, history is obvious, undeniable. The burned iron, the human skin, the shattered stones: it is all there in the newsreel footage. As film viewers, we are positioned to share her unflinching faith in the camera's inclusive gaze. We are invited to share her point of view, the pathos of having seen it all, the *frisson* of sensual immersion. But, if we assume this surrogate perspective then we, too, are left open to the charge that we have seen nothing.

Unqualified and insistent, the repeated assertion of the actress that she has seen "everything" takes on the air of spectatorial conceit.

Through rote remembrance, a recitation of visual evidence encountered in a once-infernal city, she has emotionally and cognitively incorporated the atomic bomb experience (Jackson 1994, 151).[3] The architect, by contrast, resists her desire to command total mastery over the
meanings of Hiroshima. Her sense of sureness and certainty are dis-
concerting, he suggests, because they can only be spoken through a
generic language, which too easily obliterates the particularities of this
trauma. Rejecting an easy unity between seeing and knowing, defying
immersed identification with the camera recording lens, his words
stand in as a refutation of absolute memory.

By having his two central characters' stories cast doubt on each
other, and by ensuring that their parallel narratives remain separate
throughout the film, Resnais defies the principle of narrative resolution. The dimensions of power and authenticity invested in the French
actress, as a witness, remain ambiguous and unresolved. More than
simply presenting an optical paradox (*I see everything, I see nothing*),
however, Resnais's filmic approach to the trauma of Hiroshima has
carried a powerful reminder of its own ethical limits: no matter how
much visual information he packed into the film, *Hiroshima Mon
Amour* could not ultimately answer the enormous question of what the
atomic bombs had meant to the world.

Instead, the film confronts assumptions that structure conventional films about Hiroshima—in particular, the view that there is an
intact History out there waiting to be lured into vision and spoken as
pure meaning. Resnais's "now you see it" and "now you don't"
approach to the trauma of Hiroshima disperses the task of witnessing,
openly deferring interpretation and response to viewers of his film.
Foregrounding the limits of vision, Resnais turns attention to the violence implicit in our visualizing strategies, our own complicity in
objectifying the visual field. If vision is a privileged sensory modality
in Euro-American cultures, and if as Pierre Nora once remarked, "ours
is an intensely retinal and powerfully televisual memory" (1989, 17),
then *Hiroshima Mon Amour* might allow us to pose the question: What
and how do we train our minds to picture, to know?

The question seems all the more apt when posed through the
vehicle of film. The extraordinary vividness of film media, after all,
encourages us to become quickly absorbed by its sensory field. Filmic
sounds and images are frequently taken as perceptions rather than
representations. We blush, become aroused, shiver with fear, turn
away in revulsion. As if to jar us out of deep immersion from the outset, Resnais takes us on a voyeuristic trip through Hiroshima near the
beginning of the film. This visual sweep through a city once-turned

crematoria vascillates between curious indifference and pious fascination. Circus music plays as an atom molecule dangles like a disco globe
from the Peace museum ceiling. A cheerful young woman leads a
Japanese tour bus through the downtown memory-topos. Hiroshima
could be a theme park.

Resnais's attempt to capture the elusive relationship between
vision and knowledge in *Hiroshima Mon Amour* is a way of indicting
the hubris of the all-knowing eye—a fast tourist vision that might rein
in the ruins. In questioning how our historical knowledge—our image
of the past—got to be constructed from a given perception, before the
watchful gaze of a camera, he opens a space in which to consider the
importance of perceiving anew. As such, *Hiroshima Mon Amour* provides a possible incentive for viewers to question the image repertoire
that constitutes our sense of consciousness—or what we know. In ges-
turing toward the stubborn fissures that mushroom between images
and meaning, the film registers how the perceptual experience of
viewing recorded documentation of an event may not be commensu-
rate with the intelligibility (the meanings) of that event.

Emptying Out

In many ways, *Hiroshima Mon Amour* exists as an anomaly within
the context of witness art. In challenging precepts of historical realism,
the film eludes a literalization of visual memory. In contrast to atomic-
bomb films that have been attached to notions of photographic transparency, that have attempted to reenact the experience "as it happened," *Hiroshima Mon Amour* yields the possibility of being read as a
complete testimony. Promoted by Resnais as a "false documentary"
(1961, 10), *Hiroshima Mon Amour* resists becoming "just another film"
about Hiroshima (that "other film" is there, represented as a Peace film
the actress has come to shoot). Instead, the dreamlike quality of film is
mobilized in *Hiroshima Mon Amour* to evoke imaginative associations
and memories that exceed any apparently literal codes.[4]

In her preface to the published manuscript of *Hiroshima Mon
Amour*, Marguerite Duras writes, "Impossible to talk about Hiroshima.
All one can do is talk about the impossibility of talking about
Hiroshima." The refusal to represent events directly has been a con-
stant feature of Duras's writing. In *Hiroshima Mon Amour*, we indirectly
approach the trauma of nuclear annihilation through the recurring
metaphor of fatal love. The French actress's tragic love affair with a
German soldier in wartime France, her bittersweet fling with the
Japanese architect, become provisional pathways into the immense

trauma of Hiroshima. These trysts of passion and remembrance are given added historical valence because in each instance a national border has been crossed. Reproducing the terms of war in a disquieting way, the characters are forever identified with their respective cities. Otherwise nameless, each lover is given a toponym. Identified as *Hiroshima* and *Nevers*, they become ventriloquists for larger personal and social tragedies.

Both Duras and Resnais share the view that indirection is the only way to approach these events. The great majority of us were not direct witnesses to the atomic bombings. The fictive story of a love affair between a Japanese architect and a French actress is, thus, a necessary narrative replacement. It is necessary, if mundane, because we have missed the main event of Hiroshima being decimated by the atomic bomb. We have been prevented from observing the event itself due to our belated arrival. The reduction is intended to give us a sense of the disproportionate scale of loss at Hiroshima. Whether this indirect appeal to a memory of the bombings has been sufficiently foregrounded in the film has been a central source of concern and dispute.

Some have argued that the love story comes to dominate the city's symbolic history. James Monaco, for example, states that it is too easy to read the film as "primarily a love story, one which uses Hiroshima and its history rather obscenely as background and filler to multiply the drama inherent in this supposedly intentionally banal story" (1979, 43). Others have suggested that through narrative placement and camera framing, the woman is too focally centered. The film revels masochistically in *her sad story*. Her death-tinged sadness, experienced as deeply personal, is thought to subsume the political matter of the atomic bombings within an arguably simplistic melancholia. Other writers have criticized Marguerite Duras for creating characters that are paralyzed, even destroyed, by the force of a theme-ridden allegory (Monaco 1979, 37).

While varying over time in tenor and pitch, the central issues addressed in criticisms of the film have related primarily to the risks involved in merging art and history, love and death, the personal and the public. For many critics, the strategy of postponed closure offered by *Hiroshima Mon Amour*—however aesthetically evocative it may be—is contentious, even immoral, given the weight of the disaster. Reviewing forty years of critical response, it becomes clear that something fundamental is at stake in witnessing at the limits. How we come to engage with the excesses and gaps activated by a representational practice largely depends on the viewing context surrounding that practice. *What facets of the film's narrative get foregrounded during its circulation? How do our interpretive frames allow us to engage* Hiroshima Mon Amour *toward a better understanding of the philosophical and ethical implications of attending to representational limits?*

Hiroshima Mon Amour reportedly received "thunderous acclaim" when first screened in 1959 at the Cannes Film Festival. It garnered an equally enthusiastic response from viewers and critics when it premiered in 1960 in the United States (Kreidl 1977, 55). The film's bittersweet, ambiguous ending was welcomed by American viewers. Its use of jump-cuts and layered narrative no doubt provided a contrast to Hollywood films, which were generally predisposed to melodrama and simple endings. French New Wave cinema, while eventually establishing its own customs, was a far cry from the conventions of American pop cinema.[5]

The overwhelmingly positive response to the film upon its initial release in North America raises the question of how it was marketed and billed by promoters and critics at the time. Glossing over contemporaneous reviews, it is immediately striking that critics—almost uniformly—failed to mention, let alone stress, that the film was about the "impossibility" of making a documentary about Hiroshima. Commenting on this ellision, James Monaco concludes that *Hiroshima Mon Amour* did not draw praise because "it was a sophisticated 'false documentary' trying to deal with the question of memory and history of Hiroshima, but because it was a poignant love story with a remarkable—even shocking—setting. For most viewers of the film, the tale wags the dog" (1979, 44). In short, Duras and Resnais stand accused of creating a fiction that not only uses history, but to a great extent subsumes it.

Echoing this sentiment, Earl Jackson Jr. has remarked on the dangers of presenting annihilation and obliteration through a strategy of "emptying out." Jackson questions to what extent Hiroshima, stripped of accessible historical and cultural associations, gets reduced in the film to an "ever absent-ed locus," a site of emptiness and nihilism, subsequently mortgaged to a psychosexual "metaphoric system" (1994, 150). *Hiroshima Mon Amour*, if read only as a narrative of love and loss, can thus be criticized for supplanting other dimensions of longing and mourning indirectly associated with the commemoration of mass atrocity. The allegorical doubling of the bombings with an autobiographical narrative of loss—namely the actress's loss of her German lover—means that atomic-bomb survivors never enter the frame for longer than a few seconds. Displaced from direct characterization they are presented, at most, as incarnations of absence.

Robert Jay Lifton suggests that the bodily union of the lovers and the documentary footage of Hiroshima's grotesque encounter with mass death, present themes that despite their intensity, merely coexist. Lifton faults the film for having two parallel narratives that never confront each other, concluding that in the absence of a contextual referent, Hiroshima becomes a carte blanche: open to any story. As such, he argues that the film fails to address the distinctiveness of the atomic bombings. To quote Lifton:

> Indeed, many have asked (like Ritchie): "Why Hiroshima? Why not *Yokohama Mon Amour?*" The theoretical answer is that Hiroshima represents an ultimate in man's deadly destructiveness which Resnais wished to illuminate against the starkness of physical love. Yet the formulation remains abstract, apart, because the film has recorded but not grasped its environment. (1967, 468)

Lifton further notes that *Hiroshima Mon Amour* encountered virulent opposition and criticism in Hiroshima, even while it was being filmed. Some *hibakusha* opposed the film's pervasive sensuality, claiming it was an insult to the dead (Lifton, 468). The fact that the film's title in Japanese was changed to *Twenty-Four Hour Love Affair (Nijuyojikan no Joji)* must have magnified these concerns—directing viewers towards a narrow interpretation of the narrative. In this context, the film's romantic story represents less a surrogate encounter with events too overbearing, too traumatic, to be faced head on, and more an evasion of history. In short, demons are banished from the bedroom.

The criticisms of *Hiroshima Mon Amour*, noted above, serve as a reminder that the critical and ethical potential of the film cannot be secured in advance. Here, Resnais's refusal to allow cinematic vision to master the meaning of the atomic bombs, his strategy of "emptying out," are interpreted as idioms of escape—evoking a flight from history. This contextual flight is seen to pave the way for an eroticization of death metaphors, the edification of narcissistic desire. Witnessing the impossibility of witnessing becomes an all-consuming process.[6] In postponing closure, the film has also been submitted to the charge that it integrates, even encourages, a dynamic of denial.

In light of these criticisms, the conceptual movement from a model of vision that "sees everything" to one that "sees nothing" is of ongoing concern to our practice of ethical deconstruction. As Derrida reminds us, confronting the lapses and gaps in our inability to imagine the ruins and remains need not shade over into refusal, incorporation, or the relegation of the trauma to the periphery of consciousness and concern.

Needless to spell it out here, therefore, still less to insist on it too heavily: it is not a taste for the void or for destruction that leads anyone to recognize the right of this necessity to "empty out" increasingly and to deconstruct the philosophical response that consist in *totalizing*, in filling in the space of the question or in denying its possibility, in fleeing from the very thing it will have allowed one to glimpse. (Derrida 1994, 30)

I cannot propose to offer insight into the true meaning or intent behind *Hiroshima Mon Amour*. I would, however, suggest that most of the aforementioned criticisms engage the film *solely* at a descriptive or denotative level. That is, as a narrative *about* the atomic bombings. Bearing this emphasis in mind: What happens when we begin to see the film as *about* the production of memory, vision, and knowledge more generally? It is certainly true that the film does not readily reveal its meanings, that it retains a disturbing ambiguity. But it is, I would argue, precisely this underlying tension that makes the film so compelling. The film's deconstructive approach—which engenders a realization of its own limited vision—draws back into view the layered process by which memory is constructed, and our own role in this process. The need for historical inquiry and denotative knowledge is not diminished, but surpassed.

Minding the Excess

At this point, readers might well ask whether or not *Hiroshima Mon Amour* is, in fact, actually engaged in representing the atomic bombings at all. Unlike *Night and Fog*, the film has moved away from verifiable facts and figures to register memory through evocation. *Hiroshima Mon Amour* deconstructs, leaving Hiroshima, as referent, in a ruin of representation. In so doing, the film challenges our desire to seek reconciliation with the past. It perplexes our efforts to establish closure so as to assuage the anxiety of that which eludes closure. But having acknowledged the impossibility of fully perceiving or comprehending what was experienced at Hiroshima, the question becomes: What are we left to commemorate? What is there to witness?

Flight is one of the organizing metaphors of *Hiroshima Mon Amour*, accentuated by a camera that seems at times to literally "fly" through the city. Foregrounding the false immediacy (or "thereness") of visual representation, and dispensing with the solidity of an "earth-bound" rational perspective, Resnais encourages us to move into that space of perception and thought that might be found between "seeing everything" and "seeing nothing." Through recurrent flashbacks and afterimages, which defy linear chronology, he simulates the "irrational" experience of trauma survival—conveying both "the truth of an event and the truth of its incomprehensibility" (Caruth 1995, 153). Thus, oscillating between certainty and uncertainty, *Hiroshima Mon Amour* offers a model of witnessing that may be inherited by the viewer watching the film.

Again, Marguerite Duras's words re-echo: "Impossible to talk about Hiroshima. All one can do is talk about the impossibility of talking about Hiroshima." Duras directly addresses our inevitable infidelity to these events. The limits of vision inherent to the film connote a similar crisis of representation, or more specifically, a crisis of not having adequate frames to contain historical events. There are different positions from which to engage these limits of vision and knowledge—as reflected in the varied responses to the film. Our task is to consider the different responsibilities that come with each of these positions and not leave historical representations in an "'unreconstructable' litter, thus undermining the possibility of determining precepts for moral action" (Cornell 1992, 1).

Where are there gaps in our framings of the past? Is our lack of knowledge substantive or important? Why? Would our actions in the future be different if we could exceed our present understanding? *Hiroshima Mon Amour* enables such important witnessing questions by calling out beyond its own evidential frames of remembrance.

Transmemoration

In *Hiroshima Mon Amour* signs and images of trauma appear to be held in place through a viewing relation founded on absolute certainty and order. A standpoint that "sees everything," requires configuring and absorbing Hiroshima as a particular totality of memory and meaning. This memory is derived from a perspective that arrests and universalizes trauma artifacts—in museums, peace plazas, archives. Symbols of grisly death are, thus, embalmed through a positivist tradition, which in turn serves to limit possible memorializing positions for the viewer-witness.

In an effort to discern the limits of positivist and other incorporative orders of historical engagement, this final section turns to the possibility of elaborating *trans*memoration as a process of situated historical inquiry and ethical translation. My attempt to grapple with the possibilities of *trans*memoration hinges on an understanding of experience, perception, and knowledge as historically contingent and located. Whereas the prefix 'com' denotes togetherness, unity, and completeness, 'trans' derives its associations from words such as across, over, beyond. According to the *Oxford Dictionary of English Etymology* (1986), *commemorate* means to "relate to memory together" or "recollect in unity." *Trans*memoration, by contrast, signals a coming to terms (to language) with the ways in which our identities and understandings are unevenly implicated in wider social and symbolic formations structured on power and inequality. *Trans*memoration, as such, conveys the *trans*-it between disparate experiences, knowings, languages, cultures, times, and geographies.

The work of Drucilla Cornell and Jacques Derrida is inordinately helpful to any discussion of *trans*memoration. Both Cornell and Derrida have suggested that "heeding the call of otherness" cannot be achieved through narcissistic or universalizing modes of identification. Calling attention to the limits of every historical translation, they seek to register yet-unspoken claims of otherness, which cannot be encompassed by any given narrative, and thus point to the narrative's contradictions and exclusions.

In this sense, they suggest, ethics is not about establishing a common ideal (in the name of such "universals" as humanity or national history). Nor is it about establishing a moral blueprint for how we should "behave." Herein defined, ethics focuses rather "on the kind of person one must become in order to develop a nonviolative relationship to the Other" (Cornell 1992, 13). An ethical relation, in other words, assumes a commitment to "guard" otherness "against the appropriation that would deny her difference and singularity" (1992, 62).

Derrida employs a metaphoric trinity of ghosts, hauntings, and specters to introduce us to a different politics of memory and inheritance. Breaking with a metaphysics of presence and absence, Derrida discusses the possibility of forging an ethical connection to those others who are "not present, nor presently living, either to us, in us, or outside us" (1994, xix). While the "ghost" cannot be named in any fixed manner, while the "haunt" has no concrete referent, they are still liminal members of our contemporary ethical community. As Derrida writes: "The ghost, *le re-venant*, the survivor appears only by means of figure or fiction, but its appearance is not nothing, nor is it mere semblance" (1986, 64).

The "not nothing" invoked by Derrida introduces the ghost as an excess, the unnameable remainder, which nonetheless makes ingresses into the lives and psychic unconscious of those surviving terror. The "not nothing" invokes also the importance of revisiting distinctions between the real and the imaginary. As illuminated in previous chapters, hard-line fact-and-fiction distinctions collapse in the face of trauma. For many the task of overcoming the hauntings of trauma memory, the struggle to lay the ghosts to rest, are impossibilities.

The challenge invoked by both Cornell and Derrida is two-pronged. On the one hand, it involves addressing the excessive and untranslatable dimensions of loss; on the other hand, we are asked to probe the normative limits of language and narrative which act to bar certain memories of violence, trauma, and injustice. As discussed in earlier chapters, the fear that the excess remains of collective mourning may destabilize normal language and life have resulted in efforts to isolate and assimilate the surplus significance of these events. How these traumas and testimonies get marginalized at the same time as they are written into the mythic and metaphoric structures of national commemoration and public memory is a matter that warrants ongoing scrutiny. The collective representation of death, through commemoration, may contribute to its very idealization.

*Trans*memoration, in the sense being proposed, may allow us to move the task of remembering beyond the triumphalist phase of mourning and beyond the "assimilationist's dream" of a full absorption of difference (Bhabha 1994, 224). As Homi Bhabha notes, attempts to strike homology through translation amount to a process of "naming *for*"—ultimately resecuring calcified traditions and self-same communities of meaning (Bhabha 1994, 225). In order to guard against the assimilation of difference, both Walter Benjamin and Homi Bhabha have introduced the importance of recognizing the "foreignness" or "newness" of testimonies. Surpassing our present orders of language and knowledge, this "newness" precludes the possibility of a total transfer of memory and meaning. These yet-unknown memories and experiences may, nonetheless, through a process of *trans*memoration, revisit or haunt the orders that have made their testimony *impossible*. In welcoming the ghosts of other histories and collective memories, *trans*memoration challenges the authority of progressive modern time and the foundations of national communities.

As Benjamin notes, translation marks the "stage of continued life" for a testimonial form, restoring new energy to the past (Benjamin 1968, 71). It is the realization that every act of translation involves a gesture of re-creation which makes it an ethical practice. Never *given*, *trans*memoration is always an aspiration, a life-filled task. It exposes ethics to be a fraught process of understanding our complicity and responsibility to witness, to interpret, to act, toward the cessation of violence and oppression. Bidding us to continually test the limits of vision and remembrance, enjoining us to mind the aporia between seeing and knowing "everything" or "nothing," an ethical community might herein be defined as a space where contradictions can be maintained without a hastened rush for conclusions or harmony. It is a space that yields a common field of possibility and hope through the friction of questioning and reflection.

7

Witnessing Otherwise

Toshi (Akamatsu) and Iri Maruki arrived in Hiroshima three days after the bombing to search for family members and participate in relief efforts. The married couple were professional artists living in Tokyo when they heard reports of the destruction. When they stepped off the train in Hiroshima, they became eyewitnesses to the human torment of August 6, 1945. Their lives would never be the same again. (It is a cliché that bears repeating.) The stench of death filled their senses and flies and maggots engulfed them. They carried the injured, cremated the dead, and searched for food and water. They walked through black rain, the ashes of Hiroshima caked to their clothes. Of their relatives, few had survived the blast. Those that had, including Iri's father, would soon die of radiation illness.

It could be said that the Marukis never left the rubble of Hiroshima. Rather, the experience, which had dragged them through death's corridors, was an initiation into a kind of maelstrom of witnessing. The fulcrum of their vision—the infernal slaughter of humans—found its way into everything they painted. Thus, from 1948 (the year they completed their first mural *Ghosts*) to 1995 (the year Iri passed away), the Marukis have worked collaboratively on murals testifying to the gross proportions of war. The Atomic Bombings, the Nanjing Massacre, the Shoah, and the battle of Okinawa, are among the events they have addressed—each event treated with rare subtlety and intricacy.

In 1967, Toshi and Iri Maruki opened a permanent gallery for their collected murals near their residence in Saitama Prefecture, northwest of Tokyo. Since then, the Maruki Gallery has become a pilgrimage site for flocks of school children, tourists, and international visitors. Approximately sixty thousand people visit yearly. It is estimated that ten million people have viewed the Maruki murals, making the *Hiroshima Panels* (*Genbaku no Zu*) perhaps the best known of atomic-bomb paintings. I have chosen to discuss the Maruki murals in this final chapter, believing that many of the issues and questions raised throughout this book congregate eloquently in their collected works.

Evidence of Sights Unseen

The Maruki Gallery is located in a quiet stretch of woods on a cliff overlooking the Toki River. Beyond the stream, one has a view of miles of rice paddies and foothills. Across the gallery courtyard is a shrine, built of wood from the Maruki home that was exposed to the atomic bomb in Hiroshima. For the visitor, the power of the Maruki compound resides in its surface peacefulness. Twenty-five miles from central Tokyo, the aura of calm is tangible. The gallery space is flooded with natural light. It has the sense of interiority that one might get in a temple or church.

Walk inside the gallery and you will see a permanent collection of twenty large-format murals spanning a forty-year period. They are images of the slaughter-bench of history: naked women wreathed in flames, uniformed men dangling lifelessly from barbed wire, children careening into empty space. They reflect on deaths that were frequently instantaneous—often unrecorded and unmourned.

If the gallery walls feel dense, even overpopulated, it is intentional. The artists see themselves as filling a lacunae of sorts. They want to create commemorative sites where there were none before. Thus, there is an investigative impulse presiding over the work. Yet the Marukis, contradicting a basic law governing the visible world, are looking for evidence of sights *unseen*. They are motivated by an understanding that for an event or experience to be collectively remembered—even in the crudest terms—it must be named through language.

When the Marukis began painting *The Rape of Nanjing*, for example, they found that no artist had ever depicted this atrocity. As many as 300,000 Chinese civilians were murdered in a grisly invasion of mainland China by the Japanese Imperial Army. Thousands of women were raped and mutilated. To many of us, the savagery of what happened in Nanjing and in many other mainland villages seems undeniable. Yet in Japanese official history, Nanjing is described, at best, as an "incident," and at worst, as an "inevitable consequence of war." For the most part, it is amputated from public discussion. The Marukis hoped that by naming Nanjing through a visual language they could bring the massacre into public focus. They could not define the meanings that their mural would hold for their viewers. They wanted only to give form to the silence surrounding "Nanjing"—a trauma that had no match in the image world.[1]

There can be no mistaking the urgent address of the mural. The *Rape of Nanjing* conveys halting sights of bodies hacked into fragments

FIGURE 7.1. *The Rape of Nanjing* (detail, oil and ink on paper). Iri and Toshi Maruki, 1975. Courtesy of Maruki Gallery, Japan.

of life. A tempest storms across the surface. Bodies knitted together by death can be glimpsed disappearing into a fierce tangle of brush strokes.

Significantly, the mural was completed in 1975, around the time that conservative Japanese revisionists were attempting to delete any mention of the Nanjing "incident" from Japanese school texts (Dower 1988, 7). The gulags were torn out of official Soviet history, Wounded Knee torn out of American history. What has been torn out of Japanese history are the pages concerning the brutal effects of Japanese expansionism in Asia. The space for the construction of a national history is, as it were, cleared through acts of omission.[2]

In light of the constant rewriting of trauma history in Japan, the Maruki murals create a powerful space in which to reflect on memory as a process of exclusion and foreclosure. They recall the disappearances of official history: the censors' black blottings, the deletions that allow coherent nations and identities to be formed. They represent the rifts between official and private memories, the gaps between the representable and the indescribable.

The visible, as the Marukis remind us, remains our primary source of information about the world. We orient ourselves through the visible. We translate other senses into visual terms. "The visible brings the world to us," but, as John Berger notes, it also "reminds us ceaselessly that it is a world in which we risk to be lost. The visible with its space also takes the world away from us. Nothing is more two-faced" (1993, 215). The murals speak to the ambiguity of the visible. They strive to prevent what has disappeared from falling into the negation of the unseen and, thus, the unthought of. They retain, at the same time, an awareness of what the eye cannot and will never see. And so, as we will see, it is not surprising that the murals, which contest absences, have a special relation to them.

Oil and Water

Iri and Toshi Maruki were established artists working in different genres when they began to collaborate on the *Hiroshima Panels* in the summer of 1948. Iri Maruki (1901–1995) was formally trained in traditional *nihonga* suiboku (water and ink) painting, while Toshi Akamatsu (1912–) was schooled in a Western-influenced oil tradition. Prior to their first collaboration, Iri Maruki had devoted much of his independent artistic career to minimalist and abstract renderings of landscape and nature. Working within the *nihonga* tradition, he became famous for his innovative approach to large-scale paintings. Toshi (Akamatsu) had developed a reputation for her scrupulous oil studies of the human figure.

Despite their lengthly creative and personal partnership, Iri continued to reject traditions of realism and direct reportage in art, while Toshi continued to pursue an interest in naturalistic and figurative depiction. When asked to comment on her working relationship with Iri, Toshi summarily described the two as akin to "oil and water."

> My paintings were very realistic. Iri would take a look at them and declare, "That's far too strong." Then he would grind some *sumi* and splash it on top of my painting. At first I thought, I just worked so hard on that and now you've ruined it! But when the ink dried, the original image emerged from underneath. Still, I would think he had concealed too much, and go back and paint the figure again. He would say, 'That's too clear again," and go over it. I would think he had wiped out the figure and paint it again. In this process of painting and concealing and repainting, the images gradually became deeper. Something emerged from the darkness, and we began to discover a surprisingly effective way of working together. (Dower and Junkerman 1985, 124)

Their artistic dialogue, or feud, has provided rich results. The Marukis have made virtue of animating the contradictions within and among aesthetic and symbolic traditions. Their pictorial language—simultaneously referencing medieval frescoes, social realist posters, and painted scrolls—establishes visual disharmony. The murals, they insist, do not belong to a continuous cultural heritage.

While attracted to the antimilitarist stance of surrealist and proletarian artists working in the Hiroshima area throughout the 1930s and early 1940s, both Toshi and Iri Maruki spent the war years and immediate postwar years painting traditional landscapes and portraits. Having refused to paint militarist art for the Japanese government, their artistic endeavors were curtailed by the scarcity of supply rations.

Following Japan's surrender, the Marukis joined the Japanese Communist Party (JCP) with hopes that they had found a community of activists and intellectuals committed to fighting fascism and militarism. Their eventual break with the JCP would occur on points of principle: they disagreed with the party's position that the American Occupation Forces was an "army of liberation." More significantly, they opposed the JCP dictate that rather than look backward, the JCP should focus on "Japan's bright future" (Dower and Junkerman 1985, 12). The latter appeal to progress did not sit comfortably with the Marukis.

The Marukis could not shed their images of Hiroshima. Their attempts to consider the prospect of "bright peace" were haunted by memories of human carnage. When Toshi began to suffer from radiation sickness, which plagued her for years following their participation in relief efforts, their grief was compounded. This undertow of grief would later be acknowledged by the Marukis as an integral force behind their postwar work.

In 1948, the Marukis embarked on their first collaborative project, *Ghosts*. Feeling that the atomic bomb was a particularly dehumanizing weapon, they committed themselves to painting figures rather than the barren landscape made familiar through several circulating press photos. They painted in secret, for American Occupation codes still operated to censor representations of the bombings. The censorship codes, they realized, had blocked attempts to initiate even the most rudimentary discussion of the human consequences of the bombings. The Japanese public had been permitted few graphic impressions of the devastation. Through art, they hoped to create a world where distance could be gathered back into nearness, a world that would reject the posture of detatched spectators.[3] *Ghosts*, an eight-panel suiboku screen, depicts a visual world irreparably scorched by disaster. Skin falls from limbs like cloth, arms dangle in front of ghostlike survivors. Yet, these ghosts do not belong to the realm of the spirits. They walk, instead, in a procession hovering between life and death. Their flesh has been stained white by the boric acid used by relief personnel to treat burns. Blurry, as if seen behind a veil, they nevertheless represent the survivors witnessed by the Marukis in Hiroshima: the phantoms, who, shorn from familiar surroundings, wandered like vagrants across a vaporated horizon.

Ghosts was first exhibited in the Tokyo Metropolitan Museum, five years after the bombings. While reports had begun to spread about the damage wrought to the city of Hiroshima, few images depicted the human effects. The tens of thousands of civilians who lived and worked in Hiroshima were eerily absent from official pictures. They inhabited a netherland beyond the visible world. *Ghosts* furnished many viewers with their first encounter with pictorial representations of the victims. Consequently, they elicited a range of responses at the exhibition unveiling. An elderly *hibakusha* who had lost his daughter and grandson in the blast is reported to have urged the Marukis to continue their work, stating: "These are our paintings" (Dower 1985, 15). Other survivors who viewed the murals felt that their memories were not properly substantiated: "You should have painted the shreds of skin far redder. . . . people were vomiting blood.

FIGURE 7.2. *Ghosts* (detail, oil and ink on paper). Iri and Toshi Maruki, 1950. Courtesy of Maruki Gallery.

Why didn't you show it?" Less generous were the viewers who
accused the Marukis of creating work that was exaggerated and pro-
pagandistic.

The responses to the murals over time, far from being uniform,
have indicated that their position as a documentary or evidentiary
resource is precarious. Although they are criticized on the basis of their
use of abstraction (i.e., for not being adequately "representational")
and accused of didacticism for relying too heavily on narrative symbols (i.e., for being *too* "representational"), what has been missed generally is their potential to simultaneously testify through both direct
and indirect expression. The encounter of these two energies, which I
believe occurs in the very language of the murals, produces a dialogue
vital to witnessing—directing us to consider what a work can and cannot say about atrocity.

Thus, if the murals attack the idea of a transparent subject, it is
only to foreground the subjective act of looking and the limits of
vision. In *Ghosts*, we are shown that the symbolic relation between the
image and what it represents (between the brush marks on paper and
the body these marks evoke) is an unconstructed one. For the image to
be meaningful, the viewer must lend it a past and a future. The
Marukis could only provide viewers with a trace. And the trace, here,
tells us that the dead cannot be brought back to life through physical
semblance. Only by chasing memory's vanishing point can we
approach the dead.

At the same time, the use of the human figure in the mural *Ghosts*
cannot be underestimated. The ghost is an identification *with* the body
of trauma. It gives temporary form to those "others" who have literally disappeared through acts of force or genocide. The ghost hails the
dead as a spectral presence. It signals the naming of those who died in
various states of namelessness and facelessness, heralding their potential participation in a contemporary ethical community. The ghosts of
atrocity are everywhere, the Marukis tell us, but because they are
vaporous, it is left to us to ensure that their claims on the living do not
dissipate like smoke. Challenged is the idea that the dead are simply
what is passed through as we create history.

And, thus, there is a degree of fidelity to the mutilated corpse,
but it is not of the sort to offer catharsis. In the works of the Marukis,
the hailing of dead bodies conjures an excess: a symbolic overflow, a
loss of the means to represent the damage in descriptive terms. The
way memory reworks the figure, for instance, becomes crucial to these
paintings. In several murals, the charcoal lines are bold and quite literally explosive. Bodies are contorted in alarming positions, lips

parted in silent screams. In others, the figures seem to melt into nothingness, with ink washes lending them an immaterial quality. Overall, the bodies appear incomplete, floating, not grounded in anything, somehow already elsewhere. And yet rather than detract from the place these images might occupy in living memory, these excesses lend them their incomparable energy. The most moving of the murals are, it seems to me, the most understated, those which merely hint at the vast numbers of victims, depicting a few in detail and sketching in the fading contours of the rest. On the margin of what the artists can convey, one gathers a sense of that which they cannot.

In this way, the Marukis stress the *emphatic* character of mimesis as described by Drucilla Cornell. Here, "mimesis identifies *with* rather than identifies *as*" (1992, 80). This identification *with* has an ethical thrust in that it insists on a world beyond surface appearance, beyond ontology. Nonetheless, what we gain in possibility, we lose in certainty. The figure is ephemeral. It departs from popular images of heroism. It is less magisterial than any icon of death and sacrifice. It is also less prosaic than any subject of reportage.

In fact, the Marukis bring us to the moment when the figure collapses upon itself. Layer upon layer, they reveal the debris, the fragments of the visible. They pick up the broken pieces and rearrange them together, creating a pictorial space that is, itself, fissured. In front of these murals, our eyes move from part to part, from a leg to a shoulder, from a face to a hand. The fissure is like a deep cut into the flesh. It cannot be easily mended. And, yet, there can be no doubting that something has happened.

It bears mentioning, at this point, that the Marukis departed considerably from other Japanese artists working throughout the 1950s. They were at odds, both stylistically and conceptually, with the Japanese avant-garde (associated with the Zero-kai and the Gutai movements)—and the differences were pronounced. The Marukis used the human figure to focus on the war's vestigial effects on Japanese social and symbolic life. The avant-garde artists, by contrast, worked to create an absolutely nonreferential art. The avant-garde mission was, in fact, to begin again from absolute zero—to create art that had no basis in tradition and, thus, no claim or commitment to a past. As postwar antipathy spread, academic realism, humanist painting, and traditional decorative Japanese arts all fell out of favor.[4]

The Marukis became heretics within an art world where to be an artist implied becoming either a custodian of tradition, or an innovator in the formalist sense. They focused on the figure at a time when other artists were placing diminished emphasis on the human subject.

(The Marukis saw the figure as an opening, not something to be abandoned or left behind.) They chose to critically employ tradition when many of their colleagues were posed to strike against all aspects of the old. Most significantly, they chose to appropriate a nationally defined art (*nihonga*) to critique nationalism.

The surrender speech delivered by a shaky Emperor Hirohito on August 15, 1945—telling his subjects to "bear the unbearable"—had a momentous effect on the Marukis as it did on many of their fellow citizens. Having lived through Japan's shattering defeat, the demotion of an emperor from stature of God to mere mortal, they had lost any sense of foundation. Society was wracked by upheaval and crisis. They had witnessed the overnight collapse of imperial icons and national myths. With certitude now lost, the artists saw, in the enshrined elements of Japanese culture, an opportunity to resignify tradition and, thus, a means of expressing their own sense of aesthetic and philosophical dislocation.

Marred Language

Tradition lives a ghostly life in postwar Japan. The reclamation of something amputated, rather than returning a sense of wholeness, introduces us to the wound. The wound is so important in the Maruki murals because it penetrates appearances, it reaches to something behind the surface of the visible world. The wound tells us tradition can no longer promise, let alone deliver, the eternal. Nor can it speak of a continuity across the ages. The phantom limb appears only to deny tradition's mending promise.

Applying the painterly conventions of *nihonga* to contemporary subjects, the Marukis forced a classical idiom to confront modern violence. Archetypes linked to theology and Japanese literary classics were rerouted to accord with the experience of trauma. The result is far from comforting: all direct paths to salvation have been cut off. In one mural, for example, an image of a mother with child resonates sorely with icons of Madonna and images of tenderness once we realize that the child is dead. Any sense of instant reference and recognition is left wanting. The Madonna's body has been invaded by the agony of maternal grief. In a mural entitled *Nagasaki*, Christian icons are engulfed in flames, a crucifix is turned upside down.[5] Now that tradition stands—like Christ—on its head, suffering has no absolute meaning: it can neither strengthen nor purify the soul. *Everything*, the Marukis suggest, has been disordered and corrupted by the chaos of human destruction.

There are no shortcuts into or out of Hiroshima and Nagasaki. Art itself has been tainted by disaster. Just as many post-Holocaust writers have evoked the particular density of words and images—train, guard dog, swastika—irrevocably marked by the Shoah, the Marukis tell us that the smoldering hell-fires of Hiroshima have burned new meanings into our symbolic worlds. We, as viewers, are left to reckon with the ethical implications of this change.

In *Boys and Girls*, a mural painted in late 1951, a gnarled tree is strewn alongside the misshapen remains of school children. The tree is shorn from its roots, which are a *nihonga* symbol of longevity and eternal beauty. We see cows and oxen—once a serene presence in Iri's prewar paintings—stripped of flesh to bone. In another mural, bamboo—a staple in Japanese traditional painting—is bent and listless, severed from its association with resilience and strength.

Even the representation of emptiness (*yohaku*) has a different valence when the theme is atomic desolation. In classical *nihonga*, emptiness is evoked by large unpainted, unfigured areas of paper. It is integral to the composition, the tonality, and the sentiment of a painting. Blank space permits the eye to imagine contours of form, distance, and landscape. Emptiness is not a void. In *nihonga*, that which is not painted is as important as that which is.

Emptiness has a place in the Maruki murals. It is simply zoned differently. Defined by the outline of water in one painting, it seems to stretch on endlessly—a vast expanse, a long and reverberating silence. One senses that there are no edges or borders to this emptiness. A woman holding an infant, hair matted to her face and shoulders, wades into the current. The space surrounding her has been forcefully vacated. It speaks only of her abandonment, the ravaged abyss where no living thing remains.

Nuclear weapons brought infernal death, destroying any illusion of refuge in war, or respite in a stable symbolic universe. The bucolic pasture is upturned and the bamboo forest no longer provides sanctuary or promise of continuity. Water, rather than providing baptismal relief, is *just* a current for bloated bodies. What does it mean to survive in such a place?

> Just above Urakami Cathedral
>   it exploded
> Instantaneously annihilating
>   the priests and believers
>   and all
> The cathedral at the center
> Endless concentric halo-like circles
> of dead human beings
> (Maruki text for "Nagasaki XV")

FIGURE 7.3. *Water* (detail, oil and ink on paper). Iri and Toshi Maruki, 1950. Courtesy of Maruki Gallery.

The flame of death defies the impassive shadows of gods; life plunges into an unmarked grave. What language will allow us to visualize this damaged world? How far can we veer before we are swayed into a brinkmanship of meaning?

A forest or cave can enclose and offer shelter, but the shelter is contingent. The trees have died, the caves are filled with corpses. The Marukis plunge us deeply into the symbolic landscape to register the fractures it has sustained. The stronger the memory of the symbol and its historical cadences, the more disruptive the changes will be to the viewer. Between our knowledge of its original meaning and our awareness of its new context, there exists a friction.

And, thus, the murals combine a graphic impulse with a melancholic presence. They seem urgently real while retaining a dreamlike quality. They immerse us in the power of archetypal images, but only to challenge the idea that myth can redeem us from history. Therein lies their irrefutable pathos: the way they alter our perception of the heritage of the past and tradition. We are introduced to the wound, the unnameable presence behind an appearance—be it the Madonna, a river, or the color red.

Twilight Perspective

August 6. The souls of the dead drift down the seven streams of the River Ota in Hiroshima. Lanterns bearing the names of fathers, mothers, lovers, and friends are launched from the shore. They float to sea along the shifting tide; the warm hue of candlelight reflects across a liquid mirror. The lanterns translate the flood gush of tears into a wild amber current, translate the dry throat of keening into geometrical rolls across a tranquil surface.

Floating Lanterns (1969) is a work of elegy, inviting us to see Hiroshima's seven streams as gorged arteries of memory. Yet what is most notable about this mural is its unique spatial treatment, its strewn perspective. In each lantern box, the Marukis have painted a shard of life: a sleeping cat, a human skull, a kimono pattern, an outstretched hand. Each detail is accentuated with equal care and attention. And, thus, there is no ocular center. The rivers are clogged with images—mingling life and death, the representational and the abstract—all compelling scrutiny.[6]

The visible is in continual flux. Figures scramble across the layered and ink-washed surface. They dissolve, first into watery planes of color, then into the recesses created by a partially unpainted surface. The perspective changes with each shift of the viewer's eye. This provides a contrast to conventions of perspective first established in the

172

FIGURE 7.4. *Floating Lanterns* (detail, oil and ink on paper). Iri and Toshi Maruki, 1969. Courtesy of Maruki Gallery.

early Renaissance, where everything converges onto the eye as to the vanishing point of infinity. As John Berger observes, in Renaissance painting, "The visible world is arranged for the spectator as the universe was once thought to be arranged for God" (1977, 16).

Rejecting Renaissance perspective, the Marukis make no pretense that everything within a measured and calculable space can be seen. They have broken with the deep-focus framing of classical *mise en scene* in order to convey a sense of the world as always in transition and human response as chronically unsettled, up for grabs. There is no nucleus of meaning—it can neither be located in the work itself nor in the proposed spectator as omniscient, all-seeing God. And thus, the artists have abandoned the vantage point of the pilot bomber: a vision that might produce a focal target by abstracting distance and spatial relations. *Floating Lanterns* demands visual reciprocity, that we situate ourselves in relation to others, that we be in different places at one time.

The Target and the Gun

By the late 1970s, the Hiroshima panels had been viewed internationally. Exhibitions had been mounted in roughly thirty countries, including many in the former Eastern Bloc. The first eight murals were brought on a tour of eight cities in the United States in 1970–71, where they met with heated critical reception:

> One critic denounced them as "perfectly dreadful" and a "degradation of all that Hiroshima should demand of us," while another ascribed to them an aesthetic brilliance "as vivid as Goya's scenes of war and perhaps more emotionally charged than Picasso's 'Guernica'." (Dower and Junkerman 1985, 19)

During this American tour, the Marukis were challenged by several critics to address Japan's own wartime atrocities. The bombs were but one manifestation of military trauma. Was it not conveniently simple to focus on Japan's victimization? The question stalked the artists. Upon returning from the United States, they began to do research on the American prisoners of war who were said to have been killed not only by the bomb, but also by vengeful citizens of Hiroshima who assailed them in the streets and beat them to death. They continued to investigate other suppressed stories of Japanese aggression. Problems intruded into their work: How could they disrupt narrow perceptions and claims of Japanese suffering? How could they testify to the con-

nections between twentieth-century atrocities while paying homage to
their singularity?

The challenge posed to the Marukis during the U.S. tour was not
an entirely new one. The problem of delineating perpetrators and victims had been highlighted in their earlier Hiroshima panels. *Who built
the bomb? Who dropped it? Who stood by?* The Marukis had long abandoned moral traditions based on absolute distinctions between good
and evil. They had steered into the grey zone of complicity, where
smoke and light intermingle. But their visit to the United States was a
turning point. They had presented their petition concerning the grave
of their father, the bomb's havoc, the corpse-filled rivers. Now it was
time to truly face their lost innocence.

After 1971, the Maruki murals mix memories of domination and
victimization in order to foreground problems of literal and figurative
identification. The spectacle offered is a radical one, not simply
because the testimony becomes immersed in several conflicting
events, but because it insists on a sort of chaos. Through shifting vantage points we find ourselves occupying positions of Witness,
Accused, and Potential Victim. The murals disseminate responsibility,
not to relativize the violence, but rather to suggest that relations of
subordination cannot be condensed or isolated by settling on one narrative of trauma or victimization.

They propose that the crime of inflicted suffering cannot be
causally located in the actions of one person, one group, one instru-
ment. In painting themselves into the frame of several murals, for
example, the Marukis implicate themselves in their narration. They are
painted as accomplices to the world they represent. History has
handed them the mournful inheritance of being both the target and the
gun. That they had friends and family who were killed is their grief,
that they had friends and family who killed is their burden.

The artists' fourteenth mural, titled *Crows*, was inspired by the
testimony of a Korean survivor in Nagasaki, who recounted how the
bodies of Koreans were left piled in the streets by indifferent relief
workers and medical staff. Most were dead, but some were still living,
and the crows came and gouged out their eyes. In 1972, when this
mural was painted, few in Japan acknowledged the fifteen thousand
Koreans who had died in Hiroshima and Nagasaki. Forced by compa-
nies such as Mitsubishi to perform war-related labor, the oppression of
Koreans was sustained even after the blast. They were left to die while
surviving Japanese nationals were treated and taken to hospitals. They
were granted no compensation in the years following the war. *Crows*
reflects the Marukis first attempt to envision those people remain-

175

FIGURE 7.5. *Crows* (detail, oil and ink on paper). Iri and Toshi Maruki, 1972. Courtesy of Maruki Gallery.

dered by Japanese atomic-bomb history. Significantly more abstract than their earlier Hiroshima panels, *Crows* virtually abandons proportional scale and perspective. The "crows" are a predatory force. Their raven blackness invades the surface in a wild overture of movement, conveyed through broad rhythmic brush strokes. Everywhere a dense beating of wings. Behind this, one can only imagine: life singed to ash, blood running dry under an unshielded sun, beak-pecked eyes, emptied skins. The Marukis have created a fugitive lament for the dead and dying. The viewer is left to supply the tragic narratives that are here only hinted at.

The trauma mercilessly compresses human life. The arc from life to death is compressed even further in painting, fitted into the space of a single surface. In *Crows*, the Marukis are working against compression, against the grain of painting itself. The experiences of Korean *hibakusha* represent a rupture in national history. *Crows* attempts to keep the rupture alive, suggesting that these *remains* cannot be accounted for within the same mimetic frame used in their earlier murals. The testimonies of Korean bomb victims still reside on the borders of commemoration. They represent the *forgotten*. They will remain phantom histories so long as their subjects occupy the status of outcasts in contemporary Japanese life.

Placing Hiroshima and Nagasaki on a continuum of mass violence pares away the mythos surrounding the Bomb and reinserts these events into wider histories of aggression and hatred. *Nanjing. Okinawa. Auschwitz.* When the paintings are hung together, the conversation between them is powerful. They reveal dessicated worlds filled up with silt and smoke—murderous worlds where it is next to impossible to die quietly of old age. They depict landscapes interwoven with cords of flesh, beauty laced with arsenic. And always, they present the question: How do people come to be fused in mass death?

The combined spatial witnessing of atrocity draws on connections, establishing a complex dialogue between events. Viewed together, the murals contribute to the labor of understanding how a civilian population could be exterminated by one bomb, how a fanatic state could devour its own people, how death could become an industry. As Paul Boyer notes:

[T]he remarkable Japanese artists Iri and Toshi Maruki have moved from powerful murals of the Hiroshima horror to equally powerful murals of the Auschwitz horror. Perhaps after the passage of four decades, we are ready for a more comprehensive understanding of the moral disintegration wrought by World War II—an understanding that will at least consider in the same context (without necessarily equating) the atomic bomb and the gas chamber. (Boyer 1985, 226)

There is certainly a danger in making links between very different atrocities: not least, the danger of reduction, and the Marukis know this. Their dialogue preserves the particularity of each event, protects it against the universal, by maintaining a sense of ongoing political dilemmas and contradictions. They are less interested in finding common heroes and villains than in teasing out nuances of national character. The result is both aesthetically and intellectually forceful. We are shown, for example, how memories of Japanese suffering and aggression coexist without resolution. A history of mass murder may link Hiroshima and Auschwitz, but the Marukis show us that there is also an explicitly Japanese connection to be found: Japan's wartime alliance with Nazi Germany.

Japan's postwar peace has been untidy. The murals remind us of this, and, thus, it is no surprise they have met with considerable opposition. Censored by U.S. Occupation authorities in the late 1940s and early 1950s, the murals were again subject to suppression when the Japanese government ordered their removal from school textbooks in the early 1980s. The most notable controversy occurred in 1981, when the Japanese Ministry of Education asked that two reproductions of the mural *Relief* be withdrawn from a textbook. They argued that the mural would be "too cruel" for young schoolchildren. (Dower and Junkerman 1985, 24). At the time, the country was engaged in protracted debates about remilitarization. (To this day, a growing lobby of Japanese politicians and journalists openly challenge article 9 of the constitution, which establishes a pacifist, war-renouncing identity for the country.) Thus, the 1981 decision to remove the reproductions was part of a wider campaign to delete antiwar content from the curriculum.

The Maruki murals bear witness to Hiroshima and much more than Hiroshima. They provide a dialectical terrain upon which to reflect on the renewal and ascendency of contemporary nationalisms, militarisms, and racisms. They are inimical to those guarding the power to exclude, destroy, forget. Because they go beyond narrow communes of memory, reminding us of that which has been left out of historical accounts, they are challenging. Because they return us—again and again—to the shadows of the dead and the unseen, they are visionary.

The World as It Looks

During World War II, the language of Japanese traditional culture was thoroughly infected by a rhetoric of racial and military pride. Something as seemingly benign as nature worship could slip easily into a defense of Japanese spiritual superiority. Cherry blossoms were painted on kamikaze planes. The chrysanthemum was sported by ultranationalists as a symbol of loyalty to the emperor. In light of this history, the Marukis believed art's role was to address the violence it had helped adorn. To this end, they elected to use *nihonga* painting in order to root out the symbols and ideals that at one time made Japan such a dangerous nation. Instead of verdant pastures and streaming rivers, they painted the obstructed flow of life and tradition, a damaged world of fragments.

The murals encourage us to experience the symbolic wounds left by trauma ever more acutely. They derive their power and overall potential from contradiction: they foreground the body only to de-emphasize literal depiction. They paint the congested world of death—its cruel deformations of the living—as it swarms the border between the aesthetic and the documentary. In one mural, for example, a woman is immolated by a burning bush. Off to the side, a figure, more ghost than human, beckons for us to recognize the sentience of the half-living. In another mural, rhythmic ink-lines lead inexorably to a funeral pyre. These works are rife with productive tensions, ridden with an energy that sways between poles of terror and beauty, annihilation and creativity, eros and death. These couplets resist sublation: the beauty has not softened or diluted the horror, death has not been redeemed through art, the brutal has not been made visually acceptable. The sensual way the materials (ink, oils, charcoal) have been handled remains in poignant tension with the horrific subject matter.

The result is that in the Maruki Gallery you have the feeling that catastrophic events spanning a century belong to a living legacy. You sense that the soul of every society is at stake. In an extraordinary way, the Marukis have created a signifying space for the production of collective memories. It has been created out of the pit of their own experience as witnesses in Hiroshima. And it has been sustained by their ongoing exposure to testimonies of suffering, a deep solidarity with the marginalized and the bereaved.

There is hope lodged in the very skin of the murals, in the numerous overlays of paint bleeding to the borders of the surface. The Marukis want us to cross various thresholds of witnessing in order to experience the break that comes with new seeing. The vitality of their painting practice creates a space and moment for careful and caring looking. Yet, their capacity to generate meaning and memorial commitments is not immanent. The murals promise no fixed aim. They merely provide openings.

These openings are easily obstructed. For example, critics have tended to focus on the work's ideological denotations, its links to conventions of realist depiction. Others direct the viewer toward the murals' themes of tributary peace. Most of these engagements do not stray past the evidentiary.[7] Art—and, by extension, history—is put through a sieve which winnows out conflict and uncertainty.

I realize that it is common for those who have glimpsed horror to want to guard against it. There is unrest in the unfamiliar. Anything that takes one from one's habitual grounding (in reality, in tradition) causes the depths to open up, causes a shift in perception. The murals encourage such a shift, but clearly their impact relies on our interpretive frames and strategies. The capacity to see deeper conflicts and questions, in surface phenomena, is learned. So, too, is our capacity to pursue them toward some transformation in thought and action.

The power of art, I have suggested, rests in its potential to represent the past in a moment of articulating something new. This is not a proposition that models art within a rhetoric of the "avant-garde." It is, rather, a means of seeing art as emerging with its own fissured coherence, its meanings deeply implicated in anterior times and spaces. Art, in this sense, opens us up to events whose value and meanings have not been exhausted. If art has a vocation, it is to remind us of the role we play in constructing a living memory.

More than that, art—when its language opens—allows us to respond to affliction and injustice. Despite its surface commitment to the visible world, art encourages us not to accept the world as it looks. Change is born from this paradox. For it is a sense of dissonance that prevents us from falling into passivity, into complacency which accepts mass violence as an ordained component of the human condition. Thus, art can be utopic, without denying the ponderous weight of history.

The dead and traumatized are always in need. The Maruki murals constitute a provisional reply to this need, this anguish. At the same time, they remind us that our sensory connections to the dead are fleeting and fragile. Art cannot return the disappeared. It cannot give them voice, speech, or animacy. The faces and hands that reach out from the paintings are, thus, ungraspable because so fluid. Only by remaining flexible are we able to reach toward the memory of the disappeared. Only by sustaining contradiction do we arrive at a sense of plural reponsibility. And this is, perhaps, the greatest and most active tribute to those abbreviated lives, those meaningless deaths.

Conclusion:
Memory Matters

A shaggy-haired German teenager confronts his aging father in the family living room where the father sits buried behind his newspaper. This might be an everyday domestic encounter, but it is Berlin in the late 1960s and this young son has come with a heavy heart to ask about his father's involvement in World War II. He wants to know: *Where were you?* He wants to know. And yet, he doesn't want to know.

The 1960s—a decade remembered by many for its rage and passion—were reportedly full of such family confrontations in Germany. The postwar generation was just awakening to adolescence when the Eichmann trials in Jerusalem rebroadcast the horrors of the Holocaust. Having grown up in relative peace and prosperity, many German youth began, for the first time, to reflect on a legacy for which they were too young to bear direct responsibility or claim, but for which they felt themselves to be nonetheless obligated.

A younger generation is suddenly afflicted by war memory, and a crashing sense that something vital has been suppressed. Reflection of this kind can be a wrenching and fettered undertaking. Japanese artist Yasufumi Takahashi knows this, and this lends disquieting force to his touring installation *Red Reflection I.* At thirty-seven years of age, Yasufumi Takahashi might play 1990s counterpart to our shaggy-haired teenage Berliner. Takahashi, too, has a father who served in World War II. And while a majority of his peers, faced with a contracting Japanese economy, have their eyes set on the future, Takahashi feels compelled to think about the past.

Yet, unlike his German counterparts, whose art has been sustained by several decades of postwar reflection and public debate, Takahashi has found himself joining a very nascent and often reluctant dialogue in Japan. For decades, the specific history of Japanese wartime aggression in Asia has been largely off-limits, with Japanese teachers, artists, and journalists generally observing formal and informal censorship codes. The silences surrounding the war were only really challenged in the late 1980s when the Pandora's Box—sealing off Japanese war crimes—was cracked open by former "Comfort Women" and other Asian victims of Japanese expansion who delivered searing testimonies about their experiences to international audiences. The death of the Showa emperor Hirohito in the early 1990s also prompted younger Japanese to start asking more questions about the war years.

Yasufumi Takahashi created *Red Reflection I* in the spirit of looking back and as an indictment of war and patriotism. The work is comprised of a circular quilt (approximately seven meters in diameter) made of dye-soaked clothes. It was made in 1995 to commemorate the fiftieth anniversary of the war's end, and the bombings of Hiroshima-Nagasaki. But, unlike our erstwhile Berlin teenager who may have dealt with war responsibility by electing to point the finger outward in stiff accusation, Takahashi's finger is curled inward like a question mark. He is heir to a difficult history. And he reveals a deep desire to distinguish his generation from that of the aggressors through an interrogative memory.

Takahashi's reflection takes the form of a giant red sun, which, attached to the wall by menacing saber-shaped hooks, spills across the floor like a curtain skirt. While reminiscent of the Japanese flag, the flag's usually poppy red center is now sun-faded, all dusty crimsons and worn orange remnants. The graphic and rhetorical pull of the red sun stands in contrast to the viscerally evocative clutter of clothes Takahashi has assembled.

A crooked hemline, a worn crotch, a torn sleeve, provide these castoffs with an elusive aura of personality. Those who have worn store-bought second-hand clothes may recall wondering about the previous wearer. Takahashi's red circle encourages us to look for such odd traces of individual life: it invites us to encounter unknown children, men, and women through the creases on a nightgown; the lace trimming on a baby bonnet; the pocket flaps on a dress shirt; the breastcups sproinging from a dress.

All this feels very intimate and even beautiful, which might give pause to those who feel postwar mourning should be a more structured, monumental affair. But the beauty here is intentional: a "trap" or lure for spectators. We need to understand beauty, Takahashi insists, because beauty is a seductive and ever-present companion to "death, fear, violence, armament, killing and sacrifice." One need look no further than Leni Riefenstahl and Albert Speer—renowned aesthetes and architects of fascist horror—to understand how the *lure* of beauty has been exploited with great consequence. (The memoirs of Albert Speer capture a man mesmerized by destruction. Of the bombing raids on Berlin at the end of the war, he wrote, "This apocalypse provided a magnificent spectacle.")

FIGURE C.1. *Red Reflection I* (mixed media installation). Yasufumi Takahashi, 1995. Photo courtesy of Mercer Union, Toronto.

So, if Takahashi wants to restage and reflect on the tension between beauty and terror, it is only to ask: *Why is war beautiful? How does it seduce?* Children yearn for war toys despite their fears of being hurt. Adults admire the beauty of a ripening mushroom cloud; wonder in awe as brilliant green lights streak through an Iraqi night sky in the wake of a scud-missile attack . . . The glory never dissipates entirely. It is simply reincarnated. Instead of being horrified by the wounds of war, one is seduced by its power of execution. The chaos, the din, the stench turns into *terrible* beauty. The sleight of hand by which one set of appearances replaces another (the atomic bombings become a necessary sacrifice for peace, the forgetting becomes an efficient form of social cleansing) is nevertheless an acknowledgment of a recurring dilemma: Can horror be made conceptually—or, for that matter, ethically—acceptable?

Red Reflection I is about catching those moments when beauty harbors violence, those moments when a blood-red sun descends into fathomless depths. Toward this end, Takahashi has invited us to partake in a ceaseless vigil. He wants us to look at the traditions, both national and aesthetic, that have lent meaning and justification to acts of aggression. Just as he believes that our ability to turn away from horror, our ability to normalize injustice, is learned, he believes in art's potential to teach us differently. And, thus, he works against the capacity of art to displace the past it would have us contemplate, and against the tendency of *all* images to reduce viewers to passive spectators. The hope here is that the spectacle of a rising red sun—the blinkered myths of any nation—will never again blind people to its awful wraths and furies.

I first encountered Takahashi's *Red Reflection I* in a small gallery in downtown Toronto. As I walked through the building's portal, the contrast between the busy mainstreet and the quiet gallery space was stunning. The roar of traffic receded into a background murmur. And, as often happens when one has the opportunity to step off the beaten track of one's daily life, I felt grateful. Time had slowed and my initial sense of disorientation, I soon realized, was appropriate, even portentous. For here was an artist whose sense of time delicately stretches between the vigor of contemporary life (what constantly appears new and emerging), and the spectral return of the past (what seems old and bygone). Here was work engendering the movement of memories from the periphery of Japan to the urban center of Toronto. Commemoration had become transnational. *Red Reflection I* had implicated me in a requiem for its unknown dead, its unseen others.

What does it mean to launch testimony across the void of time, so bridging the gap of distance? In this book, I have proposed to address the question of what it means to take the memories of others seriously. Like Takahashi, I believe ethical reflection begins when we challenge the national and symbolic borders which have defined and enforced our separateness from the dead and the aggrieved. The proverbial red curtains drawn across what we choose to forget or refuse to know are drenched with consequence. Yet, at the same time, our capacity to respond to the suffering of others is tantamount to understanding how we may be part of it: how we may benefit in both concrete and indirect ways from legacies of violence. That an event has occurred in a different time zone, a distant region, increases rather than diminishes the task of witnessing.

Questions of "long-distance" witnessing are, in fact, becoming more pertinent as we approach the twenty-first century. The dispersed effects of global economic restructuring are pushing us to move beyond our caged-in national imaginations. The practices of multinational corporations mean that "unlike" people and places are becoming ever more connected. For example: a manufacturing plant relocating from Detroit to Kuala Lumpur can have the dual effect of stripping hundreds of Americans from their livelihood *and* recruiting Malaysian workers into wage slavery. (In short, *one* unregulated move can undercut the rights of *all* workers to collective bargaining and job security.) On another level, new media technologies (from the Internet to satellite TV) are highlighting new issues for the field of witnessing. For instance, our sense of distance is challenged when a school teacher's account of a massacre in East Timor can travel to New Haven via fax-modem in milliseconds.

Being "global" means that many North Americans are part of an elaborate electronic community and increasingly connected to events in far-off places. *What effect will these transformations have on our relation to others (residing both within and outside national boundaries)?* It has been argued that the accelerated movement of capital, people, objects, and images around the world has produced a much more fluid sense of the relationship between particular events and their global implications. This may be the case. We may eventually experience a new kind of electronic internationalism linking the consciences of the rich to the plight of the poor. But, the promise of technology forever rolling back barriers of inequality, indifference, and prejudice still seems remote. As it stands, technology bears the marks of power differentials. A privileged elite, unfettered in their digital freedom, possess the means to influence others disproportionately—and abruptly. While those who do not have access to basic tools (telephones, televisions, computers), those who are finding it difficult to make the journey out of their bodies and histories into cyberspace, are rapidly becoming "virtual" unknowns. The growing division between haves and have-nots jeopardizes the capacity of historically marginalized communities to upload *basic* testimony—the kind of information more easily wedged onto web sites and on-line discussion groups. Testimonies which break with referential language, which chase the vanishing point of "common" knowledge, are easily short-circuited by a media discourse that wants solid hieroglyphs and click-and-open access.[1]

New technological developments, it would seem, have not so much overturned as extended and strengthened established patterns of power *and* perception. Digital and virtual media, for example, have supported habits of perspective and viewing as old as the Renaissance. Satellite news reports continue to endow appearances with immediate symbolism, transmitting messages along the channels of a familiar visual—and ideological—rhetoric. (Thus: Africa is desert, disease, and famine. Islam is veils and guns.) We are still, in the main, working against the assumption that the (white) Western viewer is a detached individual with an objective overview of the world. We are still working against the reduction of reality to pure seeing.

The canceled possibility of agency remains the greatest obstacle to witnessing. So suggest many of the artists discussed in this book. Acquiring a pictorial language through which to imagine catastrophic events, they insist, is not enough. Claude Lanzmann tells us we have to fight sophistication. Satoshi Furui warns against bland tolerance. For Alain Resnais, the enemy is absolute knowledge, because once one knows something absolutely it is hard to remain open and responsive. Oceans away, Iri and Toshi Maruki address the need to develop an ongoing connection to the disordered worlds of trauma, its dispossessed people, so that one may be pressed to reach other truths.

How, and to what ends, we choose to connect with events and people that exist outside the bounds of our immediate experience is a matter of continuing concern. The majority of the world's people (myself included) have been born since the bombings of Hiroshima and Nagasaki, the Nanjing Massacre, the Nazi genocide of European Jewry. For those of us who live in relative peace and privilege, it is easy to consider these events as part of a distant era, too far removed to be conceived in retrospective let alone contemporary terms. Only in times of extreme crisis, it seems, are we resensitized to the violence of modern civilization, the threat of ethnocide (Bosnia, Rwanda, Algeria), the possibility of nuclear disaster (Three Mile Island, Chernobyl). Only upon encountering a survivor, a testimony of violence, are we reacquainted with trauma's aftereffects.

Yet the question of whether those too young to have original knowledge of mass atrocity might be held to memory is perhaps misleading. Every generation must rediscover history for itself. This realization is not lessened by the fact that an event was never present before our eyes, never beheld as sensory experience. All events accrue layers of narrative significance and urgency over time. And every narrative of the past has repercussions. We know from the Masada to the Columbus Conquest to the Middle Passage that history is an ongoing contest of meaning in which the stakes *always* matter. The lessons we draw from these events and their representations continue to influence the way we see the world and our place in it.

Thus, we come to recognize that the idea that history is a sort of inscription that is passed on intact is itself *inscribed*. In its received definition, historical transmission not only presupposes that the student is a passive, blank slate, but also that learning is a legible and finite process. Yet is it not truer to the experience of traumatic events to say that learning is essentially disruptive and unfinished? Trauma, after all, is a deferred and recurring effect. Is it not, then, incumbent on us (who come later) to confront its reverberations in the arena of the present? That is to lay stress on how trauma persists in the context of contemporary injustices, and in relation to the outstanding claims of testimony. Moreover, it is to emphasize that the borders defining what we *already* know of an event may act as both a limit and resource for future action.

Witness art creates and resides in a boundary space, registering thoughts and memories that may not directly pertain to the concerns of the present. In art, we find occasion to consider how power and privilege constrain whose memories may be told, how they will be told, and under what conditions. We find opportunity to confront events that tear the fabric of our everyday mode of consciousness, that thrust us into a less literal and more uncertain state of awareness. We lose something in this process of initiation. Something is taken from us: our innocence, our safe and easy distance. As a witness, one leaves the familiar and safe homeground—the carapace of reason—to venture onto unknown and potentially unsettling terrain. Yet something is also gained.

Testimonial art offers choice, the courage to break out of the bondage of common sense. It offers a chance to move away from the false language of "realism," to realize that it is false not for being wrong, necessarily, but for supporting the illusion that its meanings are immanent. And worse, for suggesting that our arrival as witnesses makes no difference because everything is preordained, everything has been resolved. *Our arrival always makes a difference.* Art tells us this, especially work in which the artist is grappling not only with the substance of an event but with developing a language that might allow them to express something yet unheard. And, here, I refer specifically to work that addresses the political and historical voices of dispossessed peoples uprooted from their psychic, social, and geographical ligatures through trauma. I point to work that struggles to express experiences and issues not yet articulated in the public domain, not yet sanctified as history. This is the work of indigenous artists whose land has been expropriated and colonized, of refugee artists fleeing persecution, of so-called minority artists living in often hostile political territories.

Testimonial art survives when it is taken on, when it enters dialogue—not when it is passively accepted. Because its messages are inherently unfinished, it is disruptive and demanding. Because it awaits a change in the world, it can never be fully meaningful or politically effective in its initial moments. It cannot achieve closure because it reflects trauma—a wound in the symbolic order of its—and our—time. We cannot receive its counsel or wisdom, at least not immediately, not without structural transformation, not without reworking power, not without pulling and stretching the margins until the shape of the center is fundamentally altered.

Nerve endings continue to grow under scar tissue, moss in the cracks of granite tombs. There are wounds that go unseen despite our judicious looking, our keen powers of observation. In its moments of testimony, art invites us to trip against elements that had seemed to lie beyond recollection, outside familiar patterns or designs of remembrance. Wrestling with these loose remains becomes a way of generating a motion between prevailing narratives and their oversights, between what can be imagined (what we *do, can,* and *may* know), and what is as yet unimaginable. The utopian dimension of art and witnessing rests in our refusal to split ourselves off from the unknown, our capacity to imagine what cannot yet be.

Notes

Introduction

1. While focusing on the *unique* conditions and traumas associated with the atomic bombings of Hiroshima and Nagasaki, I am aware of the risks of normalizing other strategies of warfare. It is not the purpose here to establish a hierarchy of suffering wherein "conventional wars" (where civilians are napalmed, for example) might be considered "less" traumatic. It is the writer's view that while Hiroshima and Nagasaki introduced a disjuncture or shift in strategies of waging and *imagining* war, the relations of militarism and racism that supported the development and eventual detonation of the atomic bombs must be located alongside broader histories of violence and subordination.

2. See Makoto Kito, "Atomic Bombing of Japan to Be Featured on U.S. Stamp," *Yomiuri Shimbun*, 1 December 1994; Makoto Kito, "A-Bomb Stamp Cancelled," *Yomiuri Shimbun*, 10 December 1994; Bill Powell, "The Innocents of WWII?" *Newsweek*, 12 December 1994, 52–53.

3. The *view* that the war began with the atomic bombings was the implicit curatorial thesis of the Hiroshima Peace Memorial Museum *prior to* their recent exhibition renovations. (See David E. Sanger, "Hiroshima Journal: Museum's A-Bomb Message: There's More to It," *New York Times*, 4 August 1994.) The Peace Museum's World Wide Web site reflects these interpretive changes by offering an expanded discussion of the atomic bombings within the context of World War II. Included are references to Japan's role in perpetrating atrocities throughout Asia. Also mentioned is the plight of Korean A-bomb survivors.

4. The Japanese word *hibakusha* will be used interchangeably with the term "survivor" throughout this book. *Hibakusha* roughly translates as "explosion-affected person." The term has come to include children born to survivors, some of whom have been born with congenital abnormalities.

5. *Hibakusha* testimonies have been deployed in the symbolic arsenal of peace movements. The danger of conscripting often unarticulated or inarticulate memories into a political program has been a prevalent concern.

6. The term "visual culture" is used loosely here to describe what might be called concrete retinal images—or pictorial representations. Anxieties about the power of visual culture flare up consistently. Often adopting strict moral overtones, the media regularly features reports on the decline in literacy that

has accompanied TV saturation. W. J. T. Mitchell has suggested that these purist critiques have tended to take a reductive approach, condemning or appraising the creed of image making. He reminds us that "the fear of the image, the anxiety that the 'power of images' may finally destroy even their creators and manipulators, is as old as image-making itself. Idolatry, iconoclasm, iconophilia, and fetishism are not uniquely 'postmodern' phenomena" (15). Mitchell, alongside others, has argued for a more engaged critique of visual culture: one that can assess the myriad contexts in which images circulate and the historical specificity of their uses. Mitchell also opens up a space to consider how culturally disruptive forms need not be exclusively verbal. Focusing on the language of an image as unique challenges interpretative structures that apprise art through logocentric/verbal paradigms. (W. J. T. Mitchell, *Picture Theory* [Chicago and London: University of Chicago Press, 1994].)

7. The Japan Broadcasting Corporation (NHK) invited *hibakusha* to submit paintings and drawings, which were subsequently broadcast in a documentary entitled *Unforgettable Fire*. A book in English translation was later published (New York: Pantheon Books, 1977). Over two thousand memory pictures have been submitted over the past two decades.

8. See Kobena Mercer and Issac Julian, "Introduction: De Margin and De Centre," *Screen* 29, no. 4 (autumn 1988): 1–10. Mercer and Julien discuss the "burden of depiction and delegation" foisted upon marginalized artists. This burden is produced and compounded by the dehistoricizing "logic" of dominant narratives.

9. Paul Boyer has noted the ambivalence that marked American representations of the bombings in the 1940s, 1950s, and 1960s. He writes, "Only in allusive and tentative ways does the atomic bomb begin to make its appearance in post-1945 American literature" (247). See Paul Boyer, *By the Bomb's Early Light: American Thought at the Dawn of the Atomic Age* (New York: Pantheon Books, 1985).

10. *Hibakusha* have been marked literally and figuratively. The keloid scars that mark the faces and bodies of survivors have come to signify within a physiognomy of *disfigurement* and *otherness*. The unsightly scars literally render the bearer "unseeable." *Black Rain*, a novel by Matsuji Ibuse, addresses the desire of survivors and nonsurvivors to exorcise visible (somatic) reminders of the bombed body. In some cases, these *death imprints* may be taken as "marks of shame," while in other cases, they become "marks of honor." Interpretations of the epidermal manifestation of trauma, the *keloid*, relate to ways of resignifying *hibakusha* identity. Both the ennobling and derisive associations ascribed to the body of trauma rely on a discursive formation of othering and abjection.

11. Even sedimented commemorative icons and monuments are fragile on this official memory-scape. Lisa Yoneyama has explored the material and

rhetorical renovations currently underway in Hiroshima. The theme of "bright peace" has been introduced as an anodyne to trauma: a means of securing closure and resolution with the past, thereby paving the way for future "progress" in a postmodern capitalist Japan. See Lisa Yoneyama, "Taming the Memoryscape: Hiroshima's Urban Renewal," in *Remapping Memory: The Politics of TimeSpace*, ed. Jonathan Boyarin (Minneapolis: University of Minnesota, 1994), 99–136.

1. Atomic Visions

1. To those of us tempted to the think that the end of nuclear politics coincided with the end of the "Cold War," Ken Ruthven offers the following reminder: "Pacific and Australian peoples experience the legacy of nuclearism in material terms as the ruination of their land by activities over which they have no say, and for which the end of the Cold War guarantees no reparation" (1993, 51). Nuclearism is not a "problem of the past" even in the most mundane sense of the phrase. President Jacques Chirac's announcement (June 15, 1995) that France would resume nuclear testing in the South Pacific (*contra* the commitment made by Mitterand's French Socialist government in 1992 to abide by the terms of the Nuclear Test moratorium) indicated that nuclear talk and deed still play a significant role in the brokering of power among nation-states. Chirac's pronouncement—made on the eve of the 1995 G7 Summit in Halifax—exposes how the idea of deterrence is still all too commonplace.

2. Robert Del Tredici, "Only Five Photographs: An Interview with Yoshito Matsushige," *Photo Communique* (summer 1985): 9.

3. In early December 1994, the U.S. Postal Service announced its decision to cancel plans to issue a commemorative postage stamp featuring an atomic-bomb mushroom cloud (a composite of mushroom clouds released by the bombings of Nagasaki, Hiroshima, and the Bikini Atoll testings). The decision came in the wake of a controversy. Peace groups and Japanese government representatives denounced the stamp as an affront to the memory of survivors. The stamp carried a caption reading: "Atomic bombs hasten war's end, August 1945." The withdrawal of the stamp avoided what many considered to be a potential fiasco in U.S.-Japan diplomatic relations. President Clinton publicly announced his regret that the mushroom cloud had been used as a visual expression of U.S. victory. (Makoto Kito, "A-Bomb Stamp Canceled," *Yomiuri Shimbun*, 12 December 1994.)

4. See Robert Del Tredici, "At Work in the Fields of the Bomb," in *Photo Communique* (spring 1984): 31.

5. Joyce Nelson argues that the splitting of bomb from the human body was "immediately useful to the manufacturing of public opinion." Beyond postwar victory elation, Nelson suggests that the "two strands of imagery-

information" have helped marshall support for nuclear proliferation. She notes that the human fallout of nuclear testing was also diminished in press releases that followed the atomic explosions in the Bikini Atoll, which reported "'no visible effects' on living beings exposed to the tests" (32–35). (Joyce Nelson, "The New World of the Bomb," in her *The Perfect machine: TV in the Nuclear Age* [Toronto: between the lines, 1987].) Judith Butler offers a slightly more nuanced analysis, while still attending to the material effects of representational strategies. Butler has related the visualizing strategies mobilized during the Gulf War to the interpellation of a viewing public as patriotic subjects. Here, she suggests that the visual record of the war (mediated on TV) was "not a *reflection* on the war, but the enactment of its phantasmic structure" (11). The television screen became an extension of the smart bomb itself, conflating bomber with viewer. Yet the record of destruction was unenvisionable, the possibility of viewing the embodied human consequences detonated, with the bomb-camera blanking on impact. As Butler notes, "[T]his is a frame that effectively performs the annihilation it systematically derealizes" (12). (Judith Butler, "Contingent Foundations: Feminism and the Question of 'Postmodernism'" in *Feminists Theorize the Political*, ed. Judith Butler and Joan W. Scott [New York and London: Routledge, 1992].)

6. "Ground Zero" was produced by Ian Cameron for CBC Prime Time, January 1995.

7. It is not difficult to trace the racism that informed popular representations of the "Japanese" prior to and following the bombing. It behooves us to remember that when the decision was made to drop the bombs on two Japanese cities, Japanese Americans and Japanese Canadians were still languishing in internment camps where they were branded "enemy aliens." In late 1945, African Americans W. E. B. Dubois and Langston Hughes were among those condemning the racism which supported the decision to drop the bomb on Japan, a "colored nation" (Boyer 1995, 198–99).

8. The exception of course was the Vietnam War. Brought to North Americans as the "living-room war," a totally unique frame was constructed within the intersection of an indigenous antiwar movement and unprecedented media access to the front lines. Of course, representations of the Vietnam War were still mediated by dominant interests. There were events such as the massacre at My Lai, and repeated serial bombings of civilians in the North, that in large measure escaped the recording lens of North American journalists. But the Vietnam War broke considerably with the optics of war that preceded and followed it. Considerations of war representation and war strategy were undoubtedly present when President George Bush summoned the Gulf War as an opportunity for patriotic Americans to finally purge themselves of the legacy of their defeat in Vietnam.

9. Nuclearists continue to conduct their work in secrecy, with tests conducted in putatively "out-of-the-way" places. These often "invisible" and

allegedly uninhabited test sites have their own legacy of violence, tied as they are to histories of indigenous land expropriation and displacement.

10. The U.S. Atomic Bomb Casualty Commission (ABCC) was established by presidential decree, and placed under the direction of the National Academy of Sciences with the general support of the Atomic Energy Commission and the Armed Forces. The ABCC policy of research *without* treatment has been a focus of criticism and resentment. Survivors frequently conjure up guinea-pig imagery to describe their experiences with the ABCC. Yet as Robert Jay Lifton remarks, these criticisms are often measured with feelings of ambivalence: "whatever resentment *hibakusha* may feel toward the ABCC, their bodily anxieties often led them to place great value on the thorough examination they knew to be available to them there" (Robert Jay Lifton, *Death in Life: Survivors of Hiroshima* [New York: Random House, 1967], 351). Caught within a nexus of competing needs and interests, it is evident that knowledge production in the bomb's aftermath had multiple functions. Some survivors have openly accused the Japanese government of collaborating with American officials in surveying the destruction, and researching the effects of aggression, not for the sake of the victims and survivors, but in a bid to secure better diplomatic relations with the U.S. (see Braw 1991, 132) .

11. Lifton notes that the film now sits in a Tokyo warehouse "as an incomplete and not very accessible record" (455). Footage has been occasionally used for films about the bomb. The American copies are said to have disappeared into the deepest reaches of the military bureaucracy. In Japan, these lost reels are known as *maboroshi no firumu*: "phantom film" (456).

12. The United States government did not declassify archival information about the Occupation period until 1977.

13. It is grimly ironic that *Nisei* (second-generation) Japanese Americans, who spoke and read Japanese, were among those recruited as censor officials. Many individuals who had spent the war in internment camps branded as "enemy aliens" were now conscripted to serve the Occupation Army, and by extension the U.S. government (Braw 1991, 59).

14. See Nobuko Tsukui, "Yoshie Hotta's *Judgement:* An Approach to the Atomic-Bomb Literature of Japan," in *Arizona Quarterly* 42, no. 3 (autumn 1986): 197–212. Tsukui quotes Shoda: "I made up my mind that I would face the death penalty if I must; and despite my family's objections, I published the book secretly because I felt compelled to do so."

15. Wilfred Burchett details the events that led up to his deportation from Japan, and official efforts to suppress reportage of the aftereffects of the bombings, in *Shadows of Hiroshima* (London: Verso, 1983).

16. Georges Bataille has criticized John Hersey for reducing the recollections of survivors to the "dimensions of *animal* experience" (in Caruth 1995,

225). The immediacy of description and the concentrated focus on sensory perception bypassed the cognitive dimensions of survivor experiences. By contrast, President Truman was given intellectual (and *human*) authority to situate the significance of the bombings within history and the future.

17. *The NonViolent Activist*, January/February 1995, 20.

18. See "Review of A-Bomb Controversy Sought," *Yomiuri Shimbun*, 22 October 1994. The arguments advanced to justify the decision to drop the bomb—"it shortened the war," "it prevented further casualities on both sides"—can be used to legitimatize *any* action, however merciless. The logic of "necessary evils" can absolve *any* atrocity.

19. Reuters News Agency and Associated Press, "Controversy Threatens Enola Gay Exhibition," *Globe and Mail*, 28 January 1995, C20.

20. Graham Fraser, "Pressure Rewrites A-Bomb History," *Globe and Mail*, 31 January 1995, A1.

21. It was Laurence, who, in a press release announcing the Trinity test, first used the image of "a mushroom cloud of boiling dust" to describe the effect of an exploded bomb (Lifton and Mitchell 1995, 24).

22. In Winston Churchill's words, the bomb was "a miracle of deliverance" from a grisly war that the Japanese had themselves initiated in bombing the American Naval base at Pearl Harbor on December 7, 1941 (Ruthven 1993, 30).

2. Art from the Ashes

1. "Natsu no Hana" is included in *The Crazy Iris and Other Stories of the Atomic Aftermath*, edited by 1994 Nobel Prize laureate, Kenzaburo Oe (New York: Grove Press, 1985). Tamiki Hara committed suicide in 1951, during the Korean War, when he heard rumor that the atomic bomb might be used again.

2. Ota Yoko died in 1963. She is still among the best-known atomic-bomb writers. Her works include *City of Corpses, Ningen Ranru (Human Rags), and Yunagi no Machi to Hito (The Town and People of the Evening Calm)*.

3. Some critics have argued that imaginative approaches to the bombings become more tenable with each succeeding generation of artists (Treat 1988, 27–59). For the first generation the story is generally told in evidentiary, eyewitness terms to "be passed on" to nonvictims. The second generation (which includes writers such as Oe Kenzaburo, Ibuse Matsuji) has tended to use the bombings as a referent to raise broader ethical and existential questions. Subsequent generations have often approached the bombings more elliptically, as metaphor. Yet while non-*hibakusha* and younger artists have

been less restricted in experimenting with various ways of rendering the A-bomb experience, these artists face their own struggles for authenticity.

4. The essay Treat quotes from is aptly titled "Hiroshima ga iwaseru kotoba" (Words that Hiroshima makes us speak).

5. *Barefoot Gen*, a comic book drawn and written by Hiroshima survivor Keiji Nakazawa, employs a strategy of hyperexact rendering to vividly expose the *abject* remains of trauma (in one frame, for instance, maggots can be seen consuming human flesh). Combining a "serious" subject with a "light" genre, Nakazawa has developed a nonrealist figurative-based approach that may be taken to transgress familiar framings of the atomic bombings. *Barefoot Gen* has been translated and issued by New Society Publishers (USA 1987) and Penguin Books (Britain 1989).

4. Strange Gaze

1. Repetition may also produce fetishization and a high degree of totemic investment. In other words, repetition does not only produce habituation. In this chapter, I will be concentrating on acts of looking that promote a naturalization of the visual field, and thus, a normativization of trauma and injustice. The concept of habituation may nonetheless be extended to encompass, without reducing, other incorporative framings of the visual—including fetishization and metonymic symbolization.

2. In a famous interview with My Lai participant Paul Meadlo, which probed the massacre of Vietnamese civilians, reporter Mike Wallace asked: "And babies?" To which Meadlo flatly responded: "And babies." This exchange was transcribed by a group of American antiwar artists in the late 1960s and silkscreened on top of a famous photograph by Ronald Haeberle showing the My Lai dead lying unceremoniously in a ditch. Fifty thousand copies of this poster were distributed internationally to call attention to an event that defied normal categories of understanding and morality. Revoking explanation, these artists attempted to render legible a reality that defied understanding by depicting the moment when moral reason broke down.

3. The visual paradoxes inherent to postatomic representation need to be considered more carefully in view of the constant slippage between the real and the symbolic. These paradoxes can be seen to haunt even the most "non-representational" work. Abstract and conceptual artists working with found objects in immediate postwar Japan, for example, confronted an overturned symbolic field. Their "found objects"—reclaimed from urban dumps and refuse piles—were essentially remnants of war destruction, stranded now without purpose or function. As critic Tono Yoshiaki writes: "The blasted city had been their playground: their first toys had been bottles melted into dis-

196   *Notes*

tortion from fire bombs, pieces of roof-beams found in the ashes. Now, their shows were full of these junk-flowers, with their queer blossoms" (in Munroe 1994, 157).

Throughout the 1940s, Japanese artists from various movements were united by their "queer" context. Expressions running the gamut from abstract to realist were all being created against the lingering shadows of nuclear and military fallout. Some artists acknowledged this landscape directly, while others responded to the strange world of postatomic Japan more obliquely. Butoh dancers Hijikata and Ono Kazuo, for example, played with images of physical deformity and self-obliteration. Without directly referencing the atomic-bomb experience, many viewers were struck by the sight of seminaked Butoh dancers writhing in ghostly and grotesque movements. The gestures, because so unfamiliar, had an eerie resonance, passing through an imagination riven with thoughts of recent disaster.

4. See also Ben Brewster, "From Shklovsky to Brecht: A Reply," *Screen* 15, no. 2 (summer 1994): 82–102. Here, Brewster observes that alienation was not Brecht's only representational strategy. Working under different material and discursive constraints, he also saw the need to use more recognizable or "familiar" narrative conventions. As Brewster notes, "In the 1930's Brecht wrote a number of plays like *Senora Carrar's Rifles* (1937) which were a deliberate retreat from epic theatre to a more naturalistic theatre, because only the latter had the support of the revolutionary movement and could thus have any influence on the immediate class struggle" (99).

5. Guy Brett, "Open Only in Conditions Specified, Camino War," 1991 (excerpted for *Remota: Airmail Paintings by Eugenio Dittborn*), New Museum of Contemporary Art, New York, February 12–April 13, 1997.

6. Here the reader might wish to return to chapter 1 and the discussion of the American Atomic Bomb Casualty Commission and problems surrounding spectatorial vision.

7. *Hibakusha* artist Yamashita Sohoh lived in Hiroshima with his family prior to his death in January 1995 of radiation-related illness. I am much indebted to the Sohoh and Yonemata families for supporting this project and in particular for sending me *Traces of the Atomic Rays: Paintings in Japanese Ink by Yamashita Sohoh* (Hiroshima: self-published, 1986).

5. Mourning the Remains

1. Lest we forget that there is a political economy underwriting all commemorations, we might consider for a moment what it meant for General Electric and Westinghouse, two of the largest producers of military hardware including nuclear weapons, and respective owners of CBS and NBC, to be financing coverage of the anniversaries of Hiroshima-Nagasaki.

2. Postwar contemporary artists such as Yoshiko Shimada have partici-
pated actively in generating public dialogue on Japan's history of imperialist
aggression. Shimada, whose work has toured internationally, has focused thematically on the history of Korean "Comfort Women." Her installation-based
art poses questions about the role of Japanese women and wartime nationalist
feminists in supporting the war effort and complying with the emperor system. During a 1995 visit to Toronto, Shimada, who is now based in Berlin,
remarked on what she perceives to be significant contrasts in German and
Japanese postwar cultural reflexivity. She noted that while Germany marked
1995 with 480 commemorative art exhibitions, less than a handful took place
in Japan.

3. Nicholas Kristof, "Japan expands its role in Asian security," *The Globe
and Mail*, 25 April 1996, A11.

4. This is not to overlook the need for *containment* under some circumstances so as to diminish the risk of psychic "flooding." Educators engaging in
commemorative pedagogies, for example, should be alert to the risk of elicit-
ing all-pervasive feelings of anxiety, despair, and powerlessness among students. Nevertheless, commemorative educators should also be wary of the
losses and exclusions incurred through every attempt to delimit and confine
trauma's significance.

5. See Douglas Crimp, "Mourning and Militancy," in *Out There: Marginalization and Contemporary Cultures*, ed. Russell Ferguson et al. (New York: New
Museum of Contemporary Art and MIT, 1990), 233–46. Writing on mourning
and the AIDS crisis, Crimp critiques the tendency to see mourning and action
as dichotomous. He attributes the constructed opposition between activism
and mourning in large part to Freudian paradigms of mourning. Crimp suggests that it is precisely this model of mourning which has tended to dehistoricize and decontextualize the experience of trauma. Here, I would add,
mourning comes to be understood as separate from the sphere of social and
political relations: mourning is thus seen as an acceptable display of sentiment
colluding with constructions of survivor-witnesses as hapless victims. When
mourning, in the form of collective testimony or grief, is enacted publicly
toward political redress, it is recoded as "pathological." Mourning as a social
practice, thus, breaks polite (and in most instances politically oppressive)
codes of convention and transgresses tidy delineations of what is private/pub-
lic.

6. Here, I would refer readers back to the book introduction, dealing
with related notions of "victim art."

7. I would refer readers to the published writing of Joy Kogawa, Mistuye
Yamada, Miné Okubo, James Masao Mistui, Roy Miki, and Kerri Sakamoto.

8. Yoneyama's primary interest rests in identifying the dominant
processes of containment "that demarcate the boundaries and define the

proper territories for memorialization, prescribing whose experiences should be remembered and when, where, and how they should be invoked" ("Taming the Memoryscape," 104).

9. "According to Gallup surveys, a majority supported using the atomic bomb in Korea after China entered the conflict; in Vietnam in 1954 when the French were surrounded; and against China in 1955 during the Quemoy-Matsu crisis. . . . During the 1980s, with antinuclear sentiment rising, polls showed overwhelming support for a no-first-use pledge—but a later survey found a near-majority backing use of the bomb against Iraq in 1991" (Lifton and Mitchell 1995, 305).

10. The phrase "perpetual mourning" was suggested to me by Professor Roger Simon (personal communication). This concept is elaborated in an (as yet) unpublished article entitled "Ethics and Epistemology in the Call to Witness Testimonies of Historical Trauma," Roger Simon and Claudia Eppert.

11. Quote taken from filmmaker John Greyson, who hosted a general discussion on AIDS, memory, and art in Toronto, March 1997. An extract from this discussion, "Scoping Boys," was subsequently published in *MIX: the magazine of artist-run culture* 23, no. 1 (summer 1997).

12. I thank Montreal-based artist Devora Neumark for her thoughtful insights on the role of art in social mourning. My own thinking has benefited greatly from our conversations.

13. Dissociated from their original owners, eight thousand works of art were auctioned off by Christie's in October 1996. Proceeds were intended for victims of the Holocaust. The collection included items ranging from Old Master paintings to nineteenth-century landscapes to more decorative ceramics and sculptures. With buyers including dealers and collectors, the looted and unclaimed property was being brought back into a normal economy of consumer exchange.

6. The Limits to Vision

1. Alain Resnais, commenting on his self-reflexive film approach, once stated, "Just as with Brecht you knew you were at the theatre, so I want you never to forget in my work that you are at the cinema. What I show on the screen is filmed images which announce themselves as such" (quoted in Stephen Heath, "Lessons from Brecht" *Screen* 15, no. 2 [summer 1974]: 105).

2. "You have seen nothing" has multiple possible meanings. It may refer to those rendered invisible by national narratives of history (for example, the Korean *hibakusha*). It may evoke experiences that cannot be encompassed by visual framings of knowledge. It may address epistemic and affective distinctions between insiders/outsiders and spectators/witnesses.

3. Earl Jackson Jr., "Desire at Cross(-Cultural) Purposes: Hiroshima, Mon Amour and Merry Christmas, Mr. Lawrence," *positions east asia cultures critique* 2, no. 1 (spring 1994): 133–74. In this essay, Jackson explores the film's visual economy with a view towards understanding its gender-inverted scopophilia. Jackson further discusses the film's gendered East/West trope focusing on how *Hiroshima Mon Amour* engages (without subverting) hierarchal binarisms of gender and racial difference. It would be productive to read Jackson's thoughtful textual critique of the film alongside this chapter with an eye to questioning how Orientalist assumptions founded on notions of immutable difference may serve to essentialize the speaking subjects, fixing insider/outsider denominations—thus precluding the possibility of ethical commemoration.

4. It is of interest to note that both Robert Jay Lifton and Claude Lanzmann have remarked on the ethical responsibility that filmmakers have to attempt to ensure that the "dream-langue" of film does not erupt into a perpetual nightmare, producing an indiscriminate and sensationalist image of historical calamity and death that precludes any contemplated encounter with trauma (Lifton 1967, 458).

5. Art and cinema have been used both intentionally and unwittingly as catharsis from disturbing memories embedded in the psyches of posttrauma nations. For example, Francis Ford Coppola in seeking assistance from the U.S. Department of Defense for *Apocalypse Now*, attempted to convince President Jimmy Carter that the film would be therapeutically valuable, helping to "put Vietnam behind us, which we must do so we can go to a positive future" (quoted in Suid 1978, 314).

6. The theme of trauma beyond imagination, trauma that resists location, is prevalent in nuclear literature and art. In some cases, Hiroshima functions as a transcendental signifier of loss. The annihilation of Hiroshima as place acts as a metaphor for the annihilation of (transhistoric) memory. In the Jungian work of Michael Perlman, for example, Hiroshima takes on archetypal significance. Perlman writes: "*Hiroshima is the place of no place*, revealing a deep lacunae, a placelessness, at the heart of postindustrial culture" (*Imaginal Memory and the Place of Hiroshima* [New York: SUNY, 1988], 91).

7. Witnessing Otherwise

1. The Japanese army did not leave a visual record of their atrocities. What exists in the way of photographs and film footage were taken by Chinese witnesses and Western missionaries.

2. People who cling to the idea that Japan was fighting a war to "liberate" Asia from western imperialism and Bolshevism see Nanjing as a necessary sacrifice in the so-called "Great East Asian War" (*Daitowa Senso*).

3. The first mural, *Ghosts* (completed in February 1950), toured relatively unencumbered by U.S. censorship codes. U.S. authorities did, however, suppress *Pika-don*, a book of monochromatic illustrations of Hiroshima by the Marukis (August 1950).

4. Many of the avant-garde artists were a generation younger than the forerunning Social Realists working in Tokyo. They had not experienced the war directly, which may have led them to be less concerned with the despair and privations of postwar society and more seduced by the future and the task of rebuilding a Japanese modern identity from the charred ruins of postatomic history.

5. Nagasaki was distinguished as a "Christian City" from the mid-sixteenth century until World War II. On August 9, 1945, when the bomb fell on Nagasaki, the famous Urakami Cathedral was left in ruins; religious statuary and icons were consumed by flames.

6. The traditional format of *suiboku* painting further lends itself to a dispersal of perspective. Each mural is composed of eight strips of gesenshi paper (made with bamboo fiber). While the tableau is comprised only by joining these strips together, each section can be seen as a compositional entity with visible seams. This distinctive presentation cultivates a versatility in viewing by suggesting the possibility of different arrangements (Ishikawa 1988, 163).

7. For more on critical reception of the Maruki Murals, see *Death in Life: Survivors of Hiroshima,* Robert Jay Lifton (New York: Random House, 1967); and *Surviving Visions: The Art of Iri and Toshi Maruki,* ed. Henry Isaacs and John Junkerman (Boston: Massachusetts College of Art, 1988).

Conclusion

1. Visual artists are gradually introducing questions of perspective to the surface-driven space of digital technology. The commemorative work of Vera Frenkel, mentioned in chapter 2, provides a powerful alternative to the dominant mode of vision. Her *Body Missing* web site, for example, produces a complex network of traces relating to the Holocaust. We are encouraged to variously connect images of Nazi-confiscated art, death camp lists, and contemporary testimony. The work of reorganizing the symbolic, while confronting its limits, produces a space for other knowledge to emerge. More importantly, Frenkel makes our role as witnesses explicit.

Works Cited

Adorno, Theodor. 1985. "Commitment." In *The Essential Frankfurt School Reader*, ed. Andrew Arato and Eike Gebhardt. New York: Continuum.

———. 1967. "The Valery Proust Museum." In *Prisms*. London: Neville Spearman.

Anderegg, Michael, ed. 1991. *Inventing Vietnam: The War in Film and Television*. Philadelphia: Temple University Press.

Bakhtin, Mikhail. 1981. *The Dialogic Imagination*. Austin, Texas: University of Texas Press.

Benjamin, Walter. 1968. "The Storyteller" and "Theses on the Philososphy of History." In *Illuminations*, ed. Hannah Arendt, trans. Harry Zohn. New York: Schocken Books.

Berdhal, Daphne. 1992. "Voices at the Wall: Discourses of Self, History, and National Identity at the Vietnam Veteran's Memorial."

Berger, John. 1993. *The Sense of Sight* . New York: Vintage International.

———. 1991. *About Looking*. New York: Vintage International.

———. 1988. "The Limits of Painting." In *Surviving Visions: The Art of Iri Maruki and Toshi Maruki*, ed. Henry Isaacs and John Junkerman. Boston: Massachusetts College of Art.

———. 1977. *Ways of Seeing*. London/New York: Penguin Books.

Berger, John and Jean Mohr. 1982. *Another Way of Telling*. New York: Panthcon Books.

Bhabha, Homi K. 1994. "How Newness Enters the World: Postmodern Space, Postcolonial Times and the Trials of Cultural Translation." In *The Location of Culture*. New York and London: Routledge.

Boler, Megan. Unpublished. "The Risks of Empathy: Interrogating Multiculturalism's Gaze."

Boyer, Paul. 1985. *By the Bomb's Early Light: American Thought at the Dawn of the Atomic Age*. New York: Pantheon.

Braw, Monica. 1991. *The Atomic Bomb Suppressed: American Censorship in Occupied Japan*. London: M. E. Sharpe Inc.

Brett, Guy. 1986. *Through Our Own Eyes: Popular Art and Modern History.* London: GMP Publishers.

Brewster, Ben. 1994. "From Shklovsky to Brecht: A Reply." *Screen* 15, no. 2 (summer): 82–102.

Burchett, Wilfred. 1983. *Shadows of Hiroshima.* London: Verso.

Buruma, Ian. 1995. *The Wage of Guilt.* New York: Meridian.

Butler, Judith. 1992. "Contingent Foundations: Feminism and the Question of Postmodernism." In *Feminists Theorize the Political,* ed. Judith Butler and Joan Scott. New York and London: Routledge.

Caruth, Cathy, ed. 1995. *Trauma: Explorations in Memory.* Baltimore: John Hopkins University Press.

Caruth, Cathy and Deborah Esch, eds. 1994. *Critical Encounters: Reference and Responsibility in Deconstructive Writing.* New Brunswick, New Jersey: Rutgers University Press.

Cha, Theresa Hak Kyung. 1995. *Dictee.* Berkeley: Third Woman Press.

Cohen, Susan D. 1993. *Women and Discourse in the Fiction of Marguerite Duras.* Amherst: University of Massachusetts Press.

Cornell, Drucilla. 1992. *The Philosophy of the Limit.* New York and London: Routledge.

Crimp, Douglas. 1990. "Mourning and Militancy." In *Out There: Marginalization and Contemporary Cultures,* ed. Russell Ferguson et al. New York: New Museum of Contemporary Art and MIT.

Derrida, Jacques. 1994. *Spectres of Marx: The State of the Debt, the Work of Mourning, and the New International.* Trans. Peggy Kamuf. New York and London: Routledge.

———. 1986. *Memoires: For Paul de Man.* Trans. Cecile Lindsay, Jonathan Culler, and Eduardo Cadava. New York: Columbia University Press.

———. 1984. "No Apocalypse, Not Now: Full Speed Ahead, Seven Missiles, Seven Missives." *diacritics* 14: 20–31.

Doane, Mary Ann. 1980. "Misrecognition and Identity." *Cine-Tracts* 3, no. 3 (fall).

Dower, John W. 1993. *Japan in War and Peace: Selected Essays.* New York: New York Press.

———. 1988. "Crossing Boundaries: An introduction." In *Surviving Visions: The Art of Iri and Toshi Maruki,* ed. Henry Isaacs and John Junkerman. Boston: Massachusetts College of Art.

Dower, John W. and John Junkerman, eds. 1985. *The Hiroshima Murals: The Art of Iri and Toshi Maruki*. Tokyo and New York: Kodansha International Ltd.

Duras, Marguerite. 1961. *Hiroshima Mon Amour*. New York: Grove Press.

Felman, Shoshana and Dori Laub. 1992. *Testimony: Crisis of Witnessing in Literature, Psychoanalysis, and History*. New York and London: Routledge.

Freud, Sigmund. 1984. "Mourning and Melancholia." In *Volume II, On Metapsychology: The Theory of Psychoanalysis, Sigmund Freud*, ed. Angela Richards and trans. James Strachey. New York and London: Penguin Books.

Fusco, Coco. 1988. "An Interview with the Black Audio Film Collective: John Akomfrah, Reece Auguste, Lina Gopaul and Avril Johnson." In *Young British and Black: The Work of Sankofah and the Black Audio Film Collective*. Buffalo: Hallwalls.

Gerson, John. 1995. *With Hiroshima Eyes: Atomic War, Nuclear Extortion, and Moral Imagination*. Philadelphia: New Society.

Gillis, John R. 1994. "Memory and Identity: The History of a Relationship." In *Commemorations: The Politics of National Identity*, ed. John R. Gillis. Princeton: Princeton University Press.

Gilroy, Paul. 1993. "Not a Story to Pass On." In *The Black Atlantic: Modernity and Double Consciousness*. Cambridge, Massachusetts: Harvard University Press.

Haraway, Donna. 1991. "Situated Knowledges: The Science Question in Feminism and the Privilege of Partial Perspective." In *Simians, Cyborgs, and Women: The Reinvention of Nature*. New York and London: Routledge.

Heath, Stephen. 1974. "Lessons from Brecht." *Screen* 15, no. 2 (summer): 103–27.

Huyssen, Andreas. 1995. *Twilight Memories: Marking Time in a Culture of Amnesia*. New York and London: Routledge.

"Introduction: Nuclear Criticism." 1984. *diacritics: a review of contemporary criticism* (summer).

Irwin-Zarecka, Iwona. 1994. *Frames of Remembrance: The Dynamics of Collective Memory*. New Brunswick, New Jersey: Transaction Publ.

Isaacs, Henry and John Junkerman, eds. 1988. *Surviving Visions: The Art of Iri and Toshi Maruki*. Boston: Massachusetts College of Art.

Ishikawa,Yasuo. 1988. "Afterword: The Joint Works—Technical Aspects, Tradition, and Thought." In *The Hiroshima Panels*. Saitama: Maruki Gallery.

Jackson, Earl, Jr. 1994. "Desire at Cross(-Cultural) Purposes: Hiroshima, Mon Amour, and Merry Christmas, Mr. Lawrence." *positions east asia cultures critique* 2, no. 1 (spring): 133–74.

Japan Broadcasting Corporation, ed. 1977. *Unforgettable Fire: Pictures Drawn by Atomic Bomb Survivors*. New York: Pantheon.

Jenks, Chris. 1995. "The Centrality of the Eye in Western Culture." In *Visual Culture*, ed. Chris Jenks. New York and London: Routledge.

Kingwell, Mark. 1996. *Dreams of Millennium*. Toronto: Viking.

Kinney, Judy Lee. 1991. "Gardens of Stone, Platoon, and Hamburger Hill: Ritual and Remembrance." In *Inventing Vietnam*, ed. Michael Anderegg. Philadelphia: Temple University Press.

Kreidly, John Francis. 1977. *Alain Resnais*. Boston: Twayne Publishers.

Langer, Lawrence. 1995. *Admitting the Holocaust: Collected Essays*. New York and Oxford: Oxford University Press, 1995.

Lanzmann, Claude. 1985. *Shoah*. Paris: Editions Fayard.

Laub, Dori. 1992. "Bearing Witness or the Vicissitudes of Listening." In *Testimony: Crisis of Witnessing in Literature, Psychoanalysis, and History*, ed. Shoshana Felman and Dori Laub. New York and London: Routledge.

Lecercle, Jean-Jacques. 1992. "To Do Or Not to Do without the Word: Ecstasy and Discourse in the Cinema." *New Formations*, no. 16 (spring): 80–90.

Leo, Vincent. 1985. "The Mushroom Cloud Photograph: From Fact to Symbol." *AfterImage* (summer).

Levin, David Michael. 1993. "Introduction." In *Modernity and the Hegemony of Vision*, ed.

Levin. Berkeley: University of California Press.

Lifton, Robert Jay. 1979. *The Broken Connection: On Death and the Continuity of Life*. New York: Basic Books.

——— . 1967. *Death in Life: Survivors of Hiroshima*. New York: Random House.

Lifton, Robert Jay and Eric Markusen. 1991. *The Genocidal Mentality: Nazi Holocaust and Nuclear Threat*. London: Macmillan.

Lifton, Robert Jay and Greg Mitchell. 1995. *Hiroshima in America: A Half Century of Denial*. New York: Avon Books.

Lingis, Alphonso. 1994. *The Community of Those Who Have Nothing in Common*. Bloomington and Indianapolis: Indiana University Press.

Lyotard, Jean-Francois. 1990. *Heidegger and the Jews*. Trans. Andreas Michel and Mark Roberts. Minneapolis: University of Minnesota Press.

———. 1988. *The Differend: Phrases in Dispute*. Trans. Georges Van Den Abbeele. Manchester: Manchester University Press.

Marks, Laura. 1994. "A Deleuzian Politics of Hybrid Cinema." *Screen* 35:3 (autumn): 244–64.

Marlatt, Daphne. 1984. "On Distance and Identity: Ten Years Later." In *Steveston*, ed. Daphne Marlatt and Robert Minden. Edmonton: Longspoon Press.

Maruki, Toshi and Iri Maruki. 1988. *The Hiroshima Panels*. Trans. Nancy Hunter and Yasuo Ishikawa. Japan: Otsuka Kogeisha Co.

Mercer, Kobena and Isaac Julien. 1988. "Introduction: De Margin and de Centre." *Screen* 29, no. 4 (autumn): 1–10.

Minh-ha, Trinh T. 1991a. *When the Moon Waxes Red: Representation, Gender, and Cultural Politics*. New York and London: Routledge.

———. 1991b. "Bold Omissions and Minute Depictions." In *Moving the Image: Independent Asian Pacific American Media Arts*, ed. Russell Leong. Los Angeles: UCLA.

———. 1989. *Woman Native Other*. Bloomington and Indianapolis: Indiana University Press.

Mitchell, Stanley. 1994. "From Shklovsky to Brecht: Some Preliminary Remarks Towards a History of the Politicisation of Russian Formalism." *Screen* 15, no. 2 (summer).

Mitchell, W. T. J. 1994. *Picture Theory*. Chicago and London: University of Chicago Press.

Monaco, James. 1979. *Alain Resnais*. New York: Oxford University Press.

Munroe, Alexandra. 1994. *Scream against the Sky: Japanese Art after 1945*. New York: Harry N. Abrams Inc.

Nelson, Joyce. 1987. *The Perfect Machine: TV in the Nuclear Age*. Toronto: between the lines.

Nichols, Bill. 1991. *Representing Reality*. Bloomington and Indianapolis: Indiana University Press.

Nora, Pierre. 1989. "Between Memory and History: *Les Lieux de Memoire*." *Representations*, no. 26 (spring): 7–25.

Oda, Makoto. 1990. *The Bomb*. Ed. D. H. Whittaker. Tokyo and New York: Kodansha International.

Oe, Kenzaburo. 1995. *Hiroshima Notes.* New York: Grove Press.

Perlman, Michael. 1988. *Imaginal Memory and the Place of Hiroshima.* New York: SUNY.

Rabinowitz, Paula. 1993. "Wreckage upon Wreckage: History, Documentary, and the Ruins of Memory." *History and Theory* 32, no. 2: 119–32.

Robbins, Kevin. 1996. *Into the Image: Culture and Politics in the Field of Vision.* NY and London: Routledge.

Ruthven, Ken. 1993. *Nuclear Criticism.* Carlton, Victoria: Melbourne University Press.

Said, Edward. 1985. "In the Shadow of the West." *Wedge*, nos. 7–8 (winter–spring).

Santer, Eric L. 1990. *Stranded Objects: Mourning, Memory, and Film in Postwar Germany.* Ithaca, New York: Cornell University Press.

Sata, Ineko. 1985. "The Colorless Paintings." In *The Crazy Iris and Other Stories of the Atomic Aftermath*, ed. Kenzaburo Oe. New York: Grove Press.

Schley, Jim, ed. 1983. *Writing in a Nuclear Age.* Hanover and London: University Press of New England.

Schwenger, Peter. 1992. *Letter Bomb: Nuclear Holocaust and the Exploding Word.* Baltimore and London: John Hopkins University Press.

———. 1994. "America's Hiroshima." *boundary 2* 21, no. 1 (spring): 233–51.

Shono, Naomi. 1993. "Mute Reminders of Hiroshima's Atomic Bombing." *Japan Quarterly* (July–September).

Silverman, Kaja. 1996. *On the Threshold of the Visible World.* New York and London: Routlege.

Simon, Roger. Unpublished. "Pedagogy and the Call to Witness in Marc Chagall's *White Crucifixion.*"

Sohoh, Yamashita. 1986. *Traces of the Atomic Rays: Paintings in Japanese Ink by Yamashita Sohoh.* Hiroshima: Self-published.

Sontag, Susan. 1989. *On Photography.* New York: Doubleday.

Spivak, Gayatri Chakravorty. 1990. "The Post-Modern Condition: The End of Politics?" and "Questions of Multiculturalism." In *The Post-Colonial Critic*, ed. Sarah Harasym. New York and London: Routledge.

———. 1992. "Acting Bits/Identity Talk." *Critical Inquiry* 18 (summer).

Suid, Lawrence H. 1978. *Guts and Glory.* Reading, Mass.: Addison-Wesley.

Sweet, Freddy. 1981. *The Film Narratives of Alain Resnais.* Ann Arbor, Mich.: UMI Research Press.

Taussig, Michael. 1993. *Mimesis and Alterity: A Particular History of the Senses.* New York and London: Routledge.

Taylor, Lucien, ed. 1994. *Visualizing Theory: Selected Essays from V. A. R.* New York and London: Routledge.

Treat, John Whittier. 1994. "Hiroshima's America." *boundary 2* 21, no. 1 (spring): 233–53.

————. 1988. "Atomic Bomb Literature and the Documentary Fallacy." *The Journal of Japanese Studies* 14, no. 1 (winter): 27–59.

Tribe, Keith. 1977–1978. "History and the Production of Memories." *Screen* 18, no. 4 (winter): 9–22.

Tsukui, Nobuko. 1986. "Yoshie Hotta's Judgement: An Approach to the Atomic-Bomb Literature of Japan." *Arizona Quarterly* 42, no. 3 (autumn): 197–212.

Witek, Joseph. 1987. "History and Talking Animals: Art Spiegelman's *Maus.*" In *Comic Books as History.* Mississippi: University of Mississippi Press.

Yerushalmi, Y. H. 1989. "Postscript: Reflections on Forgetting." In *Zakhor: Jewish History and Jewish Memory.* New York: Schoken Books.

Yoneyama, Lisa. 1994. "Taming the Memoryscape: Hiroshima's Urban Renewal." In *Remapping Memory: The Politics of TimeSpace,* ed. Jonathan Boyarin. Minneapolis: University of Minnesota.

Yoneyama, Lisa. 1995. "Memory Matters: Hiroshima's Korean Atom Bomb Memorial and the Politics of Ethnicity." *Public Culture* 7, no. 3 (spring): 504–505.

Young, James E. 1993. *The Texture of Memory: Holocaust Memorials and Meaning.* New Haven: Yale University Press.

Index